Richard Wherrett is one of Australia's most acclaimed theatre directors. He was an Associate Director of the Old Tote Company, Co-Artistic Director of the Nimrod Theatre, Director of the Sydney Theatre Company from 1979–1990 and Artistic Director for the 1992 and 1993 Melbourne International Festival of the Arts.

During this time, his productions included Brecht's *The Resistable Rise of Arturo Ui*; *Cyrano de Bergerac*; *Chicago*; and *The Elocution of Benjamin Franklin*, which toured to England and America, and won him a New York off-Broadway Obie Award for Best Direction. Other productions included *Emerald City*'s world premiere and tour to the Lyric Theatre in London; *Away* and *The Summer of the Seventeenth Doll* for the 1988 Pepsico Summerfare Festival in New York; the Australian arena version of *Jesus Christ Superstar*; *Turandot* for the Victoria State Opera, which won the Victorian Green Room award for Best Production; *The Rise and Fall of the City of Mahagonny* for the Australian Opera; and *The Crucible*, which was revived three times including a 1994 national tour.

He has directed two short films, *The Girl Who Met Simone de Beauvoir in Paris* and *The Applicant*, as well as *The Girl From Moonooloo* for ABC TV and the feature film *Billy's Holiday*. In 1984 Richard was awarded an AM for his distinguished services to the performing arts.

Most recently, Richard has directed *wunnerful Liberace* for the Sydney Theatre Company; the world premiere of Katherine Thomson's *Navigating* for the Queensland Theatre Company and the Melbourne Theatre Company; and *Cabaret* for the Gordon Frost Organisation.

In 1997 Hodder Headline published *Desirelines*, which he co-authored with his brother Peter.

edited by

# RICHARD WHERRETT

*mardi gras!*

true stories

VIKING

*The editor and publisher would like to thank William Yang and C. Moore Hardy for permission to include their work in the photograph sections of this book.*

*Author royalties from the sale of this book will go to the Bobby Goldsmith Foundation.*

Viking
Penguin Books Australia Ltd
487 Maroondah Highway, PO Box 257
Ringwood, Victoria 3134, Australia
Penguin Books Ltd
Harmondsworth, Middlesex, England
Penguin Putnam Inc.
375 Hudson Street, New York, New York 10014, USA
Penguin Books Canada Limited
10 Alcorn Avenue, Toronto, Ontario, Canada M4V 3B2
Penguin Books (N.Z.) Ltd
Cnr Rosedale and Airborne Roads, Albany, Auckland, New Zealand
Penguin Books (South Africa) (Pty) Ltd
4 Pallinghurst Road, Parktown 2193, South Africa

First published by Penguin Books Australia Ltd 1999

1 3 5 7 9 10 8 6 4 2

Designed by Ruth Grüner
Cover photography by C. Moore Hardy
Author photograph by Paul Freeman
Typeset in 9.3/13.3pt Stone Serif by Midland Typesetters,
Maryborough, Victoria
Printed and bound in Australia by Australian Print Group,
Maryborough, Victoria

National Library of Australia
Cataloguing-in-Publication data:
Wherrett, Richard.
Mardi Gras!: true stories.
ISBN 0 14 027226 7.

1. Sydney Gay and Lesbian Mardi Gras – History. 2. Gays – New South Wales – Sydney – Interviews. 3. Lesbians – New South Wales – Sydney – Interviews. 4. Festivals – New South Wales – Sydney. 5. Carnival – New South Wales – Sydney. I. Title.

305.90664099441

To all Mardi Gras lovers past,
present and future.

*And with special thanks
to Corby Beard.*

# Contents

# mardi gras !

true stories

# Introduction

MOST, PERHAPS ALL, societies − primitive or advanced, ancient or modern, straight or gay − have their festivals: the one or two occasions set aside in a calendar to mark a special event. Thus Australia has Australia Day, Anzac Day and so on. We also have our religious festivals − Christians have Christmas and Easter, and these have their parallels in all faiths. But our non-religious festivals serve another function I believe, providing one or two occasions a year in which we are released from the constraints of our day-to-day lives. These events have social value in that usually, when they're over, we return to our mundane routines purged a little of our tensions and stress. Most of all, these festivals are tribal. On a small scale it's 'Saturday night fever'. On a large scale, in the straight community, it might be New Year's Eve. For the gay and lesbian community in Sydney, it is Mardi Gras.

In the Christian churches Mardi Gras was the festival preceding the fasting, the 'lean' season of Lent − one last indulgence before abstinence and body renewal. When the wise decision was made in 1981 to move Sydney's gay and lesbian march from Stonewall's anniversary in winter to a new date in summer, the parade coincided with Lent. However, I think the march was probably named Mardi Gras simply because while it was, and still is, very political, the term in popular connotations also meant 'Let's party'.

And so indeed we have.

Today, the Sydney Gay and Lesbian Mardi Gras is first and foremost a three-week Festival of gay and lesbian culture − arts, sport, debate − held in Sydney, Australia during February, which culminates in a Parade. This march, in which lies the origins of Mardi Gras, is currently watched by half a million spectators, and many more on television. The Festival is the biggest of its kind in the world, as is the fund-raising party that follows the Parade.

Mardi Gras is the Big One on the gay and lesbian calendar year. Its significance is attested to by the fact that, in this era of AIDS, people *survive* a little longer simply to attend it. I'm sure St Vincent's Hospital would confirm the increase in deaths that usually follow Mardi Gras. 'Just one more. Please, just one more.'

In 1989 I mounted a production for the Sydney Theatre Company of Shakespeare's *A Midsummer Night's Dream*. My research led me to the conclusion that the occasion which inspired the play was the traditional annual holiday held every midsummer's eve when villagers throughout England would 'play up' – that is, in simple terms, get smashed, run off into the 'woods', 'steal' someone else's loved one they fancied, and wake up in the morning with a shocking hangover and only a murky dream-like memory of what had happened. During the late 1980s when the 'dance party' phenomenon was at its height, the connection between 16th century Stratford-on-Avon and late 20th century Sydney seemed obvious. I had my 'concept'. My *A Midsummer Night's Dream* would take place at Mardi Gras. Academics usually hate concepts; audiences often love them. The production did great business, and did so I believe because the audience identified with the situation.

Shakespeare knew a few things about drugs as well as festivities – witness the potion which induces a death-like state in Juliet. *A Midsummer Night's Dream* is metaphorical – after all it is set in Greece, not Warwickshire. And there are no 'woods' just outside Athens! It follows that Shakespeare didn't want to spell out, in any literal way, the mead, mandrake root, or whatever, with which he and his fellow villagers 'got out of it'. Hence the purple flower. In my production, Puck would literally tour a nightclub called 'The World' and score a 'purple flower', the power of which could induce love at first sight. I've seen it happen.

I have a friend who once went to the Mardi Gras Party at midnight, 'fell in love' at 12.30, escorted his new friend home immediately, and remained there for the rest of the night. He never saw his 'true love' again. And I challenge anyone reading this book to argue they have never woken up one morning with little but a dream-like memory of the night before, thinking 'Did I really do that?'

Not that dance parties are about drugs any more than Mardi Gras is about dance parties. The Mardi Gras parties exist to fund the Parade, the Festival, Mardi Gras' infrastructure and its few paid positions (remembering the vast majority of work done for Mardi Gras is voluntary). Without these things, Mardi Gras would not happen. Those who have worked their butt off for six months or more have every right, at its conclusion, to party.

I have attended every Mardi Gras party and nearly every Parade. I have been privileged to serve on the Mardi Gras board, and to have experienced how Mardi Gras has grown and changed over the years. Above all, I know how important Mardi Gras is in my life and others'. This collection serves as a testament to this.

We initially contacted 150 people by letter. These letters invited others, if they had a story, to submit them directly to me. Over the next few months, with Corby Beard assisting me, we tried to spread the word far and wide. We were open to any contribution − a direct 'invitation' was definitely not a prerequisite − because I knew in my heart that there were people who were, or had been, very important to Mardi Gras who, in the initial run, we had not approached. More importantly, I wanted contributions from the bloke in the street who perhaps came upon the parade unwittingly and, like Saul, 'saw the light'. I wanted contributions from the youngest and oldest persons who'd ever attended a party. I wanted every aspect of Mardi Gras covered and in every way − the funny, the sad, the bizarre, the torrid, the inspired, the angry and the critical. I wanted stories from those for whom life had changed forever.

The stories that follow do this pretty well. But there *are* some holes. I regret there is nothing about Fair Day and very little about the Festival. The latter ten years of Mardi Gras get a disproportionate amount of space as opposed to the first ten years. And there are some very notable Mardi Gras connections missing. Promises, promises. 'But I'm very busy,' was a familiar cry. To all those who we still failed to reach, who would have liked to contribute, my humble apologies. There are many more stories to tell.

One of the few benefits of getting older is that experience helps you to recognise and exploit the blissful moments in your life *as they happen* rather than as recollections in tranquillity. I didn't know, standing outside the Rex Hotel in Kings Cross in 1959 at the 10 p.m. close with my first boyfriend, how happy I was. I've been fortunate to recognise many such moments during the years of Mardi Gras.

It has been a privilege and an honour to edit this book.

# 'Your First Time?'

## Phillip Scott

MY IDEA OF a party drug has always been Berocca, and a wonderful wonder drug it is. But you can't be an active citizen of Sydney without eventually sampling some other drugs – those without healing properties.

One New Year's Eve I was given something to keep me awake all night for the purpose of partying. It worked terrifically. I boogied until dawn, hopped brightly into a cab in the streaming sunlight at 10.30 a.m. and promptly ran up a bill of over $150 by making the driver take me from one end of Sydney to another. I was desperate to visit somebody. Anybody! We crossed the harbour bridge not once but thrice. By mid-afternoon I had become a raving lunatic with very little cash, and I also knew the life stories of the cab driver and his entire family. Taxis and drugs are now inextricably linked in my life.

Mardi Gras rolled around. I'm a late starter as far as the party scene's concerned, but I had greatly enjoyed the Big One on my previous two attendances. It's always fun to run into straight friends you haven't seen lately, except on *Good News Week*. This particular year's bash promised to be even better for two good reasons. One: the person who'd made New Year's Eve so interesting and costly had promised to supply me with A Party Drug! I arranged to meet him inside the RHI (Royal Hall of Industries) at 12.30 a.m., when we'd repair to the bleachers to complete the transition and the subsequent butterfly-style metamorphosis.

My second reason concerned my partner of four months' standing. I'd never been part of a Mardi Gras Couple before. Now, instead of wandering from one pavilion to another trying to locate companions with other agendas, I would be able to spend the entire night linked to the man of my choice, sharing the Pride, the Fun, the Communal Bonding and the Portaloo. No more would I need to scream at a total stranger, 'Is Kylie on yet? I can't see.' I could ask my partner! With the added advantage of tallness, he'd be able to describe the frocks, the choreography and everything else onstage. It seemed perfect.

So I was caught off guard somewhat when my partner indicated a complete lack of interest in the Party.

'Why don't you want to go? We'll be together!' I reasoned.

'We'll be together anyway. It's too expensive.'

'I agree, but so what? Let's go!'

'I don't like the music.'

'Nobody likes the music! That isn't the point!'

'And I don't like crowds.'

'But this crowd consists exclusively of gay men with their shirts off . . .'

'Not what I've heard.'

'. . . all crammed in together. Oh! And I forgot, I'm being given A Party Drug! Maybe we can get two.'

He didn't dignify this suggestion with an answer. Instead came the clincher.

'We wouldn't get there till midnight. It's past my bedtime.'

Perhaps at this point I should explain my partner's attitude to sleep. Put simply, it's this: sleep is like compulsory Community Service. You MUST sleep at least eight hours a night and if, for some reason, you don't fulfil this quota you MUST at some future date make up the extra time. You can imagine what kind of trouble this causes after a few dozen late nights or early rises: at the age of thirty-something, he now has about four whole years of sleep to catch up on. He is understandably loath to run up the total any further. Of course, at this early stage in our relationship, I had little idea of the seriousness of the matter. 'Past your bedtime?' I may have replied lightly. 'Oh, diddums. Poor baby.' Etc.

Finally, he grudgingly agreed to come with me, but only on the understanding that we weren't to enjoy ourselves. That was okay. I knew it was impossible not to enjoy yourself at Mardi Gras.

Which, of course, we did. It was an excellent year. We saw lots of people we knew and rubbed up against one or two we wished we knew. I drank nothing but water, as I'd been carefully advised to by Party-Drug-Friendly acquaintances. At 12.30 we ambled into the Royal Hall of Industries to the designated pick-up spot. Disaster! There was no sign of my supplier. I looked hard everywhere, except in the darkened Men's Toilet where individual identification is frowned upon. I waited half an hour, then gave up.

'Did you take your drugs?' my partner asked contemptuously.

'He wasn't there,' I answered. 'He's probably been arrested.'

'Good.'

We plunged back into the seething throng and let ourselves go. I was soon over my initial spasm of disappointment. I didn't need artificial stimuli, I was high on life. Around 3 a.m. I finally succumbed to a desire to stuff a hot dog down my throat and we made our way into the open spaces. A slight breeze had come up, chilling our sweat-soaked bodies from head to foot. It was quite a pleasant sensation. My partner took the opportunity to join the Portaloo queue. I had just extricated hot dog money from my right sock when who should I bump into but my elusive drug donor.

'Where were you at 12.30?' he moaned. 'I looked everywhere.'

'I was where we said. I looked everywhere for you!'

'Well I was there.' He reached deep into the pocket of his damp, silver shorts. 'Here,' he said with a wicked grin. 'You're lucky I've still got it.'

What the hell: down the hatch. My fairy godmother pirouetted off towards the Dome as I waited, swigging sensibly on my spring water.

'I'm tired,' my partner whispered when he returned.

'One more dance!' I cried.

'All right.'

Back on the dance floor, everything was utterly transformed . . . *not*. What had I taken: a reality pill? Perhaps we weren't dancing hard enough . . . or close enough? I grabbed my partner and dragged him further into the pulsating centre of the hall. The vortex, if you like. We didn't stop until I'd found a spot seething with skin and sweat. Surely this was where the famous rush would happen? We'd just started to become slaves to the rhythm – though, technically speaking for a moment, this kind of dance music doesn't have any, it simply has pulse – when my partner spotted an old friend he hadn't seen for a long time. We squelched over, and they had a shouted conversation from which I was completely excluded by the loudness of the dance track and my lack of height. I jostled to myself morosely while they seemed to talk forever. Far from floating into realms of unearthly delight, I felt solid and grounded. When the reunion was over, my partner screamed into my ear. 'Let's go, hey?'

'It's only 3.15! The shows haven't finished. The best one's usually at 10.'

'Well, we've missed it.'

'Ten in the morning.'

He went pale. I reached out to grab him as he swayed uneasily.

'I'm happy to leave now,' I said reassuringly. I was in no mood to argue any longer. We'd seen everyone and done everything we'd agreed to do. It had been a physical evening and although I didn't have years of sleep to make up I still felt like a bit of shut-eye. We retrieved our bags from the check out and made our way across the dark, grassy fields towards Anzac Parade. A few vacant cabs crawled past, their drivers staring intently over at the Showgrounds to see if they could spy any fares or freaks (or both).

We hailed a cab and dragged ourselves into the back seat. I gave the driver unnecessarily precise directions – I do that when I'm tired – and gazed coolly out the window as we sped off through Surry Hills, towards home and hearth. The parade had been lavish, and we'd had fun at the party. Good, clean, wholesome fun, but fun nevertheless. I looked at my partner's nodding head, his eyes gently closed. He seemed happy. I was pleased.

I sighed and began to examine the back of the taxi driver's neck. It was rough with some stray grey hairs. It looked strangely familiar. Could this be the same cab I'd flagged down on New Years' Day? Surely not. And yet there was something about that neck . . . well, actually, it was beautiful. That was it! Not conventionally beautiful, but just incredibly beautiful. Probably because he was such a beautiful man: staying up so late so he could take us home. It was a marvellous, generous thing to do. I was deeply moved. How would we ever repay him? He was an angel! A wonderful, generous angel, with a beautiful neck. How I ached to reach out and stroke it.

I shut my eyes.

'Oh no,' I thought.

*Phillip Scott is a writer, musician and performer who lives in Sydney's inner-west.*

# It Began by Accident

## Dennis Altman

IT BEGAN BY ACCIDENT. In the winter of 1978, a march was organised down Oxford Street in Sydney to commemorate the ninth anniversary of Stonewall, the riot against a police raid of a gay bar in New York which sparked off the contemporary gay liberation movement. Without any apparent preparation, the leaders of the Sydney march disobeyed police orders not to continue to Kings Cross, leading to mass arrests and the creation of an Australian gay myth. I was there but very much on the sidelines. I was with Greg Millen, then a doctor at the Sydney STD clinic, from which he drew many of the details for his film script, *The Clinic*. We followed the march up to Darlinghurst Road, not wanting to leave but wanting even less to be arrested.

Mardi Gras proper began in 1981 when the original link with Stonewall was broken in favour of celebrating the Australian summer. Five thousand people marched in the parade that year, filling the five blocks from Taylor Square to Hyde Park with floats ranging from Anglican gays to the replica of a disco. All of it went unreported by the media. When I submitted a story on the Parade to David Marr, then editor of the *National Times*, he said it wasn't sufficiently interesting to be published.

Things started to change by the late 1980s, when spectators began outnumbering the Parade's participants in large numbers. By 1987 Mardi Gras had become a firm part of the Sydney calendar.

Up to 500 000 people are now estimated to show up in Oxford Street to watch the annual Parade. Those who parade, along with some thousands of others, then go on to the huge dance party in the Show-grounds, one of the biggest lesbian/gay parties in the world. How to maintain the dance party as a 'lesbian-gay space' has been a central topic of debate in the Sydney community for almost a decade.

Mardi Gras has become one of Australia's top tourist money-spinners. Not only do large numbers of people fly in from North America, but I have seen advertisements for it in mainstream newspapers in Malaysia, aimed at 'the family' market. Increasing numbers of straight politicians march to show their support, and the program includes endorsements by civic and political leaders, including the Governor-General but not, in 1997 nor 1998, the Prime Minister, John Howard.

In late February, Sydney becomes Mardi Gras City, in a way unparalleled for gay events elsewhere in the world. A few years ago I flew in for the weekend, and the taxi driver looked at me and grinned. 'Here for the Parade, mate?' he asked in his accented English. The *Sydney Morning Herald* ran a special Mardi Gras crossword, a particular irony for me as the paper had refused to review my first book, *Homosexual: Oppression and Liberation*, some twenty years earlier.

Does Mardi Gras, then, show the success of the lesbian/gay movement in changing attitudes and winning recognition, the move in a couple of decades from seeing homosexuality as a sin, crime and an illness to recognition of it as another part of the multicultural tapestry that makes contemporary Australia? Yes – and no.

In the last piece he published before his death, gay maverick and writer Peter Blazey complained that Mardi Gras had been 'sanitised' by commercial support and mainstream press coverage. There is always a risk that the very success of Mardi Gras can undermine it as the voice of a particular community. When Susan Harben was President of Mardi Gras' organising committee, she spoke of the temptation to speak of the 'Sydney' rather than 'Gay & Lesbian' Mardi Gras.

For years, the gay community has argued whether the increasing visibility and glitz of Mardi Gras has meant the erosion of its political content. Yet in a society which is still ambivalent about homosexuality, which is far from accepting it as just another form of human sexuality and emotion, the very visibility of Mardi Gras is itself a political statement. The ABC's decision to televise Mardi Gras in 1994 was both controversial and successful, at least in terms of rating. But the opposition – including a petition from a large number of parliamentarians asking that it not be shown until late at night – showed the ambivalence of middle Australia.

The ABC repeated its coverage in 1995 and 1996, though not without criticism. In addition to the moral opponents were those who felt the broadcast itself was poorly done, a campy version of the coverage of Royal Tours from the 1950s and 1960s. In 1998, excerpts from the Parade were presented on Channel 10, on the Friday after Mardi Gras, at 9.30 in the evening. A cynic might see this as the ultimate triumph of commercialism, or what Christopher Isherwood called 'annihilation by blandness'.

And yet ... There is a Mexican festival for the dead which reminds one of the carnival aspect of Mardi Gras. Mardi Gras, which began as a liberationist demonstration, has, over the past decade, incorporated the need for a community to remember those who have died, and equally, the need for those who remain to find ways of continuing to live.

The impact of AIDS in this country, unlike much of the world, has been confined largely to two groups, homosexual men and people with hae-mophilia. While there is some ongoing infection among gay men, the rate of HIV transmission has been dramatically slowed, and the lack of much infection amongst other groups owes much to widespread campaigns for 'safe sex', and the partnership between the gay community and govern-ment. Effective campaigns around prevention, community-based support programs such as those run by ACON and the Bobby Goldsmith Foun-dation, the partnership forged between the affected communities, health professionals and politicians on both sides of politics, is one of the more extraordinary accomplishments in Australia in the past decade.

Even so, the loss from AIDS in the gay community is rarely recognised by mainstream Australia. Looking through William Yang's collection of photographs, *Friends of Dorothy*, one is reminded again of how many people have died thirty or forty years before their normal life expectancy. While there are more solemn memorial ceremonies, such as the Candle-light Vigil and displays of the AIDS Quilt, the combination of joy and communal celebration of Mardi Gras has become central in acknowledg-ing the impact of the epidemic and mobilising to meet its challenges.

As Peter Blazey wrote in his last column: 'Like all political acts, the Gay and Lesbian Mardi Gras can be a double-edged scimitar . . . I am tempted to get out there in my wheelchair, hitting Taylor Square at high speed with my whistle fully engorged to blow at our radiant, gym-toned fascist marching boys.'

Mardi Gras is now the central date on the Australian gay and lesbian calendar, an increasingly important national day. While the cameras linger on the drag queens, the dykes on bikes, the beautiful boys in leather, the Parade is really a cross-section of Australian life: suburban mums supporting their children, middle-aged men and women in gay religious and sporting groups, Asian and other ethnic community floats. Perhaps Mardi Gras' great lesson is that the more we celebrate diversity, the easier it becomes to find commonalties: that gay communities are made up of people who also belong to every other community in Aus-tralian society.

*Dennis Altman is a Professor of Politics at La Trobe University in Victoria and the author of many books dealing with gay politics, as well as his recent autobiography,* Defying Gravity.

There are many unsung heroes of Mardi Gras who certainly should have found their way into this collective memory. Most have at least been mentioned. But some notable individuals are missing. One is Ron Austin. Many people credit the idea of the first Mardi Gras march in June 1978 to Ron – a visionary man. We don't have his account of that event, but we do have David Marr's.

Dear Richard,

You mention the 'relatively small march of protest and pride in 1978' that kicked things off. In fact, it was a bizarre and violent occasion, and the over-response by police to a few hundred poofters and their dyke mates marching down Oxford Street opened the way to the freedom we've enjoyed since. It was the cop's last shot, a kind of Stonewall.

I was a furtive new journalist at the time – out to my friends and colleagues but with hardly any contact within the gay community. I'd never dared write about That Sort of Thing. But after the debacle of the march I persuaded the *National Times* to let me write a full account of what happened. So, though I wasn't on the march, I was at the outrageous police siege of the Liverpool Street court that followed – and later I spoke to police, politicians and dozens of the people who were arrested and bashed.

The following is an edited version of David Marr's article which was published in the *National Times* on 8 July 1978.

# A Night Out at the Cross
## David Marr

A PARADE OF homosexuals celebrating International Gay Solidarity Day in Sydney on the night of Saturday, 24 June, led to more arrests and violence than has been seen in the city for seven years.

On that same day in San Francisco 240 000 people turned out to celebrate. The city funded the march. There were no serious incidents. In Sydney, the march was never more than 2000 strong but ended with fifty-three arrests.

There are allegations of bashings later at Darlinghurst police station, and when the defendants turned up to court on Monday they found a massive deployment of police closing the courts. The police had their heads that weekend.

The men involved came predominantly from No. 3 Division, Darlinghurst police station, about which there is a constant stream of complaints of harassment of homosexuals.

That station's beat takes in the area of homosexual night life in Sydney. Police continue to photograph and take names and addresses of people they think are homosexual. Many see homosexuals as criminals, and to many of them that Saturday night march was a march of criminals. This is antagonism of long-standing . . .

A journalist who has been working the police rounds for years said, 'If the police were rougher than is normal for NSW coppers, it would be a combination of the category of the marchers and the fact that most of the police would have had a few drinks, it being Saturday night and all.'

The organisers of the parade – they called it a mardi gras – had picked a route that was too short, and gave the crowd nowhere to go. The organiser who applied for the permit, Lance Gowland, thought the police had agreed that the parade could stop outside the bars of Oxford Street, that singing and dancing would be allowed in the street and in Hyde Park, where the crowd would disperse. The permit did not say this – and when the parade moved off from Taylor Square at 10.30 p.m. the police kept it moving.

About 1000 people moved down Oxford Street. It was more popular than the organisers and police had expected. The crowd was euphoric. They chanted, 'Out of the bars and into the streets' and 'Ho-ho-ho homosexual'. A loudspeaker van played music. There were dancers on the van. But the police kept it moving. In only 20 minutes it had reached Hyde Park.

The police disconnected the amplifier and drove the truck away. In the confusion, two men were arrested. A chant went up, 'To the Cross, to the Cross'. Without the truck, the organisers had no way of marshalling the crowd. In what followed the police did not use loudhailers themselves or try to direct or disperse it.

At the top of William Street the police had blocked off streets opposite and to the right, but left clear the road to the left. It was the only way the parade could go. The police, in fact, funnelled the marchers into the Cross. It was about 11.30.

The steam had gone out of the parade when it got to the El Alamein fountain, but paddy wagons were drawing up, and the feeling in the crowd was to disperse and to get out of the Cross together.

The mardi gras atmosphere had disappeared. Elizabeth Bay Road was blocked by paddy wagons, but the police had cleared traffic from Darlinghurst Road, so the parade moved back along its own tracks. It was almost certainly what the police intended.

The front of the parade moved past the only side streets in Darlinghurst Road. One of the marchers said, 'Where they halted the people there was nowhere they could disperse. The footpaths were packed on either side. It was like New Year's Eve at the Cross.' What followed was clearly designed to make arrests, not to clear traffic.

'I saw those headlights. I will never forget those headlights,' said a woman at the front of the procession who saw the four paddy wagons bearing down on them, their sirens blaring. Another bystander said, 'It seemed that people would be killed by them. It was terrifying.'

Two more wagons drove through the crowd from the rear and cut off the retreat to the side streets. About 200 people were trapped, and the rest of the procession pressed up behind.

Arrests began after a couple of minutes of general shuffling and confusion. The first was a man who walked between the wagons at the William Street end. He was seized from behind, and a witness said, 'People began to protest about that because he hadn't done anything. The protest wasn't terribly heavy, but then the police began to grab people by the hair, feet, tits.'

There was a lull for a few seconds after the first two or three arrests. The centre of the road was clear and the marchers were pressed against the footpath crowds. Then someone threw a full yellow plastic garbage can on to the bonnet of one of the wagons and the garbage spilled over the truck. It was the signal for the real business to begin.

'Within five minutes it was a battlefield,' said one of the marchers. The noise of chanting and shouting was tremendous. Police dragged people from the side of the road towards the wagons. Some of these resisted.

The melee was joined by passers-by, bikies, and apparently by some residents of the Cross. 'All the windows were full. Everyone in the Cross was watching,' said a bystander. There was crying, screaming and panic.

One of the parade marshals climbed on to a garbage bin outside Woolworths. 'I saw an area of people fighting, wrestling and screaming. I thought something had to be done,' he said. He found an officer who he was told was in charge and said, 'I want to tell people to disperse, but we haven't got any PA system. Have you got any?' The officer replied, 'Don't worry about it. Leave it.'

The melee continued for half an hour. Witnesses told the *National Times* they saw a young man thrown half into a paddy wagon and alleged they saw police repeatedly slamming the wagon doors on his legs.

More wagons arrived at the William Street end and these were ferrying people to Darlinghurst police station. Fifty had been arrested. When all the other wagons were full they pulled out leaving the marchers.

A passer-by who watched the vans being driven up Victoria Street has given a barrister a statement that says she saw one of the paddy wagons go past at speed in the empty street and then brake suddenly. She heard screams coming from inside the truck.

Lawyers, doctors and bail money were fetched to Darlinghurst. A couple had been deputed to bring bail money for the night but one had gone to the opera and the other had forgotten to bring the cash. It hadn't seemed a high priority when the planning was done.

A solicitor, John Terry, was among the first lawyers to arrive at Darlinghurst. He found police blocking the entrance of the station. 'I said, "My name is Terry; I am a solicitor. I wish to see the desk sergeant." The police constable said, "Why, you can't come in here." I said, "I wish to speak to him about the arrests at Kings Cross tonight. How many people were arrested?" The officer said, "You can't come past this doorway. If you do you will be trespassing and you will be arrested." '

Terry named two people he knew to be in the cells. He said, 'You can't refuse me access to my client. You know what Driscoll's case says.' Another officer replied, 'Look, just fuck off, mate. You're not in court now.'

Terry and two barristers, Mackrell and Wynn, argued their way in, and after some lengthy obstruction began to interview clients and take instructions.

A doctor had been trying for some time to get into the station. He had heard there was an injured man in the cells. After more than an hour's argument he was allowed to examine the man.

The doctor said, 'He had bruises on the head, ribs, stomach, arms and legs. He was in shock. His left lower leg was particularly swollen to about twice its normal size. I suspected a broken fibula.' He insisted he be taken to St Vincent's Hospital for X-ray. The injured man was the first out of the station, at 4 a.m.

A crowd of forty or fifty had followed the wagons to Darlinghurst. There was intermittent chanting and cheering from them. The police made several arrests from this group which witnesses say were conspicuously brutal . . .

A loudmouth in the crowd sprang forward and beat his fists on the bonnet of a paddy wagon. A barrister has collected witnesses who say the man was grabbed by four or five police, dragged into the station garage by his hair and had his head, still held by the hair, beaten against the iron gates of the garage and the side mirror of the van. He was then dragged out of sight by the hair.

Inside the station the atmosphere remained tense. The arrested people were being processed with extreme slowness. During this, a witness alleged he saw a woman sitting in a dock, 'hit by a policeman very heavily on the left side of the face with a closed fist'.

About 4 a.m. the police decided to move the twenty-one women they held in one cell down to Central Police Station in the city. They were to load them into three paddy wagons. A policeman came to the gates of the station garage where the wagons were drawn up. He had in his hand an iron bar about 50–60 cm long.

A solicitor came up to the officer, introduced himself and asked, 'Why have you got that baton? Hasn't there been enough violence for one night? You have a baton. You are not wearing a number and neither are any of the police here.' There were by then about fifteen police around the trucks. The officer said, 'You want to watch yourself, or you'll be in, too.'

When the women drove off, the long process of bailing proceeded. It quickened when the new shift of police came on, and the last prisoners were out of Darlinghurst at 8.30 a.m.

The police had only to fingerprint and release the women at Central. They arrived about 4.30 a.m. None were released until 7 a.m. and the last was not out until 9.30 a.m. A barrister there commented, 'It seemed designed to delay their release as long as possible.'

The police had laid three charges of assault; one of malicious injury (police uniform); five of failure to observe a direction; nine of resisting arrest; four of offensive behaviour, ten of unseemly words; eighteen of hindering peace; and nineteen of unlawful procession.

Neville Wran, Premier and Minister for Police, came on Channel 10 news on Sunday evening. 'These sorts of things happen,' he said. 'I think it is unfortunate that a couple of police had to receive hospital attention, as well as some people in the parade or demonstration.

'I think what should be remembered is this, that those involved in the incident had a pretty good go and they had been given the freedom of the streets since early yesterday morning and I don't suppose that it's unexpected that the police have taken exception to a busy thoroughfare in Kings Cross being completely blocked off at midnight.'

*David Marr is a Sydney writer and broadcaster. His books include the biography and edited letters of Patrick White.*

28/12/84


Dear Jim Jenkins,

I received your letter of December 4. As a homosexual, I have
always detested the Gay Mardi Gras nonsense, particularly since
so many non-gay trendies seem to have jumped on the wagon. The
homosexual issue is an increasingly serious one. We shall be
persecuted more and more since AIDS came to stay. A lot of
screaming queens in Oxford Street will not help the cause for
which we shall have to fight. I can't give you any message beyond:
Come to your senses and call off the piffling Gay Mardi Gras.

Yours,

Patrick White

# How Can Anyone Feel Threatened by a Helium-filled Balloon?

## Lex Watson

IT WAS A balmy evening in October 1971 when CAMP (the Campaign Against Moral Persecution) staged Australia's first gay demonstration. The target was an anti-gay campaigner seeking Liberal party pre-selection for a safe Federal seat. About eighty people gathered outside the then NSW Liberal Party head office in Ash Street, just near Martin Place – eighty people, 150 helium-filled balloons with slogans on them, placards, some bemused uniformed police and, as we discovered, members of the NSW Police Special Branch – the political police. From memory, the demo was my idea.

What marked that demo, what we all noted, was the humour, the satire, the sense of fun that overlaid our collective sense of uncertainty about this new tactic. One of the balloons said 'Show me a prick and I'll bang.' I wrote at the time: 'After all, how can anyone feel threatened by a helium-filled balloon? And this is very important – fear is a strange animal and if they are frightened of us, we will never win them over, but if they are interested because it looks happy, then we can talk to people and tell them about ourselves, which is what it is about.' But it wasn't all plain sailing. The head of Special Branch, Freddie Longbottom, warned us in person that, in future, we would need a permit and we should contact him. And while it was definitely a gay and lesbian demonstration, a significant part of our crowd were straight, seasoned demonstrators from the Vietnam Moratoriums, the women's movement and civil liberties groups. The gay, let alone the lesbian, sub-cultures stayed away.

Later that evening I went for a drink at Capriccio's, to be attacked by gay – well we called ourselves camp then – acquaintances, who accused me of threatening their comfortable closets. 'You don't understand "camp",' I was told. A gay colleague was very hostile the following Monday at work. As one participant noted, 'Selling magazines the next day, and seeing the bar-queens, they were all uptight. They didn't want to be associated with anything like street demonstrations. It was as if they wanted to keep the whole thing closeted.'

Demos continued through the 1970s for various reasons, and they got bigger. One, in 1973, in Sydney, resulted in a number of arrests in Pitt Street and Martin Place. There seemed to be no particular reason for this, just some words that the police present had taken exception to. The police were also singularly unhelpful about which station those arrested were taken to, and what bail was involved. Relations between activists and the police were not good, nor were they with the gay sub-culture, the bar and disco queens, who disliked, or at best distrusted, politics.

That is how it was when the first Mardi Gras was held in 1978. Based on what was seen as a political date and event – US Stonewall and Gay Lib Day – and an imported date at that, its relevance was seen as limited by most.

I was not at the 1978 Mardi Gras, the only one I have missed. I was in Holland, taking part in Amsterdam's gay and lesbian celebrations. It was then a smallish but pleasant affair. Press clippings from home reached me in Munich and I read them with bemusement but no great surprise. When I got back to Sydney some months later, however, I was rather amazed.

It seemed that the gay sub-culture (and I say gay because lesbians were not much involved at that stage) had changed significantly. The march had started to become owned by a much wider constituency than the essentially political and activist group that had organised the first event. The barriers, the occasional hostility, that had separated the activists from the general sub-culture had started to break down. Mardi Gras had to an extent shown the salience of movement politics to a lot more people. In a curious way, it was perhaps similar to the way the New York Stonewall riots in 1969 had brought together a political movement and a gay sub-culture in the States.

Crucially, though perhaps coincidentally, two other elements of the first demonstration remained. One was the involvement of the police, which was to change over later years. The other, which has remained, was the fun. It was still politics through humour, whether openly satirical or simply 'out' and outrageous.

That year, 1978, also saw a proliferation of Oxford Street commercial activity and nightlife. Tropicana, now the Midnight Shift, opened as a gay club, as did the Palms nightclub (now gone). Most significantly for this story, Sydney got its first gay-owned, gay-run, gay-identified pub, the Beresford, followed shortly by the Flinders, and then the Oxford, Albury and so on to all there is today. Watering holes were, and remain, focal points for all sorts of communities, not least the gay one. A new sense of identification, of contact, had been established.

Along with that, the gay newspaper, The *Star*, was founded late in 1978 by Michael Glynn. It was not by any means the first gay paper or magazine in Australia. That credit goes to CAMP's *Camp Ink* which John Ware founded and edited in 1979. *Campaign* as a national monthly had started in 1975 and there were others of less note. But *The Star*, now the *Sydney Star Observer*, was the first free quasi-newspaper style publication in Australia. With it came a crucial term, and the thinking behind it: 'community'.

Important and central as Mardi Gras was, 1978 was thus a transition year for the Sydney gay scene in a broader and, in the long term, perhaps equally important sense. It was arguably the year when the gay scene established itself and defined itself on Oxford Street and Taylor Square. There had been drag shows (Birdcage, Capriccios), a disco (Patches) and wine bars (Ivy's and Enzo's – further up in Bondi and Paddington) going back to the early seventies. But the pubs were still elsewhere, and the Cross perhaps had been the hub of the scene until 1978.

The community-building that typified 1978 was to be crucial to sub-sequent events and campaigns. Without it, the law reform campaigns of 1981–1984 would not have had the impetus or impact that they had. Even more importantly the experience, expertise and involvement that we have brought to the HIV/AIDS campaigns since 1983 owe much to the processes and lessons of the first Mardi Gras.

There was another spin-off of the first Mardi Gras – one that was less positive at first. The *Sydney Morning Herald* and its then afternoon stable mate *The Sun* chose to publish the names, occupations and partial addresses of all those arrested, in both the Parade and subsequent protest marches. When the charges were thrown out, they did it all again, losing some their jobs. The papers' defence was that they always published details of people charged in demonstrations and, having done that, they were duty bound to report their innocence.

Melbourne Gay Liberation lodged a complaint with the Australian Press Council. At their request, I appeared for the complaint which was heard in Sydney. In keeping with its tame status the Press Council, as it has done in all subsequent complaints, found in favour of the media.

The episode is, however, indicative of the changes that have occurred over some 27 years. In that 1971 demo we were distinctly nervous about mass media coverage and being identified as homosexual – even though 'coming out' was definitely on the gay agenda and some of us, myself included, were already 'out'. In 1978, four years before NSW's anti-gay discrimination laws, the spectre of discrimination was very real. Being 'out' today certainly feels significantly different.

Despite such changes, working on the Parade each year, as I have done for the last eleven parades, is for me and many others a logical extension and continuation of the politics and activism with which we started the gay movement in Australia.

Gay Lib's slogan was 'the personal is political'. And this – albeit ironically for some – has characterised gay politics from that first demo through to Mardi Gras today. Camp humour, satire, a touch of vulgarity is really just openness about sex and sexuality, a sending up of stereotypes and, above all, fun! To me, Mardi Gras was, and remains, a thoroughly political event.

*Lex Watson lectures in Politics at Sydney University and has been a key figure in the politics of the gay liberation movement for nearly thirty years.*

The second Mardi Gras march, held on 30 June 1979, marked the climax of Gay Solidarity Week, which included a season of film and theatre. The parade went from Taylor Square down Oxford Street and back again, and between two and three thousand people attended. Largely incident-free, its success helped establish Mardi Gras as an annual event. The following year, people who had been nervous about taking part flocked to the 1980 Parade. The *Sydney Star Observer* enthusiastically supported the event, as did gay-owned and orientated businesses. The 1980 Parade took place on one of the coldest nights of the year, prompting its move to summer the following year. That year, 1981, was perhaps the first in which Mardi Gras began to assert its own unique identity. Key amongst those in making this happen was artist Peter Tully. As Mardi Gras' first workshop artist and later its first artistic director, Peter played an enormous role in Mardi Gras' evolution through the eighties, together with other Sydney artists, including Allan Booth. Their creative spirits have left an indelible mark on Mardi Gras today, and, indeed, Peter's spirit pervades this book.

# Allan and Peter, 1981

## William Yang

AFTER ALLAN DIED, Jeffrey, the executor of his will, placed his diaries in the Mitchell Library. Recently I went in to read them. First I had to get permission in writing from Jeffrey, because they were restricted, and rightly so, because they are sexually specific and uninhibited. I wanted to remember what the early eighties were like. Allan's diaries were not only an account of his life but an account of the times as well. Part pictorial scrapbook, he would put in everything that took his fancy, cuttings of hunky guys from glossy magazines, a theatre ticket, a postcard, a sample of fabric.

I found an image that shocked me, a photo I'd taken of him with his shirt off (he wasn't one of those people who was always showing off his chest, quite the reverse). He had decorated it with a border of tiny photos of penises and bums that he'd cut out of a porno magazine. It was powerful. I'd never seen anyone eroticise themselves in such a way.

That's what I mean when I say his diaries were uninhibited. I also discovered in those pages something I wanted to know but had forgotten: the route of the 1981 Mardi Gras. I knew we'd walked past Hoyts cinema, ended up in Hyde Park and that, at one time, we'd been in Oxford Street, but I couldn't work out where we'd gone. He'd drawn a map of the route. There was a sketch of his costume as well. Our history is often recorded in obscure places, if only you know where to look.

When I first met Allan, in 1980, I didn't think of him in a sexual way, which is usually how one views potential boyfriends. His hair was cut short at the sides with a curly mop on the top, a style way ahead of its time. He wore draw-string trousers, Adidas boots, a Walkman and a long-sleeved shirt of two fabrics which joined in a diagonal cut across his chest. He carried a Japanese fan over which he would peer seductively. I guess his sexuality didn't register on me because he was completely covered up. I was conditioned only to notice the swollen muscled bodies that were beginning to poke out of increasingly briefer singlets as the gym culture took hold of Sydney. However, his boyish charms did not entirely escape me because we arranged to meet up the next week to look at my photos.

My room was small so we sat on the bed and looked at the pictures which I had pasted in a book. He loved the images and the idea of a diary. He told me he kept one too. After we closed the book it was a small move to roll together and have sex. The photographs had been foreplay. He was twenty. I was thirty-seven.

We became once-a-week boyfriends. There were many others in his life. He saw someone practically every night. Jeffrey he saw several times a week. He said that the physical bond between them was not strong but Jeffrey was his best friend and confidante. He saw a hairdresser frequently and a lawyer and a theatre director occasionally. He spent nights drinking in bars, smoking dope with friends, visiting the sauna. He would make diagrams of the places he frequented around Darlinghurst.

All the gay people I had known before Allan had, for most parts of their life, been closeted in some way. Although we all came from completely different walks of life, there was always one common thread that made all our stories similar: we had all suffered from suppression. Ours was the love that dare not speak its name, ours had been a secret, shameful existence. Yet Allan had known none of this. He had come out when he was fifteen. His parents, though conservative, knew about his sexuality. And although they didn't know exactly what he did, they were supportive.

He lived in Ann Street, Surry Hills, in a house that had a long history of gay tenancy. There was something of a ghetto forming in the Darling-hurst and Surry Hills area, and it was possible to live a life where one could work at a gay establishment, live in a gay household, read gay newspapers and magazines, and socialise with gay people in gay restau-rants, gyms, bars and clubs. In short one could live one's life and see very little of the straight world. This situation had never existed before.

This emerging gay culture was based on the American model. We had already witnessed the Cycle Sluts in the seventies and they had left their legacy of drag with moustaches. The Village People came to Sydney in 1980 and the construction worker, the leather motorcyclist, the cowboy, the policeman and, to a lesser extent, the Indian were all popular looks.

Allan's particular favourite was the construction worker. He discov-ered, in a side street in Surry Hills, a caravan that was used as a locker room for some street workers. It was unlocked and he 'borrowed' a pair of greasy, skimpy shorts and a check flannel shirt that had the sleeves torn out. He was in such excitement over this find that he went back the next night and found his irresistible piece, a singlet that had been so worn away, it dangled like a lace curtain. The next night he discov-ered the caravan had a lock on it.

The outfits Allan made himself were arty creations. The most elabo-rate involved a chunky breast-plate which proved impractical on the dance floor. By this time, Allan had already met Peter Tully, and had bought some of Peter's pieces of jewellery. Allan made similar necklaces for himself. Peter didn't mind the imitation, they had become friends.

Peter Tully had worked as a sort of jewellery-maker in the seventies. He made necklaces out of Mintie wrappers, fruit shapes, glass and metal. Plastic was his favourite medium, and he would cut it into abstract shapes with a fretsaw. There were brooches made out of the KY tube symbol, and cutout maps of Australia with pink triangles. One of the great features of his work was a sense of humour. He gave me a plastic necklace representing three planks of a billboard. On one side it said 'Honeymoon Hotel, Colour TV, Double Bed' and on the reverse side it read 'Heartbreak Hotel, B&W TV, Single Bed'. Another of his pieces involved the plastic shapes of washing on a line. The underpants had a tiny urine stain and a pale smear of shit in the crack of the bum.

Peter had a style which was completely original and totally different from the conforming gay stereotypes of the day. He dressed in assem-blages of odd garments and collected objects, like a bandanna covered with hundreds of badges. He had always liked the costumes of the Pacific

Rim, especially the way New Guinea men would incorporate found objects into body decoration. So you might get a hurricane lamp decorated with feathers and string-binding made up into a head-dress.

In the late seventies, Peter went to America and he became inspired by Paradise Garage, a black nightclub in New York. There, people would dress up in outrageous outfits. The atmosphere was competitive and Peter pulled out all stops. 'You really had to come up with something, otherwise there was no point in doing it.' He developed elaborate body works which he called *Urban Tribalwear*. He came back to Australia in the early eighties and had a few exhibitions which sold very well. His work had become more ornate and larger in scale.

Peter had seen costume pageants around the world so when he came back to Sydney he had a vision for the Mardi Gras. Up until now the Mardi Gras had been political in nature, more like a demonstration. Peter had told me that it was very important I photograph the Mardi Gras in 1981, because he felt it was a defining one in gay history. I didn't know it at the time but he was lobbying to become the artistic co-ordinator of the parade which he envisaged as a fun event.

I have a photo of Allan at the Mardi Gras in 1981. He's carrying a satin pink triangle flag down Oxford Street. He's wearing a singlet with three myla stripes across it, a thick belt, unbuttoned jeans, a Walkman, and a necklace by Peter Tully. The piece is a choker of many coloured plastic tubes daubed with fluorescent paint. I can see from the photos that this is a subdued event, people are walking down Oxford Street as you would at a demonstration. It's certainly not a wild celebration, there is a sense of purpose. Generally people are not dressed up, although there is a nun, and a big rabbit, a cowboy, a few military outfits from the *Midnight Shift* float, and the boys from the Fitness Exchange are in Speedos. The *Lesbian Line* is the only lesbian float. The sense is of street clothes not costumes.

Only Peter Tully looks spectacular: he's wearing one of his urban tribalwear outfits. There's a vest of myla, hung with a long fringe of plastic strips, each tipped with a fluorescent piece of tape or a ring. He wears a construction worker's helmet with hornlike plastic extrusions, from which dangle tassels of beaded and synthetic strips. The pink plastic gloves that he wears are cut back and tipped with yellow nylon fur. This fake fur in fact trims much of the outfit, as do reflector pieces used by cyclists. He carries a fan with an exclamation mark and a fluoro 'Star Wars' sword.

It's difficult to describe those times now, because we've seen the

Mardi Gras on TV and it all seems so big and brilliant, but it wasn't always like that. There was a time when its brilliant colours were just beginning to shine. I pinpoint that moment when Allan and Peter Tully walked down Oxford Street: Tully, the visionary, the master, and Obi-Wan Kenobi character; Allan, the neophyte, youthful and fresh, and all of us marching. A community striding out to claim its identity, to be visible, to be what it is, and just to be. Walking down Oxford Street, proud.

Someone is actually wearing a T-shirt that says 'Gay and Proud'. And one's heart swells in this ordinary act of walking. Together. I could only think of Shakespeare, 'Oh Brave New World that has such creatures in it.'

*William Yang has celebrated Sydney life through words and images, through photographs, exhibitions, journalism and theatre pieces, for nearly thirty years. Allan Booth, a true original, died in 1990, aged 30. Peter Tully – artist, designer, jeweller and sculptor – died in 1992, aged 45.*

# Queen of Mardi Gras

## (Please don't curtsy)

## Ron Muncaster

I FIRST ENTERED the Parade in 1980. The first two I watched, thinking 'we can do better than this'. I had a group of friends and we started to make some costumes and floats, headed by Peter Tully who was my hero. I feel very proud that what was started by a handful of people, most of whom are now dead, has become such an international success.

It's amazing how Sydney has taken the Mardi Gras to its heart. I am always overwhelmed when I walk up Oxford Street and reach Taylor Square to hear the cheers from the crowd and see the smiling faces. That's the reward for all the worry and work I put into my costumes.

The work is easy, I love doing it; the worry is that something might break or go wrong. Like the day before the Parade when I had to put the Lucille Balls costume together. It took all day. Then, when my boyfriend Jacques put it on, he said, 'I cannot walk in this'. There wasn't enough room in the skirt for him to take proper steps and the balls along its hem kept hitting the ground. He spent that evening practising how to shuffle along.

The next day, we loaded a Combi van with cotton blossom and tied the Lucille Balls skirt to the roof. Halfway down William Street, the big skirt fell off the van and held all the traffic up. Not one car beeped their horn, for they saw the plight we were in, and some people got out of their cars to help. Jacques had to sit on top of the van and hold onto the skirt while we slowly drove to the Parade start.

On another occasion, I was parading down Flinders Street in my very high-heeled shoes, when I hit a pothole. A heel broke off, and I lurched forward. My polystyrene tits popped out and my hat almost fell off. I could not walk, so I asked a lady behind me to climb under my skirt and take my shoes off. She was under there for ages – we held up the whole parade. The street was empty in front of us when she finally came out with the shoes. Without them, I was six inches shorter, so I had to drag my skirt the rest of the way.

Back in 1982, I made a Carmen Miranda frock with a very long train. There were no barriers in those days, so the street was littered with beer cans. As I walked along I collected all these beer cans under my skirt and it made the most awful noise. Eventually, some kind gentleman lifted the skirt to let the beer cans out.

I never use ostrich feathers, they look so sad when they are wet, and I have seen some feathered tragedies arrive at the Showground.

I was very flattered to be named Queen of Mardi Gras, but I get embarrassed when people curtsy to me.

*Ron Muncaster has won the Best Costume prize at Mardi Gras nine times since its inception in 1984.*

By 1982 the Parade was being organised by the Mardi Gras Committee, chaired by Brian McGahen, and had a theme: On Our Way to Freedom. It also had a party. After the 1980 Parade, a small independent post-parade party had been held at Paddington Town Hall. It had proved a resounding success, and many would-be party-goers had been turned away at the door. Clearly, this was an event destined to grow. In 1982, 4000 people paid $5 each to attend the first official post-Parade Mardi Gras party. Barry Cecchini, owner and manager of the Beresford Hotel at the time, remembers.

# The First Party
## Barry Cecchini

THERE WAS SOMETHING RECKLESS about the times. We had a pub. It was exciting.

Such a trivial event. A gay pub. However, for us, it meant less restrictions in meeting people. No longer just private parties or beachfronts or parks. For those who worked nine to five, the pub seemed to be busy at a more appropriate time.

We had a pub. It was exciting.

There were the almost inevitable smirks within the straight business community.

'A gay pub?'

'Openly gay?'

'Owned by poofters?'

'Run by queens for queens?'

'That won't work!'

It did work. The pub was busy. The authorities were pleased – after all, the poofters were all in one place where they could be watched.

We were unfazed. There was beer. There was food. There was information. There was friendship. There were possible partners. There was, above all, an unstated but burgeoning awareness of solidarity.

We had a pub. We wanted to party.

The venue was the street between the Beresford and Flinders hotels. It was 1980 and our second New Year's Eve street party.

The street was packed with people. The pubs were full. There was some music. Much talk. Much laughter. A lot of alcohol.

'I need a piss!'

'You can't get to the toilets.'

'Do it here, in the street.'

'Nobody will see – we'll stand around you!'

'Did you see that drag in the silver lamé number, piss trickling down the skirt?'

No one cared. It was fun. We were with friends. No one cared, that is, other than the authorities.

Too many people!

Too much noise!

Too much mess!

Find somewhere else to party!

The Royal Agricultural Society. The Showgrounds.

A flower show – Yes!

A gymkhana – Yes!

A beer fest for our German friends – Okay!

But poofters partying – Too many unknowns!

Finally, the authorities relented and Cecchini was able to rent the cattle pavilion. In 1981, a New Year's Eve party was held.

The cattle pavilion had no sides. However, there was a show, fireworks, a bar, some lights, music and a dance floor. The pig pavilion stood adjacent with its myriad stalls. There were wonderful animal grunts. Just the place for the sexually adventurous.

The New Year's Eve party graduated to a real pavilion the following year. (Fully roofed, floored and walled.) The management of the Showgrounds were suitably impressed by our behaviour.

No fights.

No litter.

And, unlike other functions, no condoms in the grandstands! (If only we had known.)

The Senior Sergeant nodded non-committedly, and despite being grazed by an errant empty beer can, desperately aimed at the big dumpster, he smiled thinly.

The party was pumping.

Cecchini was excited in the knowledge that he had been cheeky enough to book the same venue, the same lighting, the same sound, for one month hence. The night of the Mardi Gras parade.

The Mardi Gras committee: Fortunate is the soul who can master the workings of a committee. The rumours, of course, abounded:

'Definitely no money to fund the parade!'

'Full of lefties.'

'All business interests wanting the parade to end in Oxford Street to fatten the cash registers!'

That Mardi Gras committee meeting was held in a room above a poker machine club in Surry Hills. Mardi Gras President Brian McGahen was chair. Cecchini presented the plan. He mistakenly thought it was simple!

Here is the liquor licence, the venue, the lights, the sound. The DJs are all booked and paid for.

The Mardi Gras committee was to organise the sale of tickets – perhaps repay the set-up costs – and hopefully make a quid!

Cecchini would ask all the other gay bars and clubs to participate.

The committee was at odds.

Cecchini was relieved to be dismissed, temporarily, to tackle a 20 cent poker machine.

Meanwhile whatever had to be discussed was discussed.

'We need government funding!'

'This is crass commercialism!'

'The parade must end in Oxford Street!'

'We don't want the government involved!'

The committee recalled Cecchini. (Damn – the 20-center was about to pay out.)

The verdict: You can run the party as long as all the other gay venues are involved. You have one week to enlist the support of all the other gay venues and report back to us.

Poor Brian McGahen. The strain was showing on his face.

There was a certain amount of hesitation. A cautious resistance perhaps tempered by the unknown effect of such an event on the cash registers.

Cecchini had coffee with Dawn O'Donnell.

To her enormous credit and with absolute conviction, she announced to the community that each of her venues, together with the *Beresford Hotel*, would run separate stalls at the party. Further, they would actively support this event.

Every venue in the city became involved.

The Parade played pied piper. We laughed. We costumed. And we partied. The first Mardi Gras party!

The committee seemed pleased. Brian McGahen was smiling.

For no apparent reason, Barry Cecchini placed the document that granted the temporary license on the floor in the centre of the dance area and danced upon it.

*Barry Cecchini owned and ran some of Sydney's first gay bars in Paddington and Newtown. He currently owns and runs pubs in Melbourne. Brian McGahen became the first openly gay member of the Sydney City Council and later an Independent in the NSW Legislative Assembly.*

Those gay and lesbian bars in Sydney not owned by Barry Cecchini were probably owned by Dawn O'Donnell, who recently celebrated her seventieth birthday in grand style.

# Dawn at the Awning
## Dawn O'Donnell

ON 24 JUNE 1978, I made one of my most memorable statements. As the marchers of the first Mardi Gras passed by, my comment to Aniek was, 'Well this lot is not going to amount to much.'

We were drinking and sitting out on the awning of the first Tool Shed at 42 Oxford Street (now Hungry Jacks) as they passed. Then the awning started to creak and move (much to the chagrin of the Chinese restaurant underneath).

I yelled, 'Shit! Grab the booze, Donnie.' (Donnie was my friend Mandy Smith.) And so we adjourned into the Tool Shed to finish watching the march.

Mardi Gras changed to a summer parade in 1981. The first was to be held on 24 February but it pissed down rain and was held on 24 March instead. From that, it has grown into the great success it is today.

To get a liquor licence for Mardi Gras in 1981 was not easy. All the then bar owners on Oxford Street joined together to get a function licence for Mardi Gras' first Party in 1982. Each of us set up our own bars alongside one another around the Government Pavilion hall, in line with our position on Oxford Street. It was a hoot of a night. The most money any bar made was $100. Our Patch's Bar (now DCM) took $40. Great fun was had by all.

My special highlight of the evening was 'The Cigarette Girl' (who *was* a girl). The Mardi Gras committee sent her out in the hall with a tray full of cigarettes, Tally Hos and bottles of Aroma's – heart pumpers for the elderly! (No ecstasy in those days!) On returning with an empty tray a little later, the committee asked her what her takings were. 'Oh!' she replied, 'I didn't know I had to sell them. I gave them away.'

The first ten years from 1978 to 1988 were about growth. Mardi Gras was mainly all volunteers, the Presidents and Board, the committee members, all giving their time and hearts to Mardi Gras. The second ten years, 1988 to 1998, were about making it the business organisation and huge success it has become today. It seems almost unbelievable to me that approximately 750 000 people watched the 1998 parade.

Who would have ever thought that a wake for Judy Garland in a little bar called Stonewall, in New York on 24 June 1969, would become the basis for Sydney to have the world's biggest gay parade? That year, 1969, was the opening of my first gay bar on Oxford Street, 'Capriccio's', better known as 'Caps'.

After the success of its first post-parade party at the Showgrounds in 1982, Mardi Gras held the first Sleaze Ball in October of the same year, at the Paddington Town Hall. The wonderfully named Sleaze Ball was conceived to be, and still is, a fund-raising event for the Parade, and that year Mardi Gras made its first profit: $4000. It is often forgotten that the Festival, Parade, and indeed the whole infrastructure of Mardi Gras, including a few key full and part-time positions, is supported entirely by the money made at the Mardi Gras Party and Sleaze Ball.

I think I have attended nearly all these parties. Venetta Fields was one of the first to entertain at these events and regrettably, I don't remember her. I do, however, remember weird and wonderful pieces of what I guess could be called 'performance art' by the Planet Sluts in the early 1980s – drag with moustaches and 5 o'clock shadows. Fabulous.

# Horses for Courses

## Peter Whittle

| | |
|---|---|
| **The Event:** | The 1983 Sleaze Ball |
| **The Place:** | Ford Pavilion and Surrounds |
| | Royal Agricultural Showgrounds (RAS) |
| **The Main Players:** | Tina, Blaire, Fushia and 'Mr Ed' |

THE USE OF 'ACQUIRED NAMES' in this story is in no way an attempt to hide the identities of the main players. In fact, they are intentionally used for wider recognition. A great friend once commented of Tina, 'You can take the girl out of Melbourne, but you can never take Melbourne out of the girl.' Blaire, depending on one's perspective, is the affair one has when one's not having an affair. Fushia will be portrayed as an innocent and naive 26-year-old. This is the only licence I have taken, together with the fictional naming of the horse, 'Mr Ed'.

Back to the Ball. It was the second Sleaze Ball and the first to be held at the Showgrounds. The very successful first party had well and truly outgrown the Paddington Town Hall. In the early days of Mardi Gras and Sleaze, once the main gate entry was gained, the entire Showgrounds were at one's disposal. This, coupled with almost a complete lack of internal security, made the truly agricultural areas extremely popular. The afore-mentioned Tina and Blaire had lured the innocent Fushia into one such area: The Stables.

The 3 a.m. liaison was heightened by the smell of fresh straw, mingled with raw animal aromas and then thrown sideways by Quaaludes. I leave the ensuing next ten minutes to your imagination until all tension was broken by an ear-piercing scream.

'I've been bitten! The fuckin' bitch bit me, I'm bleeding.' Tina had indeed been nipped by the occupant of the next stall. For whatever reason, 'Mr Ed' had desired a part of the action and Tina had been his chosen object. Once Blaire and Fushia had contained their laughter it was obvious that the bitten hand needed attention. However, these were the pre-medical days of the parties, before the First Aid tent, so Blaire suggested Tina get some alcohol for it.

The magic of the moment having been shattered, the threesome made their way back to the pavilion. Blaire and Fushia headed for the dance floor, while Tina marched to the bar for the prescribed alcohol. Sometime later, she reappeared.

'What's that in your hand?' enquired Blaire on seeing her.

'It's for my bite,' came the reply. Tina was drinking a bourbon and Coke. It wasn't exactly what we had in mind but no one had the heart to tell her. Tina, however, duly recovered, but Mr Ed was put down suffering from Equinia (horse pox) the next day.

*Peter Whittle was, for many years, part-owner and manager of the hugely successful Oxford Hotel.*

# Remo

## Boaz Stark

ROMANCE IS NOT HIGH on the agenda of Mardi Gras revellers. But I've had a romantic experience there, with a man called Remo.

The first time I saw him was at the 1982 Party. I was living in Melbourne at the time, and had come up specifically for the festivity. In those days, I'd go with a group of fifteen or so people, many of them straight. The women would spend all morning at the hairdresser, getting their tresses tortured into beehives that wouldn't budge in a maraca. We'd all follow the parade to the Showgrounds and purchase our tickets at the gates. That was an exciting moment because it signified the beginning of the 'magic'. Indeed, moving through the portal was, as is the case today, like entering another world: one where being gay is the norm, not only accepted but welcome. The importance of this is hard to understand unless you're gay or lesbian. Imagine being born with a big green horn sticking out of your head and having to go through life wearing a hat to cover it. Mardi Gras is an opportunity to throw the hat off for a night and dance with all the other green horns.

Only a couple of thousand people attended the first few Mardi Gras parties, and most of them would leave by 5 a.m. This allowed the few hundred die-hards who remained to embrace the dance floor with the luxury of space. The DJs would slow the music down and keep it funky for those last few hours. (Thank you Allkins, Racic, Morley et al. I remember!) My friends and I loved that time. Actually, we looked forward to it before we'd even arrived. And we stayed without the benefit of chemical assistance. Exuberant youth and innocence were more than enough.

It was after 5 a.m. when I saw Remo. He was sitting alone on the bleachers in the Hordern and once I'd noticed him from my spot on the dance floor, I couldn't help but continue to glance in his direction. He was almond-eyed and swarthy, in an Italian movie star kind of way, with a slender body. Remo noticed me back, and we enjoyed sexy eye-contact for a while. But we didn't make a move to talk to each other. He seemed content sitting alone and I was having too much fun boogying around with my friends. Besides, it was an unwritten rule that we would all leave together at the end of the night and go back to someone's apartment. Once there, we'd smoke joints and share our party adventures until, one by one, we'd drift off home or to a bedroom, or to sleep right there on whoever's couch. Recovery parties weren't even a twinkle in some clever publican's imagination yet.

I saw Remo again the following year – once again, after 5 a.m. when the masses had cleared. On this occasion he was also on the dance floor, shuffling around to the beat on his own. Inevitably we edged towards each other and even enjoyed some physical contact, occasionally stroking each other around the waist, delicious frottage. But we didn't talk. I go into a kind of trance when I'm dancing and the most I can manage is a dopey smile. Remo seemed to understand. He smiled back, and so it went on. When the party ended, we said goodbye with our eyes and I left with the beehives, eventually falling asleep on someone's lap, on someone's couch. I thought of him, though, as I lay there: his beauty.

The 1984 Mardi Gras party was to be the one when we finally spoke. Five a.m. crept up, and, as usual, pushed most of the party-goers out the front gates in its wake. On this occasion, I was on my way back from taking a piss when I came across him standing on the sidelines of the dance floor. I decided to loiter and we were soon talking.

Remo turned out to be an Italian immigrant, with *that* accent. Yum. Despite having been in Australia for a few years, his English wasn't all that fluent but it didn't matter to me, of course. He smiled a lot and made a dogged effort to get his meaning across, which I liked. Also, he remembered me from the parties as distinctly as I remembered him. Flattering, considering we'd never seen each other anywhere else. So, we flirted and chatted and danced together for the rest of the party. When it was over, we left holding hands, and caught a taxi to his apartment in Darling Point.

Remo lived alone, and his apartment had a grand view of the harbour. The first thing he did was lend me some sunglasses, since there is no glare more harsh than on the morning after a Mardi Gras party. And then we sat for a while on his balcony, having cups of tea. It was easier to understand him now, away from the lights and music. I discovered something not often contemplated in the short time leading up to inevitable sex with a new partner: that I genuinely *liked* him. He was clever and perceptive. And charming. When he learnt I was an aspiring writer, he asked me a grammatical question and I was embarrassed because I didn't know the answer to it. Remo simply rose and went into the apartment, returning moments later with an old English grammar book, the kind with a cloth-bound cover.

I assumed he was going to look the answer up himself, but instead he presented the book to me as a gift. He explained that it was too advanced for him, perhaps I would benefit from it. I was touched. Eventually, of course, we ended up in the bedroom and had a fun, dirty ol' time. We stayed there all day, drifting in and out of sex, intimacy and sleep, until I had to leave in the early evening. A few hours later, I was on a plane homeward bound for Melbourne, being teased by my friends about the dreamy look in my eyes.

Remo and I had exchanged phone numbers, but we both neglected to use them. Perhaps it was because we lived in different cities. I like to believe it was due to an unconscious desire to leave a perfect, self-contained interlude alone. I didn't see Remo at the next Mardi Gras party, although I looked for him; in fact, I never saw him again. Several years ago, however, I came across his photo in the obituaries of the *Sydney Star Observer*. AIDS related. I can't tell you how sad it made me feel. I still have the book though. It taught me a lot about grammar. I'm very attached to it.

*Boaz Stark is a television and (aspiring) film writer.*

# Mardi Gras Myth 1

*I had rarely ever gone home with anyone from the Party. You could do that anytime if it was truly a priority. It had always been much more fun to gather with a bunch of friends and swap stories from the night before, especially if you'd failed to find them all night.*

*But this guy was, well frankly, irresistible – he seemed sweet and charming, bright and original, and very insistent. But we couldn't go to his place. So just before the Party's end, when taxis were plentiful, we jumped in and headed home to my place. We held hands on the way – uninhibited too, I thought. Good.*

*The niceties of entertaining were irrelevant – we were shedding clothes, well the little we had on, en route to the bedroom. His eyes were passionate, his embraces strong.*

*Suddenly he spoke. 'Have you got a sock?'*

*'Sure,' I said, my mind racing as I pulled open the dressing-table drawer. 'What kind of sock?' I thought, not daring to voice the question aloud. I didn't want to appear sexually uptight or inexperienced. 'Does he want a thin silk sock or a chunky gym sock? A brightly coloured sock or something more tasteful and sober? A dirty or clean sock?'*

*He waited patiently as I rummaged in the drawer, erection pressing hard against the handle. And then I thought, 'Why only one sock? What have I got here? Is this some strange fetish and this guy perhaps a bit weird, maybe a bit sick?' I began to hope my friends would be home soon.*

*'Come on, man, let's get going,' he said, adorably inviting from the bed.*

*I settled for a thick, chunky, white sock from a pair I'd got in the States. It would look good against his tanned, developed calf muscle – and handed it to him.*

*'No, no, bimbo,' he laughed. 'A condom, not a sock. We need a condom.'*

*And I laughed too. The necessary drawer was beside the bed.*

# Thirteen Hours on Deck

## Stephen Allkins

IT WAS 1983 and I had been asked to DJ at what was to be the second Sleaze Ball. I had been DJing around town for a few years but this was my first 'dance party' and no one was really sure what to expect.

I was the only DJ and was scheduled to play from midnight to 8–9 a.m. I planned to start off with a fairly slow electronic disco version of Ravel's 'Bolero', and work the beat up as the party grew. Back then, it was common to start off pretty slow and also to slow down later in the night as things got sexier and there was more room to dance. I could play songs like 'Sexual Healing' by Marvin Gaye or 'Juicy Fruit' and it would still be considered dance music.

I started playing 'Bolero' which had a reasonable tempo but is really something you play when no one's there. Then they opened the doors and hundreds of people started pouring in. I was taken aback. Suddenly the hall was filling with people. They were mainly gay men and a smattering of the cool, inner-city, chic fashion crowd, and they were all dancing.

There was no real precedence for this. It was new territory. In any case, it just blew me away. It wasn't like what I had come to expect in a club where punters waited around drinking for a while before they started dancing. Now they were all mixed in together, from all over the place. Clones, leather queens and pretty boys. No longer in the familiar comfort of their favourite club where they were known and they knew what to expect, here they were surrounded by thousands of strangers doing something new.

A few minutes into the track I realised I was going to have to throw on something more up. From then on, the night just rocked and I guess it's been rocking ever since. From midnight to nine in the morning, it was magic.

There were five shows featuring drags like Leggs Galore, Miss 3D, Cindy Pastel and the Planet Sluts. They really put their heart and souls into those shows. We had no idea what to expect really and the shows just seemed to grow organically out of the night. There was no pro- or anti-drag, people applauded or just kept dancing. Things were much more fluid.

I think that in a way these party-goers were more pioneering than they are now. I think they were, on the whole, older and more confident of who they were. They had already struck out and embraced the gay scene. It was really still an underground thing, fuelled to a large degree by disco music and sex. In a way, disco and gaydom were, to a lot of us, inseparable.

Fifteen years later, I was DJing in The Dome at the 1997 Sleaze Ball. Looking around the party earlier, I'd noticed how much things had changed and how it really wasn't me. Back in Dome I was more at home. I felt that I knew the audience and they knew me. We knew what to expect. There were people on that dance floor who'd been there in 1983. Unlike the rest of the party I felt I was in the company of adults. A lot of people now are just there for one night of the year. They just take for granted their right to party and forget that a lot of people have had to fight for that right. The early 1980s was a golden age – so many things really began there.

*Stephen Allkins had been DJing for twenty years and has witnessed all the trends. He continues to be a driving force on the scene, with over 18 Sleaze Balls and Mardi Gras to his credit.*

# Since Adam Was a Boy

## Kerrin Cahill

WHEN I THINK ABOUT Mardi Gras over the last fifteen years or so that I've been involved, I can't help but also think of my son, Adam.

Adam was born in March 1983. I had become friendly with a group of gay men, many of whom were performers, artists and DJs. Through these men I became involved in the party scene, including Sleaze Ball and Mardi Gras. One of the men was to become Adam's father.

So it was that I found myself standing on the balcony of the Exchange Hotel with Dawn O'Donnell watching Cindy Pastel – Adam's father, Ritchie Finger – and the other members of the drag troupe, 'Mixed Company', performing songs like 'Hot in the City' by Billy Idol while dangling from a rope attached to the roof.

'I hope we're bloody insured for this,' muttered Dawn.

It was 1983 and I was well and truly pregnant. After the parade I went home and Ritchie went off to perform at the Mardi Gras party at the Showgrounds.

I had also been pregnant six months earlier at Sleaze Ball. Not that I'd participated that much. I was happy to sit in the dressing room, teasing wigs and chatting to Theresa Green. My ex-flatmate, Stephen Allkins, was DJing and I could look over the balcony to see Cindy Pastel and the fabulous Leggs Galore do a couple of shows.

By 1984, Adam was eleven months old and I nursed him on my lap as we drove along Oxford Street in the cabin of a truck carrying a giant Martini glass containing his father. Adam was not impressed by the fireworks at the conclusion of the parade and after a few tears was delivered to his babysitter while mum and dad went to The Party.

This was to become the pattern of Mardi Gras for years to come. Ritchie became a fixture at parties and appeared at Festival events, Fair days, etc. No event seemed complete without an appearance from Pastel. Often the entire Finger family went along.

Adam attended the Fair days and loved to toss the ball about with the boys from POOFTA (Proud Openly Out Football Touch Association). He'd get sulky when he was told he was too little to play.

Adam also loved to attend rehearsals of the Mardi Gras party shows. In fact, he was introduced to many of my performing friends at the age of three months during rehearsals for Sleaze Ball. Years later he would sneak into the darkened hall on the afternoon of the party to watch the final dress rehearsals.

He even managed to *attend* a party in 1988. It was called 'Birthday Too' and was the second half of a party at the Hordern which ran over twenty-four hours. At around midday, the three of us slipped in, flashing our security passes as we went. Adam found the music a bit loud at first but soon relaxed and even had a little dance. After a couple of surreal hours we tottered home. Adam clutched a balloon and a piece of polystyrene licorice allsort that had been part of the fabulous Brian Thomson set. We looked like a typical family leaving the Easter Show. Well almost!

Adam would also sometimes pop down to the nearby Mardi Gras workshop to ride on Ron Smith's motorbike or to give Doris Fish a hand with something. Doris was a celebrated drag performance artist, with a huge following in the USA as well as Australia. Doris once made Adam a cute little Astro Boy mask. Mardi Gras was part of our lives. It was the norm.

One of Adam's favourite uncles was Allan Booth, who (like Doris) we have since lost to AIDS. Allan designed a few Mardi Gras posters and many parties. He was great with kids, being like a big kid himself. One year, he carried Adam on his shoulders in the Parade. Adam loved watching people he knew go by and remembers that Parade as his favourite. Later we would watch the Parade, and often dad, sashay past from the safety of a first floor window.

Since the death of people Adam knew, like Allan, Doris Fish and Leggs Galore (Cliff), I think Adam is a little saddened around Mardi Gras time and no longer attends. He says he prefers to remember them how they were. In any case, he has become more interested in skateboards, video games and girls.

As I've watched Adam grow up, I've also watched Mardi Gras grow and change: from vulnerable infant to stumbling toddler, and then a confident and energetic teenager. Adam, like Mardi Gras, has grown with me and also away from me, striking out and discovering new things, new interests, new people. Sometimes I feel a little left behind and sometimes a little angry, but I still love them both dearly.

Recently, some friends of Adam's were asking each other if they were going to Mardi Gras. Adam carefully explained that when you asked if you were going to Mardi Gras, you had to distinguish between Parade or Party.

One year the theme for Mardi Gras was 'We are Family', and as a family we were privileged to appear on stage outside the Museum of Contemporary Art to the strains of 'We are Family', along with five or six other families.

As we stood there holding hands, looking out over the sea of clapping and cheering people, watching fireworks light up the harbour, I thought I was really part of something fabulous. Part of a Mardi Gras family.

*Kerrin Cahill manages Videodrama in Oxford Street. Adam is now in high school.*

By 1983, the Mardi Gras Parade was attracting more than forty floats and about 20 000 spectators. Artists such as Doris Fish, Cindy Pastel (aka Ritchie Finger) and David McDiarmid shared Peter Tully's vision of what the Parade could be, and brought their own creativity, humour and vision to the event. David, who was to succeed Peter Tully as Mardi Gras' Artistic Director, created some of Mardi Gras' most wonderful floats, costumes and posters in the eighties.

# The Big Wig

## Cindy Pastel

MY FAVOURITE MARDI GRAS was the year they asked me to be the centrepiece thing of David McDiarmid's *Big Wig* float. That was one of the few years it rained, the year we, as a community, carried on regardless. Like true blue Aussies, we held our heads higher than any raindrop.

To this day I'm not sure what the significance was for me of being plonked in the middle of a 15-foot wig! Maybe I was meant to be the bow in this magnificent hairpiece, but I felt like a drenched crab with demented attitude. Seven other crabs twirled beneath my feet. I'd had a ten-foot mirror wheeled to me on request, and a huge can of pink hairspray. And, yeah, I really needed it. Thank Christ for indelible makeup! Not a skerrick of my budgie-blue eye-shadow budged.

At the end of the Parade, a huge generator which had been thrust between my legs and which powered a giant hidden blowdryer proved to be the saviour of the night. My soggy paper-and-plastic flowers, my lurex Lycra and my tortured white daisy-fied beehive sprang back to life. I had a word to the Lord above, and was told that the rain was really Her tears at not being able to come down and join the party. Suddenly I realised what She was saying: I didn't have a ladder to help me off the float either!

I pulled myself off my blowdryer, threw my legs onto a big, wet brick wall, and shuffled across it into David McDiarmid's arms. We thanked each other and as I tottered off to my next Mardi Gras gig – compering the costume parade with Fanny and Iggy – I reflected on the first time I had met David.

I was eighteen and at a Peter Tully exhibition in Melbourne's Paraphernalia Galleries. David and I didn't say much to each other. It didn't seem like we had much in common although we both admired what the other was doing, and our relationship throughout the many years that followed had never changed. I think we were both a little in awe of each other, without either of us ever knowing, until this curious situation in which we came together and produced and achieved one of the campest, girliest, most moving Pastel experiences ever made.

*Cindy Pastel (aka Ritchie Finger) starred as Cobweb in the Sydney Theatre Company's* A Midsummer Night's Dream *in 1989. Playing a fairy in drag seemed a fitting tribute to Cindy's brilliant* career – *one that continues to make its mark.*

# Mardi Gras' First Casualty

## Tony Cooper

THE 1983 MARDI GRAS PARTY is the only one I've ever missed. Certainly, this was not due to any lack of planning or determination on my part but rather to a mishap of circumstance that left me with a very dubious honour.

Back then, I was a multi-talented member of the Boomerang Social Club – famous for running the best gigs in (and out of) town. Not only could I whip up a pretty mean party frock and hold down a dance routine, I could also handle a hammer and saw. Thus I was duly given the task of co-ordinating that year's Parade float.

No expense was spared to create a grand and magnificent spectacle to showcase the Boomerang style. It was a splendiferous, gargantuan replica of the Sydney Harbour Bridge, dazzling in red and silver, and complete with lighting, sound, special effects and, of course, lots of costumed and gyrating 'happy little Boomerangs'. Definitely a Parade highlight, it was also remarkable in that the entire structure (10m × 2m × 4m) was constructed in my first-floor living room.

As due reward for my efforts, I was given (or maybe I took) the No. 1 prime position on top of one of the front two pylons. My cohort opposite was a well-known Sydney drag identity – the Dot & Fanny 'barrel girl', Severe Inflation.

From our poll positions 4 metres up, the infectious euphoria of the crowd became more and more overwhelming. As the sight of the 20 000 strong mass at Taylor Square loomed before us, it was more than an over-happy little Boomerang could bear. To help us cope, Severe, in her infinite wisdom, whipped out the smelling salts. (Perhaps, in hindsight, not so wise.) As our own state of headiness grew to become one with the crowd, an equally mindless punter lurched from the barriers across our path. A split-second reaction by our driver most assuredly saved him from grievous harm as I simultaneously executed an impromptu backward freefall to hit the bitumen, spreadeagled, at the feet of a very shocked Tony Vickery, right on The Oxford corner.

Suffering from a little shock myself, my first thought was 'how embarrassing – in front of all these people'. I bounded back up onto the truck and into position, regaining my composure, and, in true performer style, went on with the show. Only then did the realisation of my growing degrees of pain strike me. But I was a Boomerang and this was a show we'd all worked long and hard for. Never disappoint your audience – and I did not!

It was not until we turned onto the verdant turf at Moore Park for the final victory lap that a sudden pang told me to 'get down quick or suffer a repeat performance'. Painfully scaling back down from my perch, I emerged onto the tray of the truck and, as a crescendo of fireworks burst above, I looked up at Cynthia Randall, who was nearest and croaked, 'I think I'm going to . . . faint!'

Within minutes I was being stirred back to life by flashing red lights and the wailing of an ambulance siren as it wove amongst the floats and revellers to come to my aid. I was whisked away, covered over with Cynthia's three-quarter length mink, and taken to spend my party night at St Vincent's emergency units. Their first ever overnight Mardi Gras guest.

*Tony Cooper in the late nineties is still holding down a hammer and saw, and handling a pretty mean party frock.*

Dear Richard,

The following little story/monologue is based on Brian Ross — costume-maker extraordinaire and Mardi Gras workshop artist when I worked there. He won best costume several times and is well known for these creations and his Sleaze Ball poster and other work. One of his costumes is in the Powerhouse, another was used in *Priscilla: Queen of the Desert*.

# Queen of the Road

## Gillian Minervini

BRIAN PACKS HIS BAG. There isn't much to take really. Track pants, T-shirts, cap. Plenty of room left in the bag. Plenty of him left behind. He's calm, no complaints, has hardly told a soul.

'I'll only be gone a week.'

Brian spends most of his life making things. Things that shine with pride. Nothing practical . . . much more important than that.

A queer Dr Frankenstein. Pouring life into junk. The little bits that fit together. Brushed and sanded. Painted and mylared. Intricate detail.

Hours and months go by. The gift of life takes time. He peers over his little glasses. The hands of a surgeon. He smiles. Hardly says a word.

Brian makes things . . . not costumes but creations. Things he climbs into, wraps up in, straps on. They don't hide him, they extend him. They are part of him.

*Insight. Watch closely.*

Lining the Parade route . . . we wait. Trucks with noise, flocks of drags, marching bunnies . . . Brian.

We only have seconds but are fans in a heartbeat. A burst of flamboyance . . . glaring gaiety . . . quality camp. He is different. Charms thousands with a passing glance. Queen of the road.

Year after year. Always bent. Part of him.

A sea creature of dynamic proportions. Like a crab from Mars. Shining red. Underwater holograms. Grabbing the crowd with its claws . . . brilliance with a bite.

A moving chandelier . . . gliding down the road. Lighting up around him. Shining in our eyes . . . radiating hope.

A giant bird with huge shiny white wings. A mylar angel, complete with queen-sized beak. Spanning the width of the street. Flying high above the crowds.

Part of him. He breathes life into them. Injects them with his spirit. Nurtures and loves them like children so they shine on their own. But he is their heart.

*Insight. Watch closely.*

Now his creations sit in his little flat. As empty as his fridge. Not lonely but anxious. Anxious for his return.

The hospice staff don't recognise him but they smile at his photos. I remember you. A snapshot . . . the memory is instant. Brian smiles. They try and fix the maker.

'He'll be out soon,' they say.

He needs a maker of his own.

His friends agonise. They put food in his fridge. Brian is coming home.

A bed in the loungeroom. Tubes and pills everywhere. Glue and fake fur everywhere. Brian is home. Sitting up in bed . . . giving birth to another creation.

Hours and weeks go by. The gift of life takes time. But Brian can't make that. His new child grows stronger as he gets weaker. His body closes down . . . his spirit opens up.

Slowly piecing together the new creation. Inch by inch. He slips away.

His friends agonise.

New homes are found for his creations . . . they continue his reign. Carrying his soul . . . lit from inside. Part of him.

And still, we watch as the Parade goes by.

Lining the street . . . they wait . . . the ones that don't know. Doesn't seem as good this year. Can't say why.

Year after year. New faces come to bathe in the glow of our pride. Not knowing what's missing.

And still, we watch as the Parade goes by.

There is a light that shines.

*Insight. Watch closely.*

*Gillian Minervini is a writer, director and performer. She has been a Director of the Mardi Gras Festival, which began officially in 1985, and of its Film Festival.*

# Marching for Our Lives

## Bill Whittaker

FROM THE VERY BEGINNING of Mardi Gras in 1978 to the present day, HIV has been there with us. Silently at first in those early years before AIDS had a name, and then for more than a decade as one of the most defining influences on the Mardi Gras Parade and Festival itself.

For many gays and lesbians, Mardi Gras and HIV are inextricably linked. It is impossible to remember past Mardi Gras Parades and Festivals without also remembering the faces of friends and lovers now gone. But Mardi Gras has also served as a beacon for us to rally to. Even in the darkest years of the AIDS epidemic, we believed if we could keep Mardi Gras going, we could survive anything. If we could keep on celebrating our sexuality and our community, even as we cared for friends dying around us, anything was possible.

Someone who epitomised that spirit was Bobby Goldsmith, one of the first openly gay men to be diagnosed with AIDS in Australia. I first met Bobby in 1981, on the dancefloor of the Midnight Shift. He was part of a remarkable tribe of boys and girls I partied with at the time. Bobby fought a long battle against AIDS, but even as his health worsened, his smile and love of a good time never diminished. My lasting memory of him is at the 1984 Mardi Gras Party – only a short time before he died. He was obviously very sick, but the smile was still there, as was his determination to be at Mardi Gras celebrating with his community one last time. Since then, many, many others have followed his example – most of us would know people who just wanted to live until one more Mardi Gras, it was so important in their lives. And they did, and still do.

However, if Mardi Gras was a beacon for gays and lesbians during the darkest years of the AIDS epidemic, it was also a beacon for our enemies. Quite correctly, homophobes like Reverend Fred Nile – leader of the Christian organisation the Festival of Light, and independent member of the NSW legislature – saw that if they could use the HIV epidemic to put a stop to Mardi Gras, this would deliver a devastating blow to the gay and lesbian community from which we might not recover (or so they hoped). Between 1984 and 1986, at the height of AIDS hysteria in Australia, there were calls for Mardi Gras to be stopped because our enemies said holding the event would spread HIV. There were even calls for gay men to be quarantined.

Many people are not aware that the 1985 Mardi Gras came very, very close to being cancelled. The pressure for cancellation was enormous. It was only the determination of a small band of people that prevented that from happening. If Mardi Gras had been cancelled, I doubt we would still have the event. And most certainly our community would have suffered a devastating blow to morale which would have set us back for decades.

However, Mardi Gras not only went ahead in 1985 and 1986, they were bigger and better than ever. Even at the height of the AIDS hysteria of the time, the Parade and Festival took a quantum leap in quality, diversity, and numbers of people participating. This was due to remarkable people like Brian McGahen, long-time Mardi Gras President and our first openly gay city councillor, and to Peter Tully, whose magic and vision made the Mardi Gras Parade what it is today. Quiet achievers like Parade Co-ordinator Brian Hobday struggled against huge organisational barriers put up by hostile police and other bureaucracies, just to have the Parade go ahead. Each of these Mardi Gras heroes, and too many others as well, was eventually to die of AIDS. But to use a very appropriate cliché, their legacy lives on as we march up Oxford Street each Mardi Gras night, renewing our commitment to our community and friends, our solidarity and self-esteem.

The Mardi Gras events themselves have also played a key role in saving many lives from HIV/AIDS. Countless thousands of people are reached by the HIV prevention messages that are such a fundamental part of the Parade and Festival. We've done this in many ways – from camp images of dancing skeletons, through to the angry voices of ACT UP marchers urging us to remember that Silence = Death. We also remember our friends lost to HIV with flares, with silence, and by dancing even harder up Oxford Street.

It's recognised that Mardi Gras has provided a model for other community organisations, and an invaluable training ground for lots of gays and lesbians (including myself). In the mid eighties Mardi Gras became the first large Australian gay and lesbian organisation to be truly professionally structured and run. I don't mean this in a bureaucratic sense, but in the best traditions of excellence and accountability. The relentless pressure during the early years of the AIDS epidemic forced those involved in Mardi Gras to quickly learn new skills – from doing media and negotiating with governments and politicians to managing money and staff. People and the skills they learned often transferred to other fledgling gay and lesbian – and AIDS – organisations. In very many ways, the challenges of the AIDS epidemic transformed the way we organised ourselves as gays and lesbians. It is ironic that a terrible epidemic has actually produced many benefits for our community. But at a price that is all too high. Personally, I'd give away all those achievements just to have my friends with me again at Mardi Gras.

*Bill Whittaker is a gay activist, AIDS activist and sometime party boy.*

# 1985

## Jim Jenkins

THIS ISN'T A FUNNY STORY. It inflames anger. But the end result put a lot of smiles on faces in 1985, when Mardi Gras brought one of the giants of the Fourth Estate to its knees, forcing it to publish the biggest, most humiliating retraction in Australian newspaper history. Often forgotten, it was a victory that began to turn the anti-gay tide in the media.

But before the victory, the painful historical context. 1985 was the year that the media-driven AIDS hysteria reached its peak, fuelled by that ubiquitous duo: ignorance and prejudice. AIDS-related headlines engendering fear and hate had been tearing at the heart of our community for several years. This culminated in 1985 in a cacophony of calls for the cancellation of Mardi Gras.

Those calls weren't just from the usual suspects, such as Fred Nile, who warned of a Mardi Gras-induced AIDS 'infestation'. Professor David Penington, then chief of the federal government's peak AIDS advisory body, made a plea in the national media on February 1 for 'the Sydney gay community to call off the orgy that accompanies the annual Gay Mardi Gras'.

'If the gays don't heed this warning,' he railed, 'then it's inevitable they will be rushing down the pathway to self-destruction in three weeks. There's nothing more certain than that the three-day orgy accompanying the Mardi Gras will spread AIDS right through homosexual groups throughout Australia.'

Penington's comments helped fuel the bigotry that triggered a series of crises for Mardi Gras, among them death threats against its organisers, hate mail, calls for the cancellation of individual events (such as the swimming carnival, which would spread AIDS through the water to 'innocent victims'), threats of violence against the Parade, police obstruction and intransigence, and concerted verbal attacks by the Church and political figures.

Perhaps the most serious threat was the Royal Agricultural Society's (RAS) eleventh-hour cancellation of the party booking on the Showgrounds, which would have bankrupted Mardi Gras. So serious was this that Mardi Gras committee members were advised to move their assets into friends' names. The RAS reinstated the booking only after much lobbying and the threat of legal action in the Supreme Court and Anti-Discrimination Board. In discussions with Mardi Gras director Damian Furlong, the RAS cited Penington's remarks and public health concerns among its grounds for cancellation.

The hysteria and pressure on Mardi Gras was such that at least two senior members of the organising committee began to seriously consider cancellation – triggering a deluge of opposition from their colleagues, who prevailed and pulled off the most heroic Mardi Gras in history (apart, perhaps, from the riot-torn first).

But having spectacularly leapt all hurdles, we woke the following Monday to a *Sydney Morning Herald* report on the Parade that was a litany of actionable lies, prejudice and bigotry. The journalist responsible, Jacky Archer, obviously hadn't even been present at Mardi Gras, though she wrote as if an eyewitness. Her report was published under the heading 'AIDS victims watch as the Parade passes by' and her prejudice was blatant.

'The AIDS victims . . . were "paranoid" about attention. They wanted nothing to do with the press . . . The director of the Mardi Gras, Mr Damian Furlong, who organised the street-view room, spoke for them. "They feel a lot like freaks," he said. "We have here a roomful of Elephant Men." Mr Furlong said the motel had "no idea" of its guests. "We didn't want to create more hysteria," he said.'

That day Furlong and I composed a blistering letter to the editor-in-chief of the *Herald*, Chris Anderson, pointing out the many inaccuracies, the cooked-up quotes, the anti-gay tone of the article, and the fact that Archer had never been admitted to the viewing room and had possibly not even attended the Parade. The article breached virtually all journalistic ethics. We delivered the letter, which included a threat of legal action, in person, that evening.

That Friday, 5 March, page two of the *Herald* carried a retraction almost twice as long as the original story. The apology noted:

'. . . The Herald now believes that very little of [its previous article] was true . . . To protect the people with AIDS from what was assumed would be demeaning publicity, Mr Furlong declined to allow the *Herald*'s reporter, or any other, to visit the [viewing] room. As a result, the reporter did not see inside the room and did not speak to anyone there . . .

'Further difficulties arose from some of the quotations used in the report, Mr Furlong was quoted as saying that people with AIDS "feel a lot like freaks" and that "we have here a roomful of Elephant Men". He denies ever having said such things; in particular, he strenuously denies having used the term "Elephant Men".

'The editor-in-chief of the *Herald*, Mr C J Anderson, said: "The *Herald* has decided to set out these facts because it is such an exceptional case. Reporting of this kind has no place in our newspaper . . . Obviously we regret any damage done to the reputations of Mr Furlong and the Mardi Gras committee. In this case our normal standards lapsed. We have taken steps to ensure that such lapses do not recur".'

The retraction was an important victory for a community that for too long had had to put up with fabrication, prejudice and vilification. It sent a strong message to all media – 'Don't fuck with Mardi Gras' – a message which, to a certain extent, has been heeded, resulting in more careful and fairer coverage of Mardi Gras and the gay and lesbian communities to this day.

The victory against the *Herald* was a watershed, as was the parade and the party's survival against its enemies. Had our barricades against the hysteria fallen that year, so too, most likely, would have Mardi Gras, struck dead permanently by the forces of homophobia.

It was a big night at the *Midnight Shift* that Friday, 5 March 1985.

*Jim Jenkins was elected to the Mardi Gras Board in 1984 and 1985 and became the organisation's first full-time employee in 1986. He produced* The Guide *from 1985–92.*

# Snipers

## Corby Beard

I REMEMBER ONCE reading how everybody remembers their first Mardi Gras. You know, like the moon landing or your first tongue kiss. Well, I don't remember my first Mardi Gras at all really. I do remember the kiss though. (Hello Lisa Bridges, wherever you are!) Sure, I remember incredible people like Allan Booth and DJ Stephen Allkins back in the eighties. I also remember a beautiful American model in drag showing Joh Bailey and me his passport photo in the Stables at the Showgrounds to prove to us he really was cute.

I remember bits and pieces. But what I remember most is the urge. The overwhelming urge just to be there. No matter where I was at the time. Buses from Melbourne. Trains from Byron Bay. Epic, crowded car journeys in the pouring rain. Some unspoken compulsion drove me on, every year, like a pilgrim on the road to Mecca. Party after party. Parade after Parade.

In 1985, I attended a glamorous dinner party at Bronte House, hosted by a wildly eccentric and extravagant English queen who was in Sydney for the summer. My lover and I were staying in the guest wing and were lapping up the beauty of the house and a magical summer. As the dinner progressed it became obvious, to my horror, that, à la Patrick White, it had been decided that we would not be attending the garish and vulgar Parade. Displays of this ilk apparently were uncalled for, especially at the height of the 'AIDS BABIES' headline crisis. There was much talk of blood-letting by skinheads and snipers at the parade, but the only sniping I felt was the bitching amongst the guests fearful of exposure. It was felt that we would be much better served to just sit tight, shut up, and wait for a cure and/or forgiveness.

After some protest from the host, I extricated myself from the Georgian furniture and, along with my somewhat reluctant partner, headed tipsily in the direction of Oxford Street. We had missed most of the Parade and I hated myself for letting this happen, but we stumbled onto Oxford Street, part of an amorphous crowd of locals, odd bods, gays and hippies. There wasn't a sniper in sight. Nor were there any barricades.

There were also few lights and not much music. But what there was was a lot of defiance. There was something in that joyful triumph that would change my life forever. Something that spoke to my own fear of who I was and of the HIV virus. Something about courage.

I was not infected by the dreaded virus, but I was infected by Mardi Gras. I was hooked. I was god-damned Mardi Gras positive and proud of it!

*Corby Beard is a Mardi Gras Hall of Famer for services rendered, including Mardi Gras Board Member, Festival Co-ordinator, Entertainment Co-ordinator, and Drag Bar compere. His somersaults while performing Blondie's 'I Want that Man' are legendary.*

# WHAAAM!

## Mark Stryker Meyer

I'D SPENT DAYS READYING MY OUTFIT – Y-fronts, cap, paper jewellery, socks and boots – with an entire rainbow of illuminous acrylic paints. I put my heart and soul, and some great brush strokes, into creating a look that was boyish, comfortable, arty and sexy. The cock-ring made my dick look bigger, and I'd even been to the gym four months prior, so my skinny body would look toned, brown and ready for . . . *anything*! I felt like dancing and kissing people; I think I had a lazy mongrel constantly that whole last week. I was filled with confidence! Or was I? Okay, one more check (at every angle) in the mirror. *Now* I had confidence.

I put on my party belt, reassured myself that I had keys . . . tickets . . . money (what little I had) . . . twenty reefers . . . two trips, and with a girlie little jump, hit the street.

The sidewalks were filled with bums, pecs, crotches, fluoro-green wigs, bad make-ups, laughs, screams – it all seemed so unreal. I went with the flow toward Oxford Street.

As I hadn't planned to meet up with anyone, I could take my time. The costumes and wild visions became denser and more exciting the closer I got. Onlookers, cheering and sneering, and probably wishing they were gay, too. Unsavoury groups of anti-ness were gathering, it made me think of my safety.

The Parade had already started and no matter how hard I tried, I couldn't get through the frantic crowd on either side of the street. I decided to walk on the outside of the onlookers toward the Party. Further up, past the Flinders and through the traffic lights, I saw a fairly open space in the crowd. At last, somewhere I could view the Parade from. I grabbed it. People were happy, some commenting on my 'look', others just yelling and screaming with pride and appreciation.

Suddenly, my head was flung to the right so quickly and with such force that I didn't have time to realise what had happened until my right ear hit my right shoulder. There was an instant ringing in my head like a siren. My head hurt real bad and, as I looked around for what I thought must have been the brick that had hit me, I realised I was deaf to the music and the crowd. Deaf to everything except this incredible ringing.

I tried to identify the culprit, but of course I was wasting my time. I was dizzy, very dizzy. I slumped and sat down. A girl wiped my tears with her silver glittered hands and mouthed something about my well-being – I think! Then she continued to jump and scream for the Parade, blowing a silent whistle.

I decided to walk to the Party. The Parade was still going, but I couldn't summon any interest. I followed my luminous boots across the grass. My head hurt and rang for hours during the party; in fact, I could still hear jingling for about four days afterwards.

Approximately two-and-a-half years later, I was having conversations and beers with some friends who were talking about people's misfortunes at Mardi Gras. One girl told a story of some people she knew who'd been shot by an air-rifle, sniper style. I was horrified. 'When? Where?' I couldn't believe her answer. It had been the same year and the same area where I'd been standing. *Wow!*

I was shot in the head at Mardi Gras. And survived!

*Mark Stryker Meyer is a performer extraordinaire and make-up artist who won a BAFTA award for his work in* Priscilla: Queen of the Desert. *He now lives in Perth and is living with AIDS.*

# Acid Queens

## Roger Crawford

WE WERE NAIVE. We hovered over the square bits of blotting paper in the palm of my hand like naughty schoolboys divvying up Craven As. This was our first Mardi Gras and these tabs of LSD our first drugs. Lightning Bolts. They were really quite pretty. Black squares with red bolts outlined in white. R thought he'd quite like to have a tank top with the same design. He'd had some drug experience in his deep university past, but as the moment of drug-taking truth neared, he deferred to me. I'd related tales of eating hash cookies around the camp fire at cadet camp and this seemed to give me some credibility. And I'd got the drugs. In the palm of my hand. Lightning Bolts . . .

I drank in those days. Who didn't? Beer, wine, lighter fluid. And somehow the drug instructions got confused in my mind. R was whirling round his compact kitchen making mango daiquiris with pulp he'd somehow preserved from the height of summer. That glorious summer . . . We'd spent New Year's Eve at the Shift and R had taken V and I aside and screamed in our ears: 'Enjoy every second of this . . . for it will never be like this again.' I scoffed. I wanted it to go on forever. Even the bomb scare that propelled us all down the Shift's hideously carpeted stairs and out onto Oxford Street, seemed entertaining, especially when S, a Sydney icon clad only in a jockstrap and leather cap, climbed a flagpole in the median strip and touched the hem of the Sydney Festival flag. How bold we were that summer! With our daiquiris and our drugs. We felt so very . . . American.

'Well,' said R with mango moustache, 'what do we do with these aesthetically pleasing bits of paper?'

The phrase 'three hours' popped into my head. 'We take a tab each' – I loved using the word tab – 'and three hours later we take flight.'

R's eyes expanded and he put out his furry mango tongue. V, my lover, blushed and giggled, which made us all laugh for he was macho and from Melbourne and so he seldom giggled. P, a chunky ex-priest from New Zealand who had somehow ended up a trolley-dolly, blessed the Bolts and said: 'For what we are about to receive may the Lord make us truly grateful.' Priest-like, he then placed the Lightning Bolts on our tongues – I closed my eyes (a Catholic upbringing is so hard to deny) – and we swallowed, then moved on to gin slings. It was only then that it occurred to me that my supplier (a chain-smoking grandmother who ironed our shirts, rather badly) may have said: 'The acid will last three hours.' I think she also suggested we take a quarter, not a whole tab.

I suppose none of this would have really mattered except R had invited us for dinner, prior (very much prior) to dancing the night away at the Showgrounds. And it was a dinner party for EIGHT. So, four dinner guests, who hadn't had the lightning bolt aperitif, and who would probably be home in bed by the time we were hitting the dance floor at the Mardi Gras party (what would it be like?) were about to arrive. They were all gay, of course, and good eggs, but they hadn't quite embraced the party animal ethos as enthusiastically as we had. As the doorbell chimed we, the drug-takers, decided to play dumb and act normal.

'Loose lips . . . fall off,' I quipped. And laughed. (Had I always been this witty at dinner parties?)

I was the first to go. Take flight, I mean. Shortly after we sat down for soup, Gazpacho, which was all the rage that summer. I remember finding the chunks of cucumber floating in the bowl very amusing and began conversing with them. I stuck my fingers up my bread roll and began using it as a puppet, diving it into the bowl of the stunned guest on my right. He was G, a thespian who, possessed of a fine sense of humour, also animated his knotted French roll and together we did Bert and Ernie from *Sesame Street*. Soon, we co-opted the nearby pedal-bin and dive-bombed for Muppets and empty wine bottles in there. The rest of the table looked on in astonishment . . . except for V, who seemed to have turned into a dog. He'd ditched his spoon, preferring to lap his soup up directly from the bowl.

He was the second to take flight. His right-hand man was H, a handsome rugger-bugger with a slow wit and a little dick. Fascinated by the evolutionary reversion at his end of the table, H made V beg for more soup. (I mean beg as in 'Fido, sit up and beg'.) We all watched in disbelief as V barked for joy when more gazpacho hit his doggie bowl, with the croutons serving as the dry food every well-bred canine needs.

Well, actually, I wasn't really watching. My eyes were awash with tears, so funny did I find everything V did. Then I noticed that ex-priest P and his drug-free companion, a prissy architect, who always discussed the religious aspects of Parsifal, were staring into each other's eyes. You need to know that P's party trick involved the accelerated rotation of his eyeballs, or rather, pupils . . . the right one clockwise and the left anti-clockwise. He used this specialised talent (found only on the South Island of New Zealand) to entrance prospective lovers, much like a cobra mesmerises a mongoose or vice versa.

P's rotations were, as we awaited our next course of multi-coloured pasta, phenomenal. Out of control. The Great Franquin, that renowned hypnotist, sprang to mind. And how he had used Q, a voluminous drag queen friend of ours, as a stooge, getting Q to feign hypnosis and act like a chicken.

That's what this party needed. A chicken! I jumped on my chair, clucked, and pronounced on the irresistible power of P's hypnotic eyes. V joined me, giving up his life as a dog to join the chicken revolution. M, the eighth member of our clan and a congenial chap – the type you might find in the dark corners of a sex club – cock-a-doodle-dooed and exclaimed: 'I don't know what it is you guys are on . . . but is there any of it left?' He too was perched on a chair.

'On? ON?' queried R too intensely. 'We're not ON . . .' he was travelling into the kitchen '. . . ANYTHING!'

If he couldn't control the dinner party, he would at least control himself. No Lightning Bolt would strike him down. There was a pause. We could hear nothing but the steady whir of P's eyes. Then, R screamed, 'Aaaagggghhhh! Somebody's just left the room.'

There was a cluck.

Then M said, 'Yes, R, that was you.'

Pause.

'Oh, thank God for that.'

And through the kitchen servery, we chooks watched our host enact the final drama of this drug-affected, culinary expo: the transferral of the multi-coloured pasta from the aluminium pot to the colander.

Oh the concentration! The willpower! Not since Uri Geller bent his first fork has so much effort gone into making inanimate objects do as they were told. But, much to R's chagrin, the pasta would not make that leap. Despite all his efforts and, of course, our want that our host not fail in this simplest of Italian rituals, the main course remained aluminium bound. And R's taut, strained arm (revealing how beneficial his City Gym visits actually were) could do naught to alter the stand-off.

Time froze. (I think I'd peaked.) The pasta was in danger of losing its *al dente* status.

Now, I hate stories that rely on a *deus ex machina*, but the phone rang. It was the septuagenarian drug-dealer warning us to be careful of the acid. It was strong, she said. So strong, in fact, that her tab had sent her skinny-dipping in the Raindrop Fountain at Roselands. (Did that really happen? Or was the acid kicking in again?)

In any case, the ringing set R in motion and he jubilantly poured the pasta, artistically, onto the kitchen floor. Deliriously happy and released at last from the responsibility of being our host, he took flight. By the time the unaffected got to him, R too was on the kitchen floor, playing with the fettuccine as though he were Scrooge McDuck swimming in a pool of filthy lucre. He stroked it, he wove it, he put it on his head and swore he was Robyn Nevin as Lady Macbeth.

'Is this a colander I see before me?' he asked.

'No, no! That's wrong!' he said with a vehemence even La Nevin would envy. And then, sweetly. 'The correct line is: "Out dam-ned pot!" ' Midst the streams of his own teary laughter, he threw the aluminium container skywards and collapsed.

Later, as we, the Four Musketeers, sort of floated across the dewy Moore Park grass towards the muffled music of our first big party, a jogger told us the night was quite nippy, but we didn't believe him. We were naive and still in that glorious summer . . .

Inside the main hall we found friends, including Q. He was standing in front of a stack of blaring speakers wearing, of all things, a Walkman. When he saw me his eyes lit up and he eagerly transferred the headphones from his ears to mine. I momentarily heard Ethel Merman singing 'Everything's coming up roses'. I returned the headphones.

'Isn't this great?' he screamed, staring straight ahead as though Ethel had appeared before him.

I heard myself say, 'Enjoy every second of this . . . for it will never be like this again.' But Q could only hear Ethel.

I wanted it to go on forever.

*Roger Crawford is a Sydney writer.*

# Mardi Gras Myth 2

*Marilyn was happily married with two teenage girls. But Marilyn had another family – her gay boys. And Mardi Gras was their great family gathering. She wouldn't miss it for the world.*

*So when Marilyn's husband banned her from attending her beloved party she protested. But, having seen her arrive home a little ragged, shall we say, from one too many poofter stomps, hubbie put his foot down.*

*Marilyn realised she wasn't going to win, smiled and said, 'You're right. We'll have a quiet night in and I'll cook you a lovely meal.'*

*While her other family, in homes around Sydney, were getting dressed for the party, Marilyn was cooking up something other than chicken schnitzel. During dinner, she spiked her husband's drink with sleeping pills.*

*After she'd cleared the table, packed the dishwasher, and put her drugged husband to bed, Marilyn squeezed into a sexy little outfit, and headed straight for the Party to join her friends.*

*Marilyn's husband woke from a deep sleep at 7 a.m. to discover his wife was missing. But he knew exactly where she was.*

*He got straight into the car and drove to the Showgrounds. Arriving there, in his pyjamas and dressing gown, he stomped onto the dance floor, grabbed his wife and marched her home.*

*Marilyn is no longer with her husband but never misses a Mardi Gras.*

# Chux and Chaka

## Ian Jopson

IN 1985 I went to my first party. It was like suddenly being given some Windex and a Chux after looking through dirty glass my whole life. I've died and gone to heaven, I thought. I looked around and realised, as a boy from Perth, that this was where I wanted to be. Not specifically in a never-ending dance party, but in a city where I could live within a counterculture of my own people. A place where I could walk down any street, and if I bumped into a friend I could kiss them hello, a simple right not available in other, less open-minded places. So a week later, I went home, wound down my business, cleaned up my affairs and without a second thought, moved lock, stock and barrel to Sydney.

From that moment on, my association and involvement with Mardi Gras grew steadily, although usually from an independent source not directly related to the Mardi Gras committee. My first parade involvement was through my friendship with DJ Stephen Allkins in 1986. Stephen introduced me to friends of his who regularly participated in a costume group. This particular year we were 'Card Carrying Fags', about thirty men dressed like the deck of cards from Alice in Wonderland. Everybody decorated their own cards. Stephen was the Queen of Clubs and I was the Queen of Diamonds.

I lovingly made us these boots with toes that curled up and around like a joker's shoes. They were made of felt and took me hours. This was one of the years it rained at the end of the Parade. I still have the most vivid recollection of Stephen and I walking home to get his records in what turned from light rain into the most tropical of downpours. We ran through the streets still dressed as the Queens, screaming with laughter at being caught in such a storm. And those precious boots being made of felt turned into mush that dragged behind both of our ankles.

A few years ago, when Chaka Khan sang at Mardi Gras, I was asked to help out by pushing a steel structure across the dance floor during the track before Chaka's appearance. There were four of these structures, each with a Lesbian goddess on top. All we had to do was push them from the back of the hall, through the centre of the dance floor to the stage. I thought it would be nearly impossible, but well organised Mardi Gras volunteers and security opened up a channel about 6 feet wide, right down the centre. So clad in yet another G-string we dragged this thing very slowly across the floor. If you can imagine 4000 sweaty bodies, writhing like a sea of solid flesh with this channel cutting through the centre. It was not unlike Charlton Heston parting the Red Sea in *The Ten Commandments*.

One of the fabulous things about volunteering for this was the opportunity to hear Chaka doing her sound check that afternoon. It was a private performance for twenty people, a performance held in an empty cathedral. Her voice was so strong and pure that it moved me to tears. When she hit that first big note, it was like being punched in the chest and being winded. While I enjoyed her performance that night, it didn't have the same impact as that afternoon.

*Ian Jopson, gay icon, is one of the most charming men in Sydney. Oh, and he's a very talented designer, too.*

# Maids of the Mountains

## Colin Fawcett and Bruce Pollack

**Colin Fawcett:** It was all new to me. I'd somehow managed to get onto the Mardi Gras Board at the 1986 AGM. I thought the days of initiation ceremonies were over, but I was wrong. Mardi Gras put on Sleaze Ball, the Parade, Party and Festival, wasn't that enough? At the time, it wasn't.

Dennis Lenox, Vice President of Mardi Gras at the time, thought it would be a good idea if we did something after Mardi Gras and before Sleaze. But what? Something that was away from the Oxford Street strip, something quite different to parties and something that would be fun for our members. There was a property somewhere in the Blue Mountains we could use. The facilities were very basic, but it had a dormitory style bunk house, a small cookhouse, and luxury of luxuries, a toilet. I recall someone saying that it was used frequently by the local boy scouts, so it couldn't be *that* primitive!

The one and only 'Mardi Gras Goes to the Mountains' event was born. We'd do lunch. The Board would drive up the night before and get everything ready. STA coaches would be hired to pick up our guests and drive them up. We'd wine and dine them, pack them back on to the coaches and deliver them safely back to Oxford Street and its surrounds. Easy!

Owning a ute at the time, and being one of the few Board members with a vehicle, I was given the job of picking up various items the afternoon before, including a colleague or two. We packed the vehicle and headed west. Dennis had prepared a map. You know the sort, usually written on the back of a beer coaster, but this was larger. With less detail. It was a cold, late autumn Friday afternoon, and despite leaving work a few hours earlier than usual, by the time we arrived at the base of the mountains it was getting gloomy. The entrance to the property was marked with some old Mardi Gras flags. It was at the end of a gorge. Everything was wet from the light cloud that filled the valley. The last few kilometres was a dirt track cut by a small babbling creek about 100 metres before the camp site. We crossed the creek and were met by our fellow happy campers.

**Bruce Pollack:** I do not know if Dennis had ever been in the army, but often his nature suggested that he had been a drill sergeant. Upon arrival we were all immediately instructed to start to prepare food. The first course for Sunday's event was to be pumpkin soup. For hours upon hours upon hours, we peeled pumpkins. And as we peeled, it got darker and colder. At one stage, I remember attempting to peel with gloves on. I was not the only one present to find the whole experience distressing. In a desperate attempt to overcome physical anxiety, the booze started to flow.

**Colin Fawcett:** There are some people you just can't trust with a knife – artists. Knives, to artists, usually mean amputated fingers or revenged vendettas. This automatically elevated artists up to the next rung: supervisors and storytellers. Jeff Hardy and Peter Tully assumed the jobs of rolling cigarettes, topping up the now necessary mulled wine, and entertaining us with tall tales.

**Bruce Pollack:** Having eaten dinner and finished our chores, and to avoid going to bed for the fear of being eaten alive by whatever might be living in the so-called mattress, it was decided to build a camp fire. One of the 'butch' present handled this task and, when it was roaring, we all moved out to absorb its warmth. We arranged planks to sit upon, but due to the fierce wind could only sit on one side of the fire at the risk of being incinerated. Accordingly, we were sitting on the downside of the heat. It was then decided that we should all rotate places every five minutes so that at least one of us could absorb a small fraction of warmth. I do remember that as we slowly became inebriated it became more difficult to rotate.

**Colin Fawcett:** It was during one of these rotations that Peter Tully let out a blood-curdling scream, followed shortly by a thud, as his body hit the muddy soil around the fire. The trestle, for a brief moment, had turned into a seesaw with Peter its only occupant. The four letter words subsequently expelled indicated that not only had he hurt himself, but some of his best mull had been jettisoned into the fire. This memory, remains for me, one of the only times I every saw Peter lose all artistic composure!

**Bruce Pollack:** Finally we went to bed and I passed out due to the alcohol. But, sometime in the middle of the night, I, along with all the rest of the hut was woken by uncontrollable human screaming. Peter Tully had decided to go to the toilet, and as he'd sat up on his lower bunk bed, his very long hair had become caught in the wire springs hanging down from the bunk above. The more he attempted to free himself, the more his hair was ripped from his scalp. The image of Tully's head suspended from the bed frame is one that I will never forget. He was released, he urinated and we all went back to sleep.

**Colin Fawcett:** The next thing I remember is my whole body, enclosed in its sleeping bag, rising horizontally a foot off the bed, and then crashing back down. A bugle was being played in my ear, and it was loud. Barely audible above this deafening sound was the creak of the other bunks as their startled occupants leapt into the air. Dennis had decided that we should all be woken up at 6.30 a.m. by his CD copy of reveille at maximum volume.

**Bruce Pollack:** It was a wet dawn. But our drill sergeant quickly had us running around in circles preparing contingency plans of cover for the soon-to-arrive group of eager guests and community leaders.

**Colin Fawcett:** Meanwhile, the generator had kicked in, powering the domestic blenders we had been asked to bring. Slowly and very messily we blended the soft pumpkin, and covered the cookhouse bench top with orange mush. An hour or two later, we had pots of pumpkin soup, ready for our hungry guests. But that was only the entrée.

**Bruce Pollack:** Two large rotating spits were prepared and fires lit. By now, the rain was pouring down. At some time during the morning, one of the animals decided that it did not wish to rotate any longer and dropped, unseen, into the fire. There it stayed until it was discovered some hours later, a charred lump.

**Colin Fawcett:** The coaches were due. In fact, they were overdue. The clouds had lifted a little, but it was still drizzling and cold. Finally, we saw them. Stopping short of the creek, they spewed out their passengers, leaving them to cross on foot.

We welcomed the punters with more mulled wine, cranked up the campfire and let them bond with nature for a few minutes as we ladled out containers of hot soup. The remaining lamb was carved up with a generator-powered electric knife. The rain had caused a few cancellations, so there was plenty of food. I can't recall if we attempted a dessert.

After lunch, groups started to form around the small fires that were still going. Conversations, whilst lively, had been dampened somewhat by the constant drizzle. Realising that the rain wasn't about to ease, and that Oxford Street was calling, our guests boarded the coaches eagerly for their ride back to Sydney.

We put the fires out, cleaned up in record time, packed our gear, had a quick debrief and looked forward to a warm drive home. My Mardi Gras initiation ceremony as a Board member was finally over!

*Bruce Pollack is the head of Bruce Pollack Publicity. Colin Fawcett is a computer consultant and has volunteered for a number of community organisations. They are both in Mardi Gras' Hall of Fame.*

# How Long It's Been

## John Wall

I ARRIVED BACK in Australia in September 1978 after a long 'coming out' in the UK and elsewhere, determined to create a new gay life. My first step in establishing a new life was to join the Cronulla Gay Group (CGG). The other part of my plan was to get a permanent job, get away from the parental home, buy a house and then set about finding someone to settle down with. By 1980 I'd made good progress but there was still no boyfriend. Murray and I met at a CGG meeting. A few months later, he moved in.

Looking back now, I realise that the Mardi Gras has defined my life ever since.

My first recollection of Mardi Gras is going home after seeing a movie, in the middle of winter, and walking past a few people preparing for the Parade. My most vivid memory is of seeing a nun-person in full habit, shivering. When the meeting was held to vote on a summer march, I could see the value in being warm. Although I had been in plenty of serious marches in my student days, I could see that the essence of gay was to enjoy life and celebrate that enjoyment.

The next year, a small contingent from CGG marched in the Parade. Someone took pity on us and offered us the back tray of a truck to sit on as we left from Greens Road, and paraded down Oxford Street, in ordinary clothes.

A couple of us wanted to participate again the following year. Although the form of participation was debated within the group, I knew that to be effective you had to get above shoulder height and that riding was easier than walking. So we hired a truck. We have used a truck in every Parade since.

With the help of my sister, I made Murray's and my first costumes. Our first float was simple: balloons and streamers. The theme was having a party.

The next year's Mardi Gras had its own theme: 'a new day dawning'. I decided we had to be more ambitious and with the help of a mechanically apt friend in CGG, John, we put together a rising sun over the waves of Cronulla. The waves moved and the sun was a series of lights which turned on and off in sequence, quite ambitious for those days. In the middle of the Parade, I looked back down Oxford Street and realised that the only float that stood out was Bobbie and Johnnie's station wagon, which had a couple of strings of lights above the cabin. That was the secret of success, I thought, plenty of light. (A few years later, Bobbie and Johnnie's clutch failed, and we towed them the rest of the way.) Our floats became more ambitious every year.

Over the years, we have won two-and-a-half awards. One for the *Cronulla Queen*, a large white Mississippi paddle steamer, complete with southern belles and gentlemen, and a 'mammy'. The next year, we won an award for an aquarium of underwater creatures, Queen Neptuna and her Guard of Honour. These were six well-built men wearing as little as I could persuade them to. At the other end of the float, some 'gorgeous' mermaids sat on beanbag 'rocks'. The idea came from one of our members who had seen a similar idea used in a parade in Alice Springs.

The award we shared was for our Valentine Float which had two boys in fig leaves sitting in a heart-shaped bower, with the title 'Adam and Steve'. Picking up on something Fred Nile, the intolerant one, had said I'd assured both participants that no one would ever notice them amongst all the colour of the Parade in general. It was a surprise to find they ended up starring in the Channel Nine News promo for the rest of the year.

There are memories: Of being soaking wet, of generators failing and of the roar from the crowd when, with more petrol, the generator started again, and the music and lights came back on. Then there was the year that Reverend Fred prayed for rain and the storm hit Mosman. I would like to know what the Mosmanites had done to deserve that. The most enduring memory of those early Parades is walking at the side of the truck and pushing people back so that we could get through. Now, with barriers all the way, it's almost too easy.

My house became central to CGG's Mardi Gras efforts each year. It was a convenient place to store construction materials and trimmings from year to year, and close enough to town to do the final construction on the day.

These working bees have always been enjoyable. Every weekend for the month or so before Mardi Gras, friends will come, sit and chat, while we make decorations for the float. On the other hand, several friendships have almost been lost as time and tempers got short and the float didn't seem to be progressing. Overall, we have been mostly blessed with good designers, practical constructors and willing workers.

During this time, Murray became increasingly involved in the Mardi Gras committee, and this culminated in his election as President, in 1986.

Suddenly, I was not an auxiliary member of the same committee as I had been in CGG. Murray was always at Mardi Gras committee meetings, interviews, bump-ins and bump-outs, festival events and more committee meetings. Quite understandably, I had no place at most of them.

Tuesday night was Board meeting night, me at home alone although sometimes I would join them for dinner late at night. Unlike Mardi Gras' committee members, I needed to sleep – sometimes. The last week before Mardi Gras, none of them seemed to go home at all, including Murray.

I did help out in the Mardi Gras workshop. John and I built a mechanism to mount an old Lotto ball on a bearing and stand in order to create the biggest mirror ball in Sydney. Wandering through the workshop when all the decorations have been made, from the Tully days to now, has always been fun. I couldn't get too involved, however, because of the CGG float. It was, and is, my first love: the only time in the year I get to do something glamorous.

Being a Mardi Gras spouse was not all bad. There were some advantages. I knew when all the shows were on and could dash over to the right pavilion to see them. The Worker's toilets were a little less libidinous and at their bar, the drinks were easier to get.

I am also proud of the things that Murray helped shepherd through during his presidency. Changing the name to Sydney Gay and Lesbian Mardi Gras happened while Murray was President. He was part of the committee when Mardi Gras became a recognised institution with a New Charter, a board of management and a small, professional paid staff. He was part of the Board that established full accounting procedures, putting Mardi Gras on a business footing, that restructured the Mardi Gras workshop and that, as a result of protracted negotiations with police and politicians, helped make the Parade and Party the success it is today. Later Boards may have had their problems but during that time, with a rapidly expanding Parade and increasingly popular parties, each year had unique challenges that required imagination as well as enormous will and effort to solve. All the people who managed this, year after year, only have my admiration.

At one time, CGG used to make the money for its floats by running the cloakroom at Sleaze Ball. No one will admit it but, one reason our group liked to do this was that we could watch all those men change into their party gear in front of us.

These days CGG, along with a lot of the other groups who regularly supported the Parade in the past, is finding it more difficult to participate. Our members are regrettably getting older and fewer. Money is scarcer, and we are being outstripped in size and grandeur by other, more commercial floats.

In my private life, things have changed as well. Murray and I started to drift apart. We had different interests. He had Mardi Gras and parties; I the float and CGG. The affair ran its natural course; in the end, we both changed as we got older.

The first Mardi Gras without Murray seemed hollow. All of a sudden I lost privileges like getting into the Worker's bar. It was no longer 'my' party. Over the next few years, with new people on the Board, Mardi Gras became less relevant to me. However, each year Cronulla puts in a float. My place is still where most of the preparation work is done. Everybody at work still asks me what the theme of the float is this year. The neighbours still stand outside in the street on Saturday morning to watch us put it together and, although I am usually glad when it is all over, the old thrill as we turn into Oxford Street is still there.

I wouldn't miss it for quids.

*John Wall is a long-time member of Cronulla Gay Group and an ex-Mardi Gras widow.*

As Mardi Gras grew, so did its administrative structure. In mid-1983 the Sydney Gay Mardi Gras Association was formed, and at its June 1986 AGM this association became incorporated. I was invited to join the Mardi Gras board in 1987. The invitation surprised me – where had it come from? – but I was delighted to accept. We were a very good team, with Murray McLachlan as President. In my time on the board – October 1987 to April 1989 – I was proud to be a supporter of the organisation's name change to the Gay and Lesbian Mardi Gras. Like many others, I had thought the term 'gay' was genderless, but I quickly learnt that this was not how the girls felt, and that they vehemently wanted distinguishing as 'lesbian'. To me it was simple: What the girls wanted was obviously what should prevail . . . and, happily, it eventually did.

# Three Years of Evolution
## Murray McLachlan

MARDI GRAS HAS HAD, through its twenty years, a number of defining moments which have been crucial to its evolution, and indeed its very existence. These include the decision to move Mardi Gras to summer, the 1985 committee's determination to go ahead with the Mardi Gras Parade despite community hysteria about AIDS and rumours of snipers in Oxford Street, and the adoption of a 'members only' ticketing policy in 1991.

The most important symbolic moment, however, occurred during Mardi Gras' tenth anniversary year. On 8 December 1988, Mardi Gras Association members took the decision to change the name of the organisation to include the word 'lesbian'. This moment was not, as some have claimed, a strategic coup by lesbians – it did not represent 'a dyke takeover'. Rather it was the culmination of a steadily-evolving commitment by many gay men and lesbians to coalition politics, a commitment which had begun as early as 1986. Its achievement was fundamental in ensuring the continued evolution of Mardi Gras into the organisation and events we know today.

If I can claim only one achievement during my involvement in Mardi

Gras between 1984 and 1990, it is my role in the building of coalition politics in Mardi Gras and Sydney's lesbian and gay community. This involved the evolution of the organisation to the point at which it was ready to recognise women's involvement through the powerful symbolism of changing its name. The name change proudly asserted who the organisation was for, and who was responsible for making its extraordinary events happen.

In 1978, thirty men and twenty-three women were arrested during the first Mardi Gras march – evidence, perhaps, of early gender parity! After 1980, however, and particularly with the move from June to February, women's involvement dramatically decreased. The expression 'the girls got into dogma, and boys got into drag' was only partly true for most women and men, but certainly during the early 1980s, women's involvement at the parades and parties, and within the organisation, was minimal.

That started to change in 1986, with the nomination of Cayte Latta, who had been approached by Bill Whittaker and Jim Jenkins about joining the committee. The first seeds of a new coalitionism in Mardi Gras, where many gay men confronted the issue of working with lesbians, and many lesbians confronted the issue of working with gay men, were sown.

The various Mardi Gras committees from 1986 onwards, and the individuals on them, both men and women, actively encouraged women's involvement, in the committee and on sub-committees, in organising festival events, in the Parade, and in lesbian-focused shows at various parties.

The handwritten notes I used for media interviews after I was elected Mardi Gras President on 23 September 1986 have a section headed 'Future of Mardi Gras'. I had jotted down: 'Important to involve lesbian community – gradual process – efforts made to encourage lesbian attendance at MG activities.'

The 1987 Mardi Gras Festival in particular, through a number of community events, and in its Film Festival (which was opened by Robyn Archer, who had also directed the gay play, *On Parliament Hill*, at Belvoir Street Theatre) started to see this policy put in action.

In my President's report to the Mardi Gras Annual General Meeting of 26 May 1987, I reaffirmed my commitment to including more women in Mardi Gras and its festival. The Sydney Gay Mardi Gras Festival had over the past three years rapidly increased in importance, to the point where it was the highlight of Sydney life during February. Under the careful and experienced guidance of Festival Co-ordinator Tony Crewes, the 1987 Festival had included picnics in the northern and southern suburbs, a car rally in the western suburbs and a bush dance in the inner-west – all features of a concerted effort to make the Festival more representative, relevant and interesting beyond the inner city. A number of events were specifically aimed at encouraging the involvement of women, and as I pointed out: 'Such events are significant if the Festival is to be truly representative of the broad range of Sydney's homosexual life. However it is essential that such events are not seen as being merely tokenistic. Their real success can only lie in their being organised by lesbians to meet the expressed needs of lesbians. In this regard, the steadily increasing involvement of women in the association bodes well for the future.'

Despite the best intentions, the Mardi Gras committee that was elected in 1987 included only one woman, Heather Grey. Throughout 1987, the Festival continued to be the focus for building coalitionism within Mardi Gras. At the all-male Festival sub-committee meeting of 23 June 1987, the agenda item 'Women's involvement' declared:

'It was agreed that interested women be invited to the next sub-committee meeting to present their views. Robyn Archer has expressed interest in being involved again, and will be contacted. New events for women were suggested, including wrestling and a four-wheel drive rally.'

Clearly these men – myself included – had something to learn about lesbian interests!

I also spoke with another Robyn, Robyn Laverack, who was the single most important influence on my thinking about lesbian involvement in Mardi Gras. She said to me at work one day, 'Well, Murray, if I'm going to be critical of Mardi Gras, I'd better get involved!' Between 1987 and 1989, Robyn's involvement expanded from instigating a garden competition during the Festival to working on the Parade and Party. She eventually joined the committee in March 1989. It was my hope by that point that Robyn become the first lesbian president of Mardi Gras.

On 21 July 1987, I jotted down the names and telephone numbers of all the women who had accepted our invitation to attend the Festival sub-committee meeting and 'present their views'. They were (as I recorded them, some incorrectly): Sue Perry, Kimberley O'Connell, Chris Westwood, Naomi Britten and Kathy Phillips (sic). I would get to know these names much better over the next two years!

In parallel with the Festival sub-committee, other Mardi Gras' developments during 1987 were also helping to build coalitionism. Mardi

Gras' Executive Director, Ralph McAllister, travelled to the USA in June 1987 on a promotional trip. Perhaps the most important aspect of Ralph's trip was the invitation he proffered, on Chris Westwood's suggestion, to Robin Tyler to perform during the 1988 Mardi Gras Festival. Robin and Vito Russo brought the message of coalition politics to Sydney, and Robin's season of nine performances at the Trade Union Club was a major influence in changing both men's and women's thinking. For a lot of gay men, it led to the realisation that 'Dykes can have a sense of humour!' I suspect Robin's message to many lesbians suggested just as strongly that 'working with the boys' was the only way to go.

The 1988 Parade, renowned for its Aboriginal float in the Bicentennial year, was equally significant for the momentous, first-time appearance of 'Dykes on Bikes'.

Mardi Gras' commitment to lesbian involvement was reinforced when the now all-male committee appointed Alma-Mary McFarland as Administrator in April 1988. Mardi Gras was the first community organisation to appoint a lesbian to its most senior staff position. Then, in April 1988, Bruce Pollack and I initiated a meeting with Cath Phillips which was designed to ensure that lesbians would be elected to the incoming committee. During the meeting we brokered a deal that saw three women, identified by Cath, included on the incumbent group for the 1988 AGM. They were Celia Hutton, Kimberly O'Sullivan, and Cath herself. Twenty-four nominations, of which four were women, were received for fourteen positions, and the 'Mardi Gras' group was elected. This election was the most significant achievement to that point in the evolution of women's involvement in Mardi Gras.

Mardi Gras discussions and events throughout the remainder of 1988 included strong evidence of gay men and lesbians working together to ensure women's visibility. Richard Wherrett suggested at a committee meeting on 16 August that Sandra Bernhard be considered as an overseas act for the Festival; Mardi Gras' first Winter Party, *Cool with sunny periods*, also in August, included Dykes on Bikes as the opener of the major show in the Hordern Pavilion; and, at a function to launch Sleaze 1988 I referred to the party as being 'for gays and lesbians'. Sleaze Ball's Solitary Moments entertainment would include strong female images, including some sleazy lesbian phone sex, while two extraordinary dyke violinists accompanied Jeff Duff's live performance of 'Walk on the Wild Side'.

Between May and September 1988, the committee also looked at the issue of changing the organisation's name to reflect what had been happening during the previous two years. By now many gay men had become more comfortable working with women. A growing number of men on the committee found that the word 'lesbian' didn't stick in their throats. I can recall, however, several lengthy conversations with some male committee members in an effort to persuade them that 'discussing the association's name' (as Cath Phillips had suggested at a committee meeting of 4 June 1988) would not be the end of the world, let alone the end of Mardi Gras!

Formal discussion of the issue eventually took place during the committee's 'weekend away' at Leura from 2 to 4 September 1988. The official record of the discussion makes illuminating reading:

'Richard Wherrett proposed a straw vote up front. The proposal was that the name be changed from Sydney Gay Mardi Gras Association to the Sydney Gay and Lesbian Mardi Gras Association. Richard Wherrett acknowledged that words change their meaning over time, for example 'camp' to 'gay' and we should be aware of this. The result of the straw vote was for the name change, with only two votes against it. Peter Macdonnell had reservations about the name change occurring before the Sleaze Ball, and hoped for a groundswell of support from the lesbian community. Murray McLachlan proposed that an Extraordinary General Meeting (EGM) be held in November, and that any alterations to the Constitution could be put at the same time. He spoke of the need to educate gay men and lesbians about the reasons for the name change, as it needed a 75% pro vote to change the Constitution and name.

'Peter Macdonnell wanted the Parties to remain apolitical – they should not be 'heavy' but fun. Alma-Mary McFarland, Kimberly O'Sullivan and Cath Phillips spoke about Mardi Gras and the dyke community and coalition politics and the name change with the conclusion that women like to party too.

'Colin Fawcett in speaking about the proposed name change and publicity for the Parade, said that it was possible for the association to change the name of events to 'Sydney Gay and Lesbian Mardi Gras' on publicity now, without changing the name of the association. But he felt that the members of the association should know of the proposal to change the name at a November EGM, and that proper procedure must be seen to have been followed.'

Process queen that I am, I ensured that correct procedure *was* followed, and that association members *were* aware of the reasons for the proposal! I used Mardi Gras' second-ever newsletter (October 1988) to announce the committee's decision to hold an Extraordinary General Meeting to propose the name change. The proposal *was* controversial. Much debate occurred in bars, restaurants and bedrooms, and numerous 'Letters to the editor' were written. This issue was perhaps not *quite* as controversial as the DJ selection for Sleaze that year. It's comforting that some things about Mardi Gras don't change!

The *Sydney Star Observer*, in an editorial of 25 November 1988, supported the proposal, as did organisations such as the recently re-formed Gay and Lesbian Rights Lobby. In that same *Star* issue, in response to Tim Carrigan's question 'How much is the proposal a recognition of something that has happened and how much an invitation to lesbians to join in Mardi Gras' activities?' I replied that it was both, pointing to the growing lesbian involvement in Mardi Gras, with lesbian membership of the association being between 20 and 25 per cent. I argued that 'Mardi Gras as a whole . . . stands to benefit from greater lesbian involvement. It will have a broader political base. Changing the name of the association will allow us to point out to the critics of Mardi Gras – to the Fred Niles of the world – that this is an event for both men and women. The change will allow us to undercut their linking of Mardi Gras to gay men alone and from that to AIDS.'

In response to Tim's bizarre question as to whether lesbians had earned the right to be included in Mardi Gras I replied, 'Of course they have. Who's going to decide whether deaf people or Aboriginals or leather queens have the right to be part of it?'

The Extraordinary General Meeting of 6 December 1988 was attended by over one hundred members of the association. As chair of the meeting, I chose not to move the motion, much as I wanted to. Instead it had been agreed by the committee that it would be moved by Colin Fawcett and seconded by Cath Phillips, as evidence that the position was supported by both the gay men and the lesbians on the committee. The motion proposed an amendment to the first sentence of the Mardi Gras Constitution to provide for the change of name.

Given the level of controversy that had emerged from the proposed change, I felt it important that a debate be conducted which enabled all those wishing to speak to do so. Therefore, after Colin had spoken to the motion, I called on alternating speakers for and against the proposal. Seventeen association members, men and women, spoke. Cath Phillips was the final speaker.

Clearly a number of the men at the meeting struggled with their position during the evening, and many probably changed their view as a

*Top:* Oxford Street pre-parade.

*Bottom:* Where it all happens – the Mardi Gras workshop.

*Clockwise from top:* Sister of Perpetual Indulgence and Sailorboy escorts at Mardi Gras Opera House launch; Fair Day; bowling ladies entertain the crowd pre-parade.

*Facing page.*
*Top:* Parade night on Oxford Street.
*Bottom:* Dykes on Bikes get ready to roar.

*Clockwise from top:* Richard Wherrett
with Brett Sheehy, Mark Robinson
and David Franklin watch the
Parade; Corby Beard aka Corabeth;
Cindy Pastel and Corabeth rest their
feet; Bob Downe aka Mark Trevorrow
entertains the crowd; Pip Playford
celebrates the wet years.

*Clockwise from top:* Marching lemons;
in drag for the big night; its better in
beads.

*Clockwise from top:* Parade entrant; urban tribal wear; Queens of the Orient.

*Clockwise from top:* Lesbian brides; Aids float; taking off.

*Top:* The shows! Four a.m. at the Horden. *Bottom: I Am What I Am* returns in 1998. (The bearded boy in drag was our sign language interpreter.)

consequence of the debate. When the vote was taken, it saw 88 in favour and 20 against, comfortably over the 75 per cent support required for the change. My feelings as I sat on the podium with Cath and Colin were amongst the warmest (and most relieved) I was to experience during my entire Mardi Gras involvement.

Unfortunately, given production deadlines, it was not possible for the 1989 Mardi Gras poster to announce the change of name. The poster did, however, for the first time, incorporate strong lesbian images, and other promotional material was produced which used the new name.

My President's message in the 1989 Festival calendar stated that:

'This year, Sydney will see the first Sydney Gay and Lesbian Mardi Gras, presented by the Sydney Gay and Lesbian Mardi Gras Association. Lesbians have been significant contributors since the early years which led to Mardi Gras as we now know it. The change of name recognises this involvement, and is designed to encourage greater lesbian participation and greater lesbian visibility.'

The word quickly spread into the wider community. John Stapleton's *Sydney Morning Herald* article of 18 February 1989 was titled 'Women Join the Mardi Gras as Equal Partners'. The extent to which coalitionism had strengthened Mardi Gras was also seen in Alana Valentine's assessment in the *Sydney Star Observer* of 24 February 1989:

'The Gay and Lesbian Mardi Gras was, in 1989, what it started out to be in 1978 – a mind-blowing chaos of colour and imagination and excitement that defies all homophobic hatred and denial.

'This is a Parade that sticks out its tongue and its tits and its dicks and dares the bigoted straight world to tell us we don't have something to contribute.

'And because lesbians are becoming more and more involved in that message of gay pride and gay community, they were represented more widely and more diversely than ever before. There was a lesbian presence and visibility in this Mardi Gras that testifies to the growth of co-operation in our community.'

Mardi Gras was ready for its second decade.

*Murray McLachlan uses skills learnt from Mardi Gras in his job at Workcover NSW.*

# Snapshots for a Memory

## C. Moore Hardy

AS A SERIOUSLY queer/bent photographer I have been involved with Mardi Gras at various levels, from documenting the Parade and Party since 1983 to a position on the Board in 1992. My most vivid recollections and impressions are visually recorded on film. Other than that, I have a bad memory.

I have, however, a vague recollection of my first Mardi Gras Parade, and it was probably 1982. I'd heard about it through friends and decided to wander down to George Street where it went past the Hoyts cinema complex. Suddenly, caught in the middle of it all, I found myself joining in. Having been brought up in the sixties on a staple diet of anti-nuclear marches, I considered an opportunity to walk in the middle of the street with like-minded souls fun. It was never my intention to be a part of the rally so I simply followed the Parade along through to Park Street and then stood on a street corner as the last of the marchers went by. On the opposite street corner was a tragic old theatre queen, waving, shouting and enjoying himself immensely. I had seen him before, he was a well-known bex'n'beer regular on Saturday afternoons at the Albury, where I spent time socialising with my gay boyfriends. He was so thrilled to see all those 'out' homosexuals. (I imagine he had lived a life restricted and closeted.) In those days, I was a fag-hag.

My most thrilling night was in 1988 when I cruised up Oxford Street on the back of a Harley Davidson with the Dykes on Bikes (DOB). This was in the days when the DOBs led the Parade from start to finish. It was the first time I participated in the Parade, even though I had photographed it on a number of occasions. The screams, cheers, and pure adulation from the crowd was a drug in itself.

One of my favourite Mardi Gras nights was the first year that it rained. Strange you might think, as rain is a photographer's nightmare. The workshop had been planning to do more dyke-specific floats, in recognition of the increasing number of lesbians getting involved in Mardi Gras. I had been invited to the initial planning meetings, which David McDiarmid, the Artistic Director of the Workshop, was orchestrating. He was consulting lesbians on what they thought would be appropriate and humorous images, as well as offering his creative experience from previous years.

From that meeting a number of lesbians and community artists banded together and created one of the most memorable floats that I can ever recall. It was a magnificently constructed 15-foot high yellow-and-blue tartan dog with automated leg movements. Constructed by Ian Oliver and Mandy Smith, its left leg lifted up – the intention being to spray the crowd with refreshing jets of water. Had it not been for the downpour that year, this doggie would have gone down in the Parade history as the wettest canine on Oxford Street.

Self-saucing puddings, the lazy lesbians watching TV, the matadors, the marching lemons, Pip Playford's creations, lesbian brides, the 120 Xenas, and the other larger groups of lesbian-specific designs are cherished moments.

From a political viewpoint, my most treasured memory is the night at the Mardi Gras' Rushcutters Bay headquarters when the word 'Lesbian' was included in the name of the then Sydney Gay Mardi Gras. I heard many men come forth with reasons why it shouldn't be included, such as the fact that their 'Gay Lady Friends' didn't like the word 'lesbian'. It is still significant to see who cannot bring themselves to say the word, and to watch media presenters stumble over it when they do.

I love the political mixed with humour that is Mardi Gras. In 1998, the largest roar and claps of approval from Parade-watchers went to the policewomen and men who marched in uniform for the first time, as well as to the Queers for Reconciliation and Native Title. Although some of the wit and humour has gone with the major artistic talents of our community who have died from HIV/AIDS, the spirit lives on.

*C. Moore Hardy is a professional photographer.*

# The Birth of a Legend:
# Dykes on Bikes, 1988–1990

## Kimberly O'Sullivan

EVERY YEAR THE ROAR of their engines signals the beginning of the Mardi Gras Parade. Dykes on Bikes (DOB), the perennial crowd favourites, make it their business to titillate the hordes pressed against the barricades with a mixture of leather, sex and hard core attitude. Both seriously butch and glamorously femme (and every shade of personal expression in between) these girls look like they were born on a bike, their connection with the machine is so seamless and natural. The great irony of DOB is that it was begun by two women who had never ridden a motorbike, let alone owned one.

For me DOB really began in the American summer of 1987, when I watched the San Francisco Lesbian/Gay Freedom Day Parade being led by many hundreds of dykes on bikes. Standing on Market Street, I stared in awe and lust, having never seen such a spectacular demonstration of lesbian power, sex and visibility. Back in Sydney I raved to my friend Cath Phillips who was equally enthusiastic, having herself seen dykes on bikes in San Francisco a few years earlier.

We were both then on the periphery of Mardi Gras, attending Festival and Parade meetings and walking a fine line – trying to encourage the boys to include lesbians and trying to encourage lesbians to include themselves. After a lot of bluff and persistent lobbying on our parts, the Mardi Gras Parade subcommittee agreed that DOB should not only be in the parade, but lead it. Although we had won an important victory for dyke visibility, Cath and I now had a new problem: where were we going to find all these motorcycle-riding dykes?

At this time I was managing a lesbian bar, The Playground, in Surry Hills and Cath urged me to use the bar to recruit women for the Parade entry. Deb Thompson, who was later to become a major DOB organiser for many years, remembers first hearing about the proposed Parade entry at the bar.

'I was at The Playground in January 1988 when one of the barmaids said to me, "Did you hear this year there are going to be women riding bikes in the Mardi Gras Parade? They are looking for girls to ride. I am going to go in it, why don't you?" I was really keen, but heard no more about it until the night before the Parade, when Kimberly asked me if I was going and told me where the Parade was leaving from.

'As I had never seen the Parade, I had no idea how big it was. I thought the Mardi Gras was a political parade, and so the last thing I expected to see was tens of thousands of people cheering and screaming. I had ridden a bike for years and never had that reaction from the general public! We started playing to the crowd: revving our engines, racing each other off and hooning around. The girls who were pillions stood up on the foot pegs of the bike, gesturing to the crowd, showing their tits and posing for the photographers who surrounded us. Nothing we did was planned, because we had no idea what to expect, we just let our heads go and improvised as we went along. At the end of the Parade I was on such a high, it had all gone much too quickly and I wanted to turn around and ride down Oxford Street again.'

Although only eight bikes turned up on the night, the reaction of the crowd was extraordinary. Dykes with a biker look and a larrikin attitude proved to be a potent mix and many gay men, who thought of lesbians primarily as highly political animals, saw a very different kind of lesbian subculture.

Buoyed along partly by the success of DOB, which showed that a strong lesbian presence at Mardi Gras was possible, Cath Phillips, Celia Hutton and myself were elected to the Mardi Gras Board. The new Board was committed to raising the profile of lesbians in Mardi Gras and as the response of the crowd to DOB had been so enthusiastic it was not difficult for all to agree that DOB should lead the Parade again the following year.

(Mardi Gras and DOB would later have a dispute about their placement in the Parade. After the exhilaration of leading in 1988, DOB wanted to continue to do so, but the Mardi Gras Parade subcommittee wanted them behind the traditional lead vehicle. Mardi Gras won out and heated discussions continued for a number of years over DOB's Parade placement. This was not resolved until many years later, when DOB officially became part of the pre-Parade entertainment.)

After its triumphant debut, it was clear that more bikers were needed for DOB's return performance, and Deb and I, who were by now in a relationship, took on the organising. We decided to take a direct approach and made up a handwritten leaflet which read 'Are you a dyke who rides a bike? If so – we want to hear from you!' We did the rounds of every lesbian venue for a month before the parade, putting them in the hands of every dyke we could find. Every bookshop, coffee shop and venue had our leaflets and, in an inspired move, we took to sticking them to the seat of every motorbike we saw parked outside a lesbian venue.

Our phone rang hot and a meeting was organised at the Cricketer's Arms hotel at Alexandria, then a popular drinking place for lesbians who rode bikes. Deb stressed to this undisciplined group that they had to be on time (the Parade wouldn't wait for them!), organised a meeting place on the night, briefed them on how to service their bikes (so they could ride slowly without their bike overheating) and encouraged them to dress up – particularly in fetish, leather or SM clothing. Twenty-six women rode that year and the following year, 1990, fifty women took part despite the pouring rain. Mardi Gras' 20th Anniversary Parade in 1998 was led by over 200 bikes.

Deb organised the DOB parade entry for eight years and later formed The Vixens, the first lesbian motorcycle club in Sydney. She still feels strongly about DOB, believing the entry makes dykes visible and powerful in a still largely male parade. 'It is men who have traditionally owned motorbikes, particularly Harleys, and DOB challenges that because lesbians have always had amazing bikes, such as vintage British ones and American classics. DOB is a great way to show dykes as diverse, strong and powerful women in control of their sexuality and their lives.'

*Kimberly O'Sullivan is an author, archivist and sex activist.*

# Waiting for Goddess

## A phone conversation pre-Mardi Gras

## Deborah Cheetham

OKAY, SO SHE'S MARRIED. What? What do you mean AGAIN? This is completely different. Yes, there are children involved . . . it was never meant to go this far. Well how was I to know! I never thought we would fall in love, well not like this anyway. Listen don't give me a hard time, I rang you for support . . . No, I'm not just talking about sex. It's about everything you think, everything you feel, thoughts you've lived with for a long time, what you believe but can't even put into words.

She is my soul mate, she says.

I'm the first woman she has ever loved, perhaps the only person, male or female, she has ever loved in this way. Oh! To have touched a life in that way. To have made love with someone who . . . Is that your call waiting? . . . No get it, I can't think with it beeping away like that.

*'Are you going to Scarborough Fair? Parsley, sage, rosemary and . . .'*

Who was that? Are they meeting us after the Parade? No, she can't be there. I honestly can't imagine her on the back of my bike. I'm not sure you'll ever get to meet her . . .

At home of course with the husband and kids. She says she wants to leave him. Oh yeah, she'll bring them with her, I want her to. They like me, I like them, that's a good start isn't it?

I know you don't want to see me hurt, but it's a little late for that now . . .

She has this smile – and a look, it . . . it makes me so wet I can't think of anything but her kiss, her tongue inside my mouth possessing me, her nails down my back and inside me when she slowly . . . Oh, not again . . . Well, see who it is . . .

*'. . . she once was a true love of mine . . .'*

I love her so much. She *says* she'll leave but she isn't ready to. She's worried that the news will kill her mother . . .

Hang on my battery's running low, I'll have to put you on speaker phone . . .

*'at the third stroke it will be eleven twenty-five and fifty seconds'*

*Deborah Cheetham is an indigenous Australian performance artist and director of Short Black Productions.*

# Gayworld

## Jane Becker

MY FIRST MARDI GRAS was some time in the early eighties. I was a young dyke and went to watch the Parade with some other lezzo friends. We decided it was pretty much for the boys (except for those few leather dykes chained to the back of that leather float) and that our commitment to our community lay elsewhere – collectives or some other such serious undertaking.

Then, in 1989, a friend and I went to hear Vito Russo speak about his book, *The Celluloid Closet*. He spoke a lot about coalition politics and AIDS, and moved us to tears with his sadness, courage, intelligence and passion. It was clear that the boys were where it was at, and coalition politics was A Good Thing, and that it really was time to get involved somehow. So we decided to go in the Parade with Dykes on Bikes: joining the boys, but as strong, strident lezzos. In leather.

That year was my first Party as well, and I was totally blown away – the Showgrounds, full of people like me! Sort of. My first experience of feeling a sense of strength, pride and togetherness as a lesbian within a larger community. Gayworld!

Over the next few years I religiously took part in Dykes on Bikes until my bike wouldn't make it up the street any more and the marshals had to move the barricades at Crown Street aside to let me and my poor overheated machine through. I went to Mardi Gras parties, and Sleaze as well, and got involved in Festival events like Word of Mouth. Eventually, in 1993, I landed a job as a workshop artist at the Rushcutters Bay home of Mardi Gras.

This was, I think, the beginning of the end, what everyone had warned me about, and what I had laughingly disregarded as an impossibility: the beginning of Mardi Gras Taking Over My Life. I swore blind that I would never join a committee. I knew beyond the slightest doubt that my life was complete, even without Mardi Gras. I couldn't understand how other people could let an organisation so overwhelm them. I knew that I could keep my critical distance, and never succumb.

Now, I'm Mardi Gras' Workshop Manager, I sit on three committees and a few million subcommittees. I work at the weekend more often that I even want to think about. My friends think it's no wonder I don't know what's going on in the rest of the world, because I (and I quote) 'spend so much time in the rarefied atmosphere of Gayworld, associating with the likes of Kabi, and the Chiefs'. This strange many-headed monster that is Mardi Gras has somehow become very important to me, even though I swear about it quite often, and would love to make just a few little changes, if only things worked that way. I don't really understand how it happened. Certain of my colleagues just lean back and smile knowingly. They've been resigned to it for years. I'm only just waking up to it. The complexity, the uniqueness, the crazy stressful pressure and the excitement; the sheer fantastic lunacy of what the gay and lesbian community does for the gay and lesbian community.

Gayworld. Who would have thought?

*Jane Becker is the Workshop Manager for Mardi Gras, now located in Erskineville.*

Politics and personalities notwithstanding, there have probably been more column inches in the gay press given to letters and articles about music at Mardi Gras parties than any other single issue. Over recent years, by far the biggest complaint – and one with which I have great sympathy – has concerned the reluctance of younger DJs to slow down the beats per minute at some point towards the end of the Party to a funkier, sexier, groovier mode. Along with DJ Stephen Allkins and many others, I always looked forward to that part of the night. It was a time to share emotionally with lovers and friends, before facing the blinding white glare of daylight at the far end of the pavilion through which figures vanish into the light, as if lifted up by angels.

It is worth remembering that the Mardi Gras Party and Sleaze Ball are for us all, regardless of age and taste differences. No one has brought this point home with more force than DJ Bill Morley whose music selection for Mardi Gras in 1987 put any other event – before or after – in the shade.

# The True Blue Danube Story

## Bill Morley

TO BE ASKED TO DJ at a big dance party is both a joy and a privilege, and it is even more so at a big gay dance party. I had been involved with Mardi Gras since its inception, so it was with some exhilaration – and a significant degree of nervousness and apprehension – that I approached the Mardi Gras of 21 February 1987. My previous biggest gig was the Sleaze Ball of the year before. This had been especially memorable for me, as the Guest Artist was Sylvester – the first Big Time Star to appear at a Mardi Gras event.

These were the days before the parties had publicised 'themes'. It was left up to the DJs and lighting people to create the 'atmosphere'. Imagine!

The party was to be in the Hordern Pavilion (the last time it was big enough to hold the crowds).The lighting designer, Robert Lake, chose 16 mm movie projections as part of the design. These would be rear-projected onto a screen that hung over the edge of the dance floor.

Those sitting on the tiered seating above the entrance could watch the movies and the dancing. The control room was way at the top of that seating, and I remember the dance floor seemed miles in the distance.

We decided to co-ordinate specific visuals with certain songs, such as Monsoon's 'Ever So Lonely' with clips by 'Bollywood' star, Helen of India and when Robert said he was going to project some underwater sequences with a blue wash, I immediately thought of 'The Blue Danube' – please don't ask me how or why! I had already decided on as diverse a programme of songs as possible: I ranged through disco, funk, twist, Motown and pop. Remember, this was pre-House, even pre-Handbag! (Was there ever such a time?) I surmised that, in a group of six to 7000 gay people of varying age groups, there would have to be a significant proportion who knew how to waltz. And why (pray tell!) should these people not be catered for as well? Also, as I had the last half of the party, I felt I had more musical leeway.

Call me foolish, naive even, but it *was* the GAY Mardi Gras, and it *was* 1987! If it couldn't be done there, where could you do it? And what could be more 'camp' than waltzing to 'The Blue Danube' at a gay dance party?

Half-way through my set, I realised it was now or never. I started to play the full 6'55" version from *2001: A Space Odyssey* soundtrack by the Berlin Philharmonic conducted by Herbert von Karajan. I like the idea of all these conflicting resonances: underwater, 2001, waltz, disco, classical, etcetera.

My main memory is that, one minute into the track, someone yelled out from the corridor: 'You've just fucking ruined this whole party!'

Well. You can't please everybody.

What happened on the dance floor, I have only pieced together from many, many discussions with people from then until this day.

Apparently, the music at first cleared the dance floor. Then, a few people started to dance, until eventually 500 or so were dancing. Everyone else just watched, which was part of my plan.

What a scandal it turned out to be! People were outraged by that song, and indeed by my whole approach. There were, naturally, more outrageous clangers during the set – but that's another story. Funnily enough, playing 'The Blue Danube' wasn't one of them!

I'm often asked if I'd do it again, and I always reply, 'Of course not!' We are all so much more 'cool' and 'hip' these days, and dance music is so relentlessly 'now'. Also, the drugs are so specific that I don't feel it would work. And besides, it's already been done!

There have been so many Mardi Gras parties and Sleaze Balls that it's often difficult to pinpoint what happened at which one. But when somebody says, 'You know, the one where they played 'The Blue Danube', the reply is invariable: 'Oh yeah, THAT party!'

Oh, and the song I played after it? It was 'Blue Monday' by New Order, of course. Two 'classics' with almost 100 years between them.

*Bill Morley is one of Sydney's longest lasting – and bravest – DJs.*

Upon joining the Mardi Gras board in 1987, I discovered that I had been nominated by Peter Macdonnell who wanted some professional input into their parties. Many contributors recall the very special experience these parties provide. I've always thought that, apart from the outlandish fun of it all, the experience has something to do with the release of endorphins that accompanies six or eight or ten hours dancing, rather like running a marathon. And in the early eighties, when there were only two such events to look forward to each year – the Mardi Gras Party and Sleaze Ball – it was also an occasion to catch up with friends and share the joy of one special night together.

Of course, it didn't take long before commercial entrepreneurs got on the band wagon and the mid-eighties marked the arrival and explosion of the 'dance party' in Australia. Soon there were RAT parties, Dance Delirium parties, Boys Own and Summer and Attitude and Locker Room parties, Bacchanalia parties, Black parties, White parties and many more, held at diverse venues around Sydney including, of course, the Showground. With one or another of these parties happening almost every Saturday night of the year, it was no wonder that nearby residents started getting stroppy!

Shortly after I joined the Mardi Gras party committee, we agreed that it was pretty silly for Mardi Gras, which had originated the giant 'dance party' in Australia, to miss out on all this additional revenue. So we decided to add another party to our schedule. *Cool with Sunny Periods* was held in late August 1988. The party attempted to take us through the four seasons in the course of the one night, but I suspect that it was simply high summer all night inside the Hordern and deep winter all night outside.

One memory from that night stands out vividly – one which I recall with great pride. I directed a show with the current hit 'High Energy'. It began with the acoustic roar of powerful engines, then headlights pierced a thick fog as fifteen dykes on bikes with their female dancers on pillion, stormed up a ramp and slowed to a stop at the front of the stage. Heart-stopping excitement. It was, I believe, the first time dykes had participated in a performance. About time.

# When EGO Lived with TALENT

## Ian Robinson

I HAVE A TERRIBLE MEMORY for dates and years, however I never forget major 'eclipses in time' that were simply meant to happen. When Richard Wherrett once said to me, 'I think you'd be interested in Mardi Gras – take a look', I phoned and was invited to be an observer at a couple of party committee meetings.

Around a long, low, stained and ashed coffee table, surrounded by a daggy mixture of chairs in a well-used meeting room at the Rushcutters Bay warehouse sat a group of men and women whom I still regard as some of the finest brains within Mardi Gras and within a lot of today's professional arts and performance scenes.

There was no apparent order in their seniority – it appeared to me that Richard, Murray McLachlan, Brad Golesworthy, David Wilkins and Peter Macdonnell were *all* obviously in control – a true co-operative of professional men who gave freely of their expertise and who actually knew what they were doing. Oh, yes! I really wanted to be a part of this!

I'd worked with Richard on three productions as a theatre designer. He's a man who I've always thought eclectic, eccentric, extremely knowledgeable and very sexy. What I didn't realise was the extent of his commitment to Mardi Gras.

Murray has become over the years a very close and dear friend – a great humanitarian, and, as President of Mardi Gras, I found him considered and magnetic in his calmness. I fell in love with him instantly.

David 'Dot' Wilkins was a powerhouse and artistic stormtrooper at these meetings. He has never changed. He freaked me with his diva attitude and then, as now, is a man whose talent and driving force have won my huge respect. Dot's place within the community and Mardi Gras is legendary.

Brad – well, he was the magician. I will never forget his eyes and his succinct and charming sluttish style – hot and horny!

But it was Peter Macdonnell for me who had the vision, the divine sense of seeing. I understood *exactly* his images and wanted to be part of them. He had a great feeling for music, atmosphere, sensuality in performance, dance and all of life's drugs.

It was as a result of these meetings of awe-inspiring minds that I was drawn deeper into the brilliant Sydney gay culture. (I was to eventually design the three lead floats for Mardi Gras in 1993 and the 'Priscilla' float in 1996.) Immersing myself in this whirlpool of creative magnetism, I entered a submission for Sleaze Ball, producing full concept designs for a mirrored, chandeliered, decadent *Phantom of the Opera* – well before Andrew Lloyd Webber had started his rewrite. Then my problems began.

That my concept wasn't accepted by those involved with the Mardi Gras workshop at the time was due, I believe, to a lack of vision and, dare I say it, a touch of envy – rather than a supposed 'lack of storage'! When I went to retrieve the designs, I found them lying on the floor of that same room with footprints all over them. 'Fuck you Mardi Gras! Is this the way you treat designs and designers?' I thought. I also recall Brian Thomson's model for a party design being hacked to pieces in his absence by the same Mardi Gras workshop personnel. It was the early days when theatre designers (or anyone) who did not belong to the small clique of 'MAGs' (Mardi Gras Artists Group) were dismissed as not possessing the 'community' creativity necessary for major contributions to the Mardi Gras Party and Parade.

So Peter Mac and I joined forces after he too had fallen foul of this cabal and set up a partnership. Many years before, I had worked as a stage manager on the musical *Promises, Promises* at the old Theatre Royal. This is where I'd first met Peter, who had been working for J. C. Williamson's for some time. Now here we were again. Our new partnership developed into a friendship and working relationship that remains the major landmark of my designing career.

As I was soon to find out, there were many people who disliked Peter: too tall, too big, too much ego, too insecure, too principled, too argumentative. Well, to me he was a good producer with a rare inspiration, a man of courage and an artist. On the evening of a Hordern dance party, we talked of our future working relationship and agreed we'd never have an argument. We never did!

Our team was completed when I introduced a brilliant young lighting designer and operator to Peter. I'd met Tony Rossiter at NIDA when he was a student (I was a lecturer) and had been impressed by his great understanding of music and classical music theatre. He was a fine stage manager who had worked for the Sydney Theatre Company, and who'd been designing and operating lights at the Midnight Shift for some time.

Tony and Peter were both Sagittarians. Oh! Now there were two huge egos and two sets of broad shoulders with insecurities to match. I was the ham between two slices of Sagittarian bread!

Both Peter and Tony spent their last energies on parties at Alexandria Basketball Stadium and Sydney Tower. The 'Boys' Own' and 'Summer' parties, with Les McDonald, were huge hits. Peter continued his Mardi Gras tradition of making a dance party a true 'event'. He took punters on a voyage through a series of experiences and then gently brought us back to earth. He had a great spirituality which I celebrated. It was always my job to anoint the outer, middle and inner circles of the dance floor and raised seating areas with nature's amyl, 'Oil of Wintergreen'. This, as the night heated up, produced a natural high.

Once, Peter brought in his vast collection of acquired bathers to 'decorate' the toilets and showers with an extra set-dressing of towels and massage tables. With the added bonus of another bottle of Wintergreen and special lighting, these were a huge success. The chill-out spaces were always lit and decorated – trees with pea bulbs and even koala bears in the branches. All these parties raised considerable funds for World AIDS Day benefits and other Sydney priorities.

Peter was the first to light up and put fireworks on Centrepoint's Sydney Tower. When he died, they dimmed the Tower in his honour. For Mardi Gras' 20th Anniversary in 1998, it was lit pink – always his dream. He would have been thrilled.

So much of the dance party culture has arisen and grown from these fabulous days. In my view, the giant events we witness nowadays have lost their finesse and the driving edge that artists like Peter could produce. In the Government Pavilion, Peter was ahead of his time. He would still be looking and searching within our huge and talented artistic community for originality and new stars in the making, whom he could spot a mile off. He would always surprise his party audiences with something fresh and spontaneous. He was never into formulas, or repeating old successes.

I have met so many incredibly gifted people who made our earlier Mardi Gras parties special, original and relevant. Peter Macdonnell's creativity and influence is still felt – the hum of his great powerhouse lives on.

*Ian Robinson is a Sydney-based theatre, film and events designer. Peter Macdonnell was a consummate party and events producer. He died in October, 1993. Tony Rossiter was a lighting designer and a much admired follow-spot operator. He died in November, 1994.*

The two performances I directed which I am most proud of were both in 1988, when Peter Macdonnell, David Wilkins and I were working well as a team.

The 1988 Mardi Gras Party was the tenth anniversary of the first 'parade'. To mark this occasion, we devised a huge birthday cake with ten enormous candles. We cut it in half, and put each half on either end of the Government Pavilion. The curved 'sides' faced the audience, thus providing us with two great performing stages.

The current hit was Diana Ross' 'Chain Reaction', so the notion was that there would be a 'chain reaction' of Dianas emerging one by one from the candles and momentarily upstaging the one already on. 'Upstaging' in drag performances can be very physical and fiercely competitive – here we would make a deliberate joke of it. Our Dianas were choreographed by Ross Coleman, who added the great touch of having the Dianas at each end 'mirror' each other, so that they 'reflected' the opposite gesture or step.

The thrill for me, standing in the middle of the Pavilion at 2 a.m. was hearing people around me discover our Dianas. 'Look, there's another one up that end.' The number ended with each candle 'going off' like a giant Roman Candle. This was the first time I'd ever directed something on such a scale. The chain reaction of ten thousand people's enjoyment was one of the greatest theatrical moments of my career.

That Party also introduced the first indoor fireworks – a spectacular display over the heads of dancers – and the first Mardi Gras party 'snow' storm to Viola Wills' rendition of 'Stormy Weather'.

# Mark

## Brett Sheehy

**1988**

I'm at the Party having a dance with my best friend Mark Robinson. It is around 4 a.m. and slowly the flashing reds and golds of the lighting design have turned a cooler blue. The air, too, feels colder. We dance on. Slowly the light becomes an even cooler bluish-grey, and a faint breeze begins to blow.

In the distance, just over the top of the music's beat, we can hear the wind.

Then the music changes. The first hypnotic bars of a new tune come in. With that the breeze intensifies. A chill air whips around us, and a frosty light picks out the bemused and amazed faces of thousands of people on the dance floor.

Finally, as the song comes crashing in, so too does the miraculous effect of a whirling snowstorm. Mark beams at me in total awe as the light cuts through a blizzard of what appears to be dazzling white snow, falling, rising and swirling above us.

It is the dance version of 'Stormy Weather' and 5000 people are swept up in one of the most exhilarating, glorious and surreal moments Mardi Gras has ever delivered.

I am looking up into the cavernous roof, really a night sky now, and am transfixed by the effect. I am in heaven.

When the song ends, I look around for Mark but have lost him . . .

It is 8 a.m. and I haven't seen Mark for some three or four hours. I know I'll find him at the end, but I was hoping we'd catch up for a last dance. I wait for the crowd to clear and then there he is, sitting against a wall. I rush up to him and ask how his night has been.

'Lamb, thank God you're still here, I've been sitting against this wall for the past two hours!' (Mark always calls me Lamb – a long story.)

'Why, what's wrong?' I reply.

'It's these shorts, I can't let anyone see me! I saw people laughing at me before when I tried to cross the floor to go outside!'

Mark's shorts boast an outrageous leopard print. They're pretty wild, but look terrific, and anyway, I can't believe that in the midst of a Mardi Gras party of 18 000 people, they'd draw a second glance. Besides, Mark is a clothing designer par excellence, he knows fashion like the back of his hand, and if the three hours of pre-party preening and costume changes didn't deliver an outfit he's comfortable in, God knows what would.

'What's wrong with the shorts?' I shout at him. 'I think they look great!'

'I don't mean the shorts, it's what they show! It's my legs! People are laughing at my skinny legs!'

Mark's legs are more marathon-runner's than league-player's, but they're even less likely to draw a laugh than the shorts. I realise that what he's actually suffering from is a serious dose of over-stimulated, paranoiac vanity.

I laugh, help him to his feet, escort him across the floor and out into the sunlight, assuring him he looks fine, and that frankly no one could give a shit how his bloody legs look at this hour of the morning.

'Are you sure?'

'I'm sure.'

A lightning mood change flashes across his face and then out of nowhere he beams. 'Okay, let's do the recoveries!'

### 1990

I am working at the Sydney Theatre Company and, for the third year running, Richard Wherrett (STC's founding Director) has agreed that the company should be represented in the Mardi Gras Parade by a float promoting an STC production. It will be *Rome Tremble* – Bill Harding's bio-play about Maria Callas, with the extraordinary Wendy de Waal miming to Callas' greatest arias. Graham Wills, STC's ingenious head of wardrobe, designs and decorates the float on a shoestring, with Wendy as La Divina aloft in a cherry picker. A group of adoring male fans, on foot behind, strew rose petals in the float's path and, with an eye to the box office, hand out leaflets promoting the production.

We want the 'adoring fans' to look great – black tie, groomed, a night at the opera – and so I recruit Mark to join me and five others. Mark is perfect for the role, much more so than the rest of us. He is terrifically handsome, six foot two, jet hair, a style guru, and he can carry a suit like Cary Grant.

All day long the clouds are gathering, and it looks like Fred Nile might actually get his wish, after years of unanswered prayers. Sure enough, just as we head out of STC's loading dock for the Parade grouping area, the rain falls. By the time the Parade gets under way, it is teeming.

What the heck. We're soaked to the skin in black-tie and we don't give a damn. We reach the Showground, eight drowned rats, but Mark is in seventh heaven. For him, his first Mardi Gras Parade is an unqualified triumph.

### 1996

Mark has been sick for a while now, but there's no way he's going to miss Mardi Gras. I am waiting for him in the guest bar, as arranged, anxious not to miss the next show downstairs.

A middle-aged man approaches in a dishevelled dirty-blonde wig, granny sunglasses, vinyl bag and an outfit that sits somewhere between Miss New Zealand's 1950s patterned dresses and a Woodstock poncho.

This is either very bad drag or a hippie throwback. He steps up to me and I uncomfortably give him a wan smile. Who the hell is this? And what's he coming up to talk to me for?

'Hello, lamb!'

It is Mark. I have never seen him in any kind of drag before, and I'm completely shocked. Is this the same Mark who wouldn't step out the front door unless he looked like he was stepping out of *GQ*?

I burst out laughing. 'What are you?'

To this he flashes back that dazzling smile and says, 'You know what, lamb, I haven't got a clue – but who cares?'

In that one line Mark takes a leap a mile long, and I realise for the first time that there is a new order here, a restructuring of priorities, a fresh spin on what matters and what emphatically does not.

Mark tires easily now. He stays for another couple of hours, a sterling effort given that he's been in hospital more often than out these past four months. Then he announces it's time to leave.

I take him to the front gates, hug him gently goodbye, and put him in a cab.

## 1997

It is the night before Mardi Gras. Mark is in hospital and we are reminiscing about Maria Callas, 'Chain Reaction', the leopard print shorts, 'Stormy Weather, I Am What I Am', Tina, Kylie, 'Go West'. He is contemplative, funny, fatalistic, hopeful. It's the first time in ten years I'm going to a Mardi Gras party without him and I tell him I'll miss him. 'Have a dance for me, lamb.' I do, and in less than ten weeks Mark is dead.

## 1998

I'd like to say I can feel him watching, that his spirit is floating somewhere over the dance floor, that he's still with me somehow. But the truth is I feel none of that. All I feel is a sense of waste, loss and longing. I miss him. I wish he was here. Happy Mardi Gras, Mark.

*Brett Sheehy is Deputy Director of the Sydney Festival.*

# Trash

## Vanessa Wagner

BACK IN THE DAYS when the Mardi Gras parties were held in different pavilions, life seemed simpler. People were only just starting to whinge about the music, costume was still an important part of people's night (all night), and the ecstasy was really good (every time).

It must have been 1988 and there I was with ten thousand of my closest friends 'cuttin' the rug' in the splendiferously voluminous Government Pavilion Hall. The slightest turn of one's nut would reveal a unique vista, whether it be the magnificent industrial arches of the hall or a huge laser snake dancing at one end as if appearing out of nowhere. Then, of course, there was the memorable snow storm preceded by the spooky chopper-like sounds of the enormous fans firing up to distribute all those Tally Ho offcuts for the masses to enjoy.

I was in fine form that night, flying high and free from all of life's complications and anxieties, just meditating on the beautiful beats, smells and sights. Nothing was to prepare me for my one and only dance floor astral travelling experience. In what seemed no time at all, I had travelled about 75 metres from one end of the hall to the other and I didn't spot no travelator. Somehow I had been swallowed up just like Jodie Foster in *Contact* and transported to another place, except my new place was still on earth and not far from where I'd begun, but just as vexing.

The night was over before you could say 'have you got a light' and I found myself showing off my borrowed Pam Hogg lamé body shirt/dress courtesy of a forty-four gallon garbage bin which I was in. I revelled in that bloody bin sparkling away knowing that I held the true meaning of trash. I proudly sashayed out of freak show alley, unlocked my unisex bike and swished up Anzac Parade under a canopy of Moreton Bay Figs waving to confused families in their sensible cars out on a Sunday drive. *Vive la revolution!*

*Vanessa Wagner (aka Tobin Saunders) is . . . is . . . well, is just EXTRAORDINARY.*

# A Nice Night's Entertainment

## Pete Nettell

FOR LAWRENCE AND I, that year's Mardi Gras was a quiet affair. We'd just returned from a ten week whirlwind trip to Europe to visit my parents and had decided that, really, we didn't *need* to go. Our finances would be in ruins. So the justification went.

Having survived a Northern Hemisphere winter and the gorgings of many family Christmas dos, we were exhausted and out of shape. But as our return to Sydney in early February neared, the ghost of Mardi Gras Past started haunting us. When you've had a good few experiences at the Party, there's no denying its temptations. But Lawrence and I are hardly big on the scene. Two cats and a comfy house take their toll on your tolerance for shouted conversation and fag smoke. So the big outing can be especially important, a time to feel connected to something bigger than a household.

Unfortunately, we'd already rationalised our situation (a dangerous thing, logic) and decided there'd be no tickets left anyway. And we hadn't organised any party essentials, outfits, etc . . . Disturbingly, I kept hearing of friends who'd had excess tickets and who, of course, had passed them on, as we obviously didn't want them.

To compensate, we decided on the next best option: a gay pub. Maybe not very exciting for some, but an event for us. Come the evening, the desire to actually be at the party was maddening. To cope, we didn't even go to the Parade, but stayed locked inside the house with a video and takeaway. Besides, I've been crushed too many times at Taylor Square and seen enough bizarre episodes of straights getting on down post-Parade to do that again.

By 11.30 p.m. the video was finished and it seemed safe to go out. I was actually quite excited! Dressed in our casual bests, we sauntered down a strangely quiet King Street. On Saturday night there's usually a tide of men walking towards the Newtown Hotel. That night we were the only ones. When we arrived, I understood why. It was shut. Feeling naive in your thirties is a humbling experience. Lawrence was ready to call it quits and return to the cats. 'The Imperial,' I insisted.

So we headed down to the Imperial and even spotted several other 'Couldn't Be Bothered' and 'Can't Afford Its' venturing in the same direction.

Once inside we bought a drink and settled in with the lesbians playing pool and leaning against the bar. We looked around and tried to summon the ghost of Mardi Gras into the pub. In came more lesbians. I felt like we were in a women-only space. The boy from behind the bar came round collecting glasses. He was very nice. He came by several times and we began to look forward to it. Each time we gathered more information about him. He'd been in the Mardi Gras Parade. He was on one of the Christian floats. He didn't want to go to the Party. He was going to New Guinea to be a missionary.

I felt like we *were* missionaries. There had to be something that could transport us, at least partly, into that blissful state of euphoria and bonhomie. More drinks. Lawrence and I looked at each other expectantly. In a classic case of confusion between couples, neither of us had brought any money with us. Our Mardi Gras was over.

We didn't have a hangover and we didn't waste the week recovering. That's about the best I can say of it. We'd learnt our lesson. From then on, we resolved that we would either be in another country (out of sight, out of mind), or at the Party. There really isn't any in-between.

*Pete Nettell is a Sydney-based theatre director whose credits include the stage adaptation of Dorothy Porter's* The Monkey's Mask.

During committee meetings for the 1988 Sleaze Ball, it became clear that we all felt that the party had perhaps lost some of its 'sleaze' factor. We were determined to reintroduce this. Sleaze was to be held in the Royal Hall of Industries which, at that time, would allow no lighting rig to hang from the ceiling – all lights were to be grounded stands. A double solution to this problem was arrived at. A series of six or eight scaffolding towers were erected which could take some of these lights. At the same time, these towers would provide small stages on which an 'act' could take place. Each act would involve one or two people and be representative of some of the things we do in private – hence its name: 'solitary moments'.

One man, Ian Jopson, 'shaved' his body from head to toe (with a bladeless razor of course). One recalcitrant 'schoolboy', Corby Beard, was bare-bottom spanked by an outraged schoolmaster. A suited business man, Greg Conrad, got 'home' and changed into full drag. Another man in silhouette did a strip and 'masturbated'. His orgasm – in reality a large tube of lubricant in a pump action tube – lasted five minutes or so! And a bunch of dykes 'performed' the most alarming S & M scene! Amongst other acts, these small shows happened at random through the night, with no introduction – happily surprising whosoever was nearby at the time.

# Recollections of a
# Sleazy Lighting Designer
## Peter Neufeld

IF YOU CAN'T BEAT THEM . . . I was waging a losing battle. I don't know at what point I decided to give up but it was probably about 7 a.m. The magic of the night was slowly being turned into the morning after. At last, my job was over. After all how or why should a lighting designer compete with the sun? So I joined them.

There were still thousands of the hard core left and the energy on the dance floor was glorious. From 93 million miles away, parallel rays of sunlight stretched into the Royal Hall of Industries, dissolving my lights into the air. The Sleaze Ball was almost over. I'd had no previous connection with the Mardi Gras until that year. Now I was dancing at the Ball!

It was 1988 and the revolution in moving lights (ones that could change colour, position and focus, as well as project various patterns) had only been in Australia for a short time, and then only as the domain of really big shows. I'd already done several shows with them and thought they'd be mind-blowing for a party. Not that I'd actually been to a party at that stage. So I approached the Mardi Gras committee with my idea and got the go-ahead to incorporate some of these new lights into Allen Parkinson's design for the *Cool With Sunny Periods* Party. I recall Peter Macdonnell later wondering why 30 per cent had failed during the twelve hours of continuous use. It was early days but at least everyone could see the possibilities. And the pitfalls. We were all learning.

However, the budget for the following Sleaze Ball was tight and I was lumbered with conventional lighting. I was promised that the money for moving lights would be there for the Mardi Gras Party in five months time. After all, Sleaze is the fundraiser for the main party. It seemed a long time to wait before I would get my wish again.

Meanwhile, the magnitude of the job in hand was apparent. We were categorically told that the ceiling in the Hall of Industries was not capable of suspending a lighting rig. (A fact that's since proved wrong.) Sleaze Ball's set designer, David Martin, then produced a scale model of scaffolding in various forms with seven stages throughout the hall for the Seven Deadly Solitary Moments. At least I had somewhere to hang the lights. I can't think how we got all the technical drawings done without the help of the computer software that's now commonplace. There were a lot of them. It took forever.

In those days there were only two lighting companies capable of taking on the task of rigging up the Sleaze Ball. We decided on the one with the best attitude. For the next few weeks, I squeezed as much as I could out of my budget. There'd never been a party quite as big or complex. Certainly not on that budget! Finally, one week in late October, the scaffolding crews erected the set. In spite of the strange, bizarre shapes, they finished on time, and, at midday Thursday, it was the turn of the lighting crews.

There were kilometres of cables to be run to hundreds of lights. None of the digital technology that is conventional now was available then, and there were lights in the most awkward and far-flung places. We struggled throughout the following two days and nights. Before we knew it, it was Saturday – the day of the party. There was barely time to go back home, shower and change. We were all tired but excited. We had completed the fit-up. Everything was ready. It was on!

I had an hour to programme the lighting desks. I had to get to know the beast intimately and there was no time for pleasantries. I had to come to terms with it very fast to have total control over the entire space for every atmospheric possibility, all my combinations, chases and effects.

There was no turning back now. It was 10 p.m. and the doors were open. I had to pray that I had everything covered. The bare dance floor reflected the lights as the music thundered. Within an hour, there wasn't an empty space to be seen. Within two, the space was bursting with 8000 expectant and exultant people. Now it had a life of its own and we were swept along with it.

At midnight, the shows began: 'The Seven Deadly Sins'. Some happened at once on all seven stages, others just occurred on their own. Boys being 'whipped', girls being 'whipped'. Fearless performances. All through the night. Now I understood why it was called the Sleaze Ball! It was outrageous and wonderful. I could hardly keep up just looking at the seven stages, let alone lighting them. Meanwhile, the floor was pumping.

The greatest pressure on the lighting was one act which took place at about 4 or 5 a.m. A very athletic man was going to 'masturbate' his erect and monstrous penis to the point of ejaculation, and beyond. However, the only way to do this legally was to show it in silhouette. It was incumbent on me to light this man as he performed on a tiny stage, surrounded on all sides by white cloth, seven metres up on a tower, in the middle of the dance floor. No messy shadows, please, just a sharp silhouette. This one little show was a highlight for me as it worked so well. And boy, what an ejaculation!

I did fail in one duty. I'd been asked if I could floodlight the toilets at the back of the hall so they remained bright, and stayed on, throughout the night. We tried in vain – and so it still remains today. No matter how hard Mardi Gras tries to achieve this aim, they are always thwarted.

The installation of the lights had taken sixty hours with meagre sleep. I then undertook twelve hours of continuous operation. It was a mighty effort. But, for the 1989 Mardi Gras Party, I got everything I needed . . . except perhaps a laser! What a night that was! We finally proved that moving lights worked.

The next year the party had a laser. By then, every knees-up was determined to use these revolutionary moving lights that nowadays we are all so blasé about.

The 1988 Sleaze Ball was the last time a conventional lighting rig was used for a big dance party. It had served its purpose, it hadn't broken down and it had looked quite good, if I might say so myself. When I finally joined the dance floor I was exhausted but finally a real part of it all. At the next Sleaze Ball, I elected to dance to someone else's lights! Much more fun!

*Peter Neufeld is a lighter of theatre, concerts, trade shows, whatever.*

# All Those Wonderful People, Down There in the Dark

## Mark Trevorrow

FROM ARTHUR STACE to Bea Miles to the Martin Place Shouter, Sydney treasures its eccentrics, gleefully swapping stories and sightings. To its great credit, and true to its central place in the city's psyche, Mardi Gras has added to the pantheon. After a few short years everyone knows, or has seen, or has (ahem) encountered Troughman. And if you *don't* know about Troughman ... well, I'm sorry, but I'm not explaining. There's got to be a William Yang photograph you can look up.

Put it this way: once seen, never forgotten. Troughman is worthy of a piece all his own, as the subject of a play, a documentary, or at the very least an installation ... placed, perhaps, next to a Duchamp urinal. Or, more appropriately, under it.

But compelling as he is, this is not about Troughman. Something has always struck me as even more interesting. How does it happen that Troughman gets to ply his trade, year in and out? How are the right conditions achieved? All right, all right, I'll get to the point:

*Who is it that always turns out the lights in the Showground's toilets?*

Have you seen him? Is he an inspired individual with an electrical background, ancient blueprints and a purse-sized Phillips screwdriver? Or is it a highly organised gang, on a roster, with links to the very topmost levels of the Mardi Gras board, the Royal Agricultural Society and Fox Studios? Is it ... gasp ... a WOMAN?

It's a delicious mystery, really, this unsung, unidentified dark horse, whose efforts make 'Eternity' look like mere chalkmark on the pavement. Under continuous fluorescent lighting, Troughman would be left standing as helplessly as everyone else, forced to use the vast RHI or Hordern underground Men's for something no wilder than a quick slash, a furtive glance and a splash on the face from a cold tap over a hand basin.

In the dark, of course, it's a different story.

Unspoken of in polite gay society, slyly hinted at in the fag rag gossip columns, this recurring, unofficial Mardi Gras event bears all the hall-marks of ritual. Indeed, under any other circumstances it would be called a tradition. The lights *always* go out some time between 2 and 3 a.m. This is *always* greeted with the same muted but delighted reaction from an assembled, pretend-not-to-be-waiting-for-it, just-happen-to-be-here throng. One or two fainthearts always storm out in a hissy. An outraged party official *always* endeavours to turn them on again – sometimes more than once – and is *always* foiled, to yet more muted applause. Frisson is the only word for it.

Even more wonderful, to me, are the wickedly camp anecdotes gleaned from this forbidden but well-attended phenomenon. You've never heard any? *Darling, you need to get out more* ... Or perhaps just find some more forthright friends.

Shameless as it may sound, I collect these little gems. Why do they sparkle so? Is it because they illuminate all the hilarious paradoxes of gay existence? Is it because they're even funnier than that parlour game where you work out your drag name by taking the name of your first pet and coupling it with your mother's maiden name? Whatever, Miss Pussy Aspinall.

I must confess that I was actually there, deep beneath the Hordern Pavilion, for two of my favourite stories.

I stumbled, slightly innocently, into my first Mardi Gras lights-out. It was years ago now, of course, back before the war. (The Gulf War.) Against a far-away disco thump, the atmosphere grew quieter as a sil-houetted throng, already scantily clad, grabbed at the nearest unex-pected opportunity. I recall it was relatively early in the party, which merely added to the excitement. Old hands knew the likelihood of a sudden restoration to normal illuminations, and were *going for it.*

The inevitable happened. Suddenly, in the blink of a hundred eyes, the lights came blazing back on. Everyone looked down, did up, slinked out. And a single, anguished cry emanated from a locked cubicle.

*'Oh my God, I've been doing it with a drag queen!'*

A few years later. The same setting, only much later in the party. Five a.m. or so. The starting-to-get-slightly-silly-hour. In the midst of that extraordinary dark and fetid silence that descends upon such occa-sions when fingers are doing the talking – *so I'm told!* – a high pitched voice sings out.

'Steph ... Steph! ... Are you there, love?'

A slight pause. Then a reply, from the opposite corner of a packed, dark room.

'Yeah, love.'

'How's yours?'

'Bona, love. How's yours?'

'Bona.'

*Oh, God, shutup shutup shutup!* It's getting funny. And we know what a passion-killer THAT is. A few minutes pass. Back to business. Then . . .

'Steph . . . Steph . . .?'

A few groans. A few muffled titters from those of us who appreciate good timing when we hear it.

'Yeah, love?'

'I'll get you to do my tax on Tuesday.'

The lights stayed off, but the erotically charged atmosphere popped like a party balloon amid laughter and guffaws. It *is* funny being a queen, isn't it?

*Mark Trevorrow (aka Bob Downe) began his performing career as a Globo. As far as possible, he arranges his international work schedule around Mardi Gras and Sleaze.*

# A Sight for Bright Eyes

## Joh Bailey

MY FIRST MARDI GRAS, which was 18 years ago, when I was 18, is my most memorable.

As nature was calling, I innocently took myself to the men's bathroom. While at the urinal relieving myself, I noticed out of the corner of my eye that some poor party-goer had fallen *into* the urinal. My immediate reaction was to offer help.

As I leaned over to 'fish him out' I realised his positioning, *lying on the urinal trays*, was voluntary.

Not only that, he seemed to enjoy being pissed on.

I was mortified.

This person has since been elevated to 'gay icon' status and we now all know and love him as 'Troughman'.

*Joh Bailey's hairdressing salons spread widely across Australia. After work, Joh likes to slip into something more uncomfortable.*

# Mardi Gras Myth 3

*The party boy just* had *to go to the toilet. An empty cubicle – what relief! He retrieved the little 'dilly bag' containing all essentials for the evening – keys, money, VIP pass, lip balm and little brown bottles with white stuff in them – from his crotch where it also served to enhance the apparent size of what, at this stage of the evening, was a very shrivelled dick.*

*Mission accomplished, he decided to grab the opportunity to 'top up'. He could manage to get a little toot onto the end of the key-ring, but it persisted in falling during the shaky journey from bottle to nostril. Just as he was about to give up in disgust, a man popped his head over the door of the cubicle.*

*'Are you all right there, sir?'*

*'No. I just can't get this stuff up my nose.'*

*'Sir, I think you should know I'm a security officer.'*

*'Oh, great! Then you can come and help me!'*

# The Lone Ranger

## Maggie Kirkpatrick

IN 1988 IT WAS DECIDED by the board of Mardi Gras to invite donations from the Parade spectators for distribution amongst various char-
ities. This required a band of volunteers to hold out canvas bags attached
to the end of long poles over the heads of the screaming hordes into
which money could be dropped. These brave volunteers accompanied
the lead float out – the 'Collection Float' as it was called. A number of
celebrities were asked to join the volunteers, and cajole and bully the
crowd into parting with a few bucks or loose change.

The 1988 collection was graced by only one such foolish celebrity
volunteer – ME! It consisted of a very small truck driven by a brake-
happy dyke, who was obviously not used to travelling at a mere 5
kilometres per hour. I was constantly being thrown violently forward as
she slammed to a stop yet again. Sometimes this was to my advantage,
as it allowed me to dodge the coins which some eager beaver spectators
chose to throw at *me*, rather than *in* the *sack*.

My only companion was a nameless old dear sitting on a throne
looking like a very tired old Royal waving to the crowd. I never did find
out who she (if she really was a 'she') was. We raised $20 000 for our
efforts – not bad for a first go.

I had the great joy of participating this way again in 1989, with Geraldine Turner and Ron Handley, aka Fanny Farquar; and again, in 1993,
with Julian Clary and Wendy Harmer, who looked like a beardless Fidel
Castro complete with cigar. This was also the first year of *Shop Yourself
Stupid*, organised by the Bobby Goldsmith Foundation, which has continued to be one of the great highlights of the Mardi Gras Festival. Again,
I volunteered to encourage shoppers to spend. I worked my arse, or tits,
or both, off – yelling at prospective customers to come and spend. It
was great fun. Meanwhile, the crowds of spectators at the Parade had
become too big for the collectors to reach them, and the practice of
soliciting donations was eventually dropped around 1994.

I have also, on two other occasions, judged the Costume Parade, once
with Leo Schofield, and I was invited once to judge the Parade entries.

I am very proud of those years and my involvement with the gay and lesbian community. While always in awe of the huge efforts in glitz and glamour of the big, often political statements in the Parade, I have also been deeply moved by the smaller organisations that participate – especially the parents and friends who march, and also the country and smaller town gays, who have braved what is often a 'red-neck' background to make their statement. These have brought tears to my eyes.

*Maggie Kirkpatrick is a great actress. She once agreed to leave a message on a friend's answering machine in the voice of 'the Freak' from* Prisoner: *'Now listen, leave your message quick and then get straight back to your cell.'*

# Sequence of Sequins

## Lana Turnip

DEARIE, DEARIE ME. Where do I start?

I remember first meeting Cindy Pastel at the Albury in 1989 during a power failure and in total darkness. When the lights came on she told me I would look fab in one of her skinny muumuus. Thus began my dubious, maybe even infamous life in drag and consequently my involvement with Oxford Street and Mardi Gras.

I recall my first Mardi Gras in 1990 to the strains of: 'Here Lana, go buy a bevvie love, and I'll start your face.' Suddenly it was all happening – off to my first Parade. The greatest show on earth.

It was raining (thanks to Fred Nile and cohorts) and my make-up was running and my wig was falling to pieces. 'Oh what a feeling.' I'll never forget it. It was heaven.

Since that night of a million sequinned, screaming queens, I have not missed a Mardi Gras Parade. I have wobbled and blubbered my fat arse up Oxford Street, often in front of the Marching Boys. I have been on other floats but believe me, the wonderful buzz of that first night has never left me.

The most amazing thing about Mardi Gras for me is the feeling of community and unity – not just from the participants in the Parade but also from spectators. Everyone wants to be involved. It makes me feels like a shining star, people touching me, cheering, smiling – a lovely night. Chookas!

*Lana Turnip is more than a drag queen. She's an experience.*

# Pom-Pom Cut Offs

## Di Henry

FROM 1989 TO 1991 I performed the role of Art Director for the Sydney Gay and Lesbian Mardi Gras – supervising workshops and artists, producing Parades, organising party sets and props, etc. It was an enlightening experience – being a straight woman while being completely enveloped in the gay community.

In the first year, Corby Beard and I dreamt up the mad concept of the Marching Boys – a parody of the American parade marching girls. Only sheer persistence and determination on Corby's part ensured that he was able to recruit the team and put the scene together. He allowed me the delight of watching rehearsals outside my office, day after day after day. Memories of the tons of pom-pom off-cuts that covered the floor still haunt me!

I should have realised that working for Mardi Gras was going to be exciting and controversial. Shortly after I arrived, Fred Nile announced that he was going to tread the gay turf and walk the magic mile up Oxford Street – much to the chagrin of the community. A less than peaceful protest followed with the majority of the Mardi Gras acting as marshals – a task well practised by the team. One image I will always carry is that of the giant rump of a mounted police horse bearing down on me whilst, sashes on and two-way radio in hand, I endeavoured to protect a horde of spectators behind me! It was a sight to behold! It was pouring rain too and in the middle of the night! It continues to surprise me how much stamina one can maintain in situations such as these.

Working for Mardi Gras meant that I experienced how it must feel to be gay in mainstream society. I am sure, however, that my colleagues treated me with a lot more respect than they, at times, received from the majority. For that experience, I will be forever grateful.

*Di Henry now works for SOCOG.*

# Scrap Foam Rubber

## Corby Beard

IT WAS 1989 and I was serving (an appropriate description) on the Board of the Sydney Gay and Lesbian Mardi Gras. As Mardi Gras approached, this required almost taking up residence in the run-down, overcrowded, hot/cold, leaky, draughty workshop-come-offices at the bottom of Boundary Street in Rushcutters Bay. When not catching fitful snatches of booze-affected sleep in my bomb-site of a bedroom, or working for the long-suffering owners of Café 191 in wildly unpredictable shifts, I could be found stumbling from Party meeting to Board meeting to Festival Launch. At other times, as I was on this day, I would be chatting with the ever-patient and stoic workshop crew as to how I was going to make the first seventy-five Marching Boys costumes out of a few baseball hats donated by the Australian Ballet and some scrap foam rubber.

It was while returning with my fix of grease and flavoured milk from the nearby take-away 'Food Fantasy Café' – re-dubbed by Mardi Gras regulars as the 'Food Nightmare Café' – that I noticed a swarthy man looking a little lost at the entrance of the workshop. Part of me wanted to glide past, head down, high on adrenalin and my own projects, and leave him to work out who to talk to and where to go. Like the first night of football training or the first day of school, it is never easy, and always a little daunting, entering the fast-moving lap-pool that is Mardi Gras during February.

Anyway, I stopped and, with a mouthful of schnitzel sandwich, asked if I could help.

His name was Sam, I think! Or Con, or Nick, or one of those generic Anglicised Greek names. He was, to put it in the vernacular, very 'straight-acting'. But he wondered if he could help in any way as he was on holidays for a few weeks.

'What do ya do for a quid?' I asked in my butchest tone.

'I'm a sparky . . . an electrician,' he beamed back.

'Well I'm sure we can put you to some good use,' I said as I began to introduce him to the workshop manager. Then I escorted him on a whirlwind tour of the lavish premises at our disposal, before returning to the Marching Boys' drawing board.

Over the next few weeks, I would notice Sam involved in various non-electrical tasks around the place: painting, gluing, shredding, teasing, glittering and the all-important sequining. He had become one of the real daily volunteers, and was usually there crowded around a case of beer at the end of the day with the staff and the other volunteers who had earned their stripes.

Occasionally I would wave hello as I scurried past, nursing my burgeoning ulcer, and 'Sam' would look up and smile contentedly as he studiously beavered away.

'How's it going Sam?'

'Not bad, mate.'

The day of Mardi Gras arrived. My seventy-five marching boys, resplendent in their mock tin soldier outfits and pom-poms, were all gathered at the Showground for our final, and only, dress rehearsal. It was around two in the afternoon and we were all like skittish three-year-old colts, chaffing at the bit before the big race. We were all anxious to get on with the last minute shopping, waxing and preening that always consumes those last few hours before one assembled at the beginning of the Parade route.

I was a wreck. I had well and truly come to the end of what was, by then, a threadbare tether. Anxiously I waited for the damn music to start from the ute containing our sound and lights. All I got was much fiddling by the official technical types with our amplifier and generator, accompanied by the odd deafening blast of feedback and the hysterical chatter of seventy-five queens.

'Listen mate,' a stern roadie type finally informed me, with a grave and foreboding sense of finality, 'you're fucked! These two ain't compatible. Better get another generator.' And with that he strode off, his face obscured by a chattering Madonna-esque headpiece.

At that moment I felt like John Wayne in *The Alamo*, as my gay soldiers pleadingly stared at me, eager for their general's solution. When the earth failed to open up and swallow me, I decided the best tactic was to run.

'Don't worry,' I said. 'I'll be back in a flash with another generator.'

Another generator, I thought. Where the fuck would I find another generator at three o'clock on the Saturday afternoon of Mardi Gras? SHIT!

In full panic mode, I retreated to the control room. Frantically I began flicking through *Yellow Pages*. G for genuflect . . . genocide . . . generators. As the pages of generator adds stared defiantly at me from the page, I noticed large wet spots of tears, slowly blurring the type. I had failed at the last post. I had convinced everyone I could pull this off and now I had to go out there and tell them all . . . 'Maybe next year!'

I slumped weepily in a corner, the *Yellow Pages* abandoned in my lap, and the phone discarded forlornly by my side. My sobbing had failed to attract the attention of the attendant Cath Phillips (President) or Richard Cobden (Party Director). I upped the volume and intensity of the sobbing until Richard dragged himself away from his own daunting schedule to embrace and comfort me. I was a broken little boy. Shell-shocked in the trenches. For a moment, I had lost it. Richard got me a drink and assured me that everyone would understand. I really should let people know that it was over as soon as possible.

Like a condemned man, I took a deep breath and began the long walk across the burning asphalt of the Showground towards the now desperate group of young men huddled around the pathetically crippled vehicle which had once, not so long ago, promised so much.

Suddenly, without warning, as I neared them, a booming chorus of Kylie Minogue's 'Step Back in Time' rent the air.

I ran toward the source of this heaven sent refrain.

'Thank you, God,' I thought. 'I'll never masturbate again.'

In the centre of the now cheering and dancing crowd was the calm and happy face of Sam.

'How ya goin', mate? They are buggers sometimes these things. Someone forgot to adjust the level on the blah . . . blah . . . blah . . .'

My electrician angel, I thought, as his technical description faded away in the wake of my delirium.

'You're a saint,' I cried, as I smacked a big kiss on his moustached lips.

As the marching boys pumped off on their final joyous rehearsal around the Showground, I thought to myself of the delicious synchronicity so often evident in such magnified human activities as Mardi Gras, shipwrecks and war. A lesson for us in life.

Always be kind to strangers – you never know when you might need them.

And, if you are out there, Sam or Con or Nick?

'Thanks, mate!'

*The Marching Boys debuted in 1989, and became one of the Parade's most popular entrants.*

# Planes, Trains and Hairy Dames

## Marie-France Stockdale

I'D BEEN AWAY FAR TOO LONG. I'd left Sydney just after the Mardi Gras. My friends had dragged themselves with me to the airport, direct from Recovery. As they waved goodbye, I was still too euphoric to realise just how much I would miss them. The real trip was about to begin.

Living in Japan, I learnt how cruel an unpermissive society can be. You can get into all kinds of strife just for being open and friendly. It didn't help that western women are chiefly seen as the victim/vixens in *manga* porn magazines. I'd changed a lot of people's minds, but it was hard going. By the end of my stay, I was guarded about everything I said, did and wore. I had an extensive wardrobe of ankle-length office clothes and sharp pointy boots.

My physical body was flown back to Sydney a year later. Someone picked it up and took it to a safe house. It was hard to believe that anyone could really relate to me. It was hard to believe that women in Darling-ghurst dared to wear leopard skin bras out to lunch, let alone the guys! The last time these things had seemed possible was at the Mardi Gras twelve months ago. That time and place where you can't be too brazen or freaky to fit in. A celebration of respect and acceptance. It was just what I needed.

Happily, it was that time of year again. Desperate to see familiar faces, I invited some old friends to meet me at the Parade. At 6.30 I left my sensible travelling armour in the suitcase where it belonged, and stepped out the door armed with a water bottle and a milk crate. My outfit would have seen me stoned at Mecca and felt up on a Tokyo train.

As I walked up to Oxford Street, people laughed. For once they weren't laughing *at* me. People were skipping. They were showing off skin and giving out hugs for free. A gorgeous seven foot drag queen sang an ode to his own beauty as he swept along the sidewalk in a fantastic red beachball of a dress.

The crowd thickened as I neared the Parade route, so I darted through back streets toward my favourite corner. The alleyways were strewn with feathers, stray sequins, glitter and confetti. Finally, I reached the partying masses on the main street. I plunged in. It was the kookiest, happiest crowd I'd seen in a long time, so it took a while to realise: I was lost.

How was I going to find my friends? I'd told them to look out for me in a loud outfit at Taylor Square. It was hard to pick out any familiar features among the thousands of spectators dressed up as Mardi Gras oddities.

Some boffin always claims that there 'couldn't possibly have been however many spectators watching the Parade, because you can't fit that many people on Oxford Street'. I'm telling you: that street becomes a *Tardis* on Mardi Gras night. There are expert wrigglers, roof-perchers, tree climbers, window ledge walkers, shoulder riders and milk crate hang fivers . . .

I'm a veteran of several Ramones concerts, and so I managed to negotiate my way to the crowd-restraining barricade. The girls next to me had organised a posse to defend their prime location for the last five hours. I smiled and chatted to them, to avoid any resentment about my territorial infringement.

As we heard the distant rumble of the Parade approaching, a tough looking girl with a camera tried to shove in next to us. I was happy to share my spot, but the ogling girls got quite self-righteous.

'We were here first!' they screamed.

'I'm from a gay magazine, so I have more right to be here!' came the isolationist inner-city response on my left.

Both sides looked to me for support. I was wedged in the centre of a fully-blown bitch fight. Appropriately, the Dykes on Bikes roared past at this point, wielding whips and chains.

I started to wonder: strictly speaking, what right did any of us have to be here? A bunch of oglers getting a free Chippendales show. A journalist who couldn't be bothered to get to her assignment on time. And me. Why was I squashing myself between a collection of petulant arguing strangers and a wobbly metal road barrier?

Just then the Marching Boys appeared on the horizon. Everyone could see what they'd come to see. The Boys were beaming out brotherly love and strutting it in vibrant Bondi lifesaver cossies. Look at them! Ooh!

The one in red, the one in blue. My God! Nick! My high school buddy! He'd always seemed a bit reserved about *something*. Now he was proud and I was proud too. More than that, he'd heard my shrieks over the hysterical thousands. Looking round, he picked me out, squashed against the metal bars. And, after five years, ran straight over and kissed me!

'Was that your brother?' asked one of the girls on my right.

'No. Just a friend.' I knew that would leave them wondering.

Who's the bitch now?

*Marie-France Stockdale is a Sydney-based architect.*

Letters to the Editor
*Sydney Morning Herald*

Dear Sir

Regarding the repeated media claim of 600 000 to 700 000
spectators at the Gay and Lesbian Mardi Gras:

1. The route is 2500 metres long
2. The entire roadway is 30 metres across
3. Total space – 75 000 square metres including the roadway used
   by the Parade itself.

Therefore, if eight people crammed into every square metre,
there would still be no room for the Parade.
For the available footpath space to accommodate 600 000 people,
there would have to be about 29 people to every square metre.

A more realistic (yet still generous) figure, at six people per
square metre, would total around 180 000 to 200 000 people.

Cameron Horn
Research officer for Fred Nile, MLC, Sydney

# Eyes Wide Open

## Harry M. Miller

I REMEMBER CLEARLY THINKING on the night, 'I'm sure I know that face . . . Isn't it . . . God, yes it is!'

It's just that when you are used to seeing people in a particular surrounding, somebody who you have perhaps been dealing with during the week before, in shirt, tie and Armani suit, it does take a bit of refocusing when they have on that rather special Mardi Gras outfit with a touch of make-up here and there. Dear reader, I'm not pretending that I have led a sheltered life, nor am I asking you to forget that I've been deeply involved in the theatre and entertainment business for thirty years, but you do get thrown by a different persona in a different context.

I might add that the he, with whom I'd been doing business earlier in the week, now made a pretty gorgeous gal.

That first Mardi Gras year, for me, began when a very longstanding and dear friend, Frank Marcovic, phoned up and asked me if I would like to come and watch the Mardi Gras from a very special viewing stand, virtually right in Taylor Square. I accepted in a flash, and invited Josephine Greaves, a friend of mine who had just returned from Paris as Fashion Editor of *Harper's Bazaar*. I also decided to take my two youngest daughters, Brook, aged 12, and Lauren, 10. It seemed like a great opportunity to widen their horizons and add to their general education. My third daughter, Justine, had just returned from college in America, and she too, I believed, would benefit from coming out of the eggshell of a pretty WASPish educational and social background.

I have always had the view that we are enriched by being exposed to all of the patterns that shape the world in which we live, and certainly the Mardi Gras fitted into that matrix. I can imagine the conversations at Ascham School when Brook and Lauren told their classmates on Monday where they had been on the previous Saturday night.

The major domo of our night was Vitek Czernuszyn (now Director for the National Aboriginal Cultural Centre). Vitek had cleverly worked out that the real way to see the Mardi Gras was to hire a large table-top truck, pay the owner of the truck $200 for the hire, and arrange for him to park the truck early in the day in Flinders Street – just where it leads away from Taylor Square. Vitek would, of course, generously reimburse the driver the statutory $60 parking fine that would be attached to the truck's residence there on the night.

Vitek then invited a number of friends to join him on the viewing platform, and me and my crew were lucky to be included. A waiter served refreshments, including Piper Heidsick champagne. Frank Marcovic, who is always a man of style, had his long-time chef/valet in attendance, and he stood near the truck with a constant supply of the fresh iced Perrier water and special club sandwiches that were part of Frank's diet regime. The truck had a steel grill about a metre and a half high around its sides to ensure that nobody fell off and, just as importantly, to prevent any of the uninvited from climbing onboard. A beautifully crafted, temporary staircase allowed access from the rear, if you'll pardon the expression.

THIS WAS A HELLUVA WAY TO START THE NIGHT. But more importantly, it was the ultimate invitation and viewing venue. In 1989, it was as hard to get on Vitek's list for his tabletop truck stand as it was to get an invitation to the Cointreau Ball. (Lady Mary Fairfax wasn't even in the hunt.)

I remember laughing the night away on the truck with old friends, amongst whom were Graham Murphy and Janet Vernon, as well as frocksters, Mel Clifford, Jonathan Ward, Stuart Membery, Trent Nathan and John MacArthur, who wore a sensational turban around his head that somehow, magically, wound down to the rest of his body. Also there were Deborah Thomas; former work colleague Warren Fahey; the late Brad Robinson; film maker, Jim McElroy and his wife, Marta; Mark Cavanagh; snapper, Robert Rosen; James Mollison; Lesley Walford; and Peter Chadwick.

My daughter, Brook, remembers the night not just as her first Mardi Gras but as her first can of beer. I think my three girls certainly came away with their eyes opened a little more, and were enriched by the experience.

Lauren, now twenty-one, remembers that her first Mardi Gras was 'a bit bewildering for a country girl who attended a Catholic school in Manilla'. She had, after all, just returned to Sydney from our property at Manilla, in Northern NSW. In these last eight or nine years, Mardi

Gras has become one of the 'must attend' events of her year, as it has been for me.

The whole event is a reminder of the madness and mystery of life – if you are open to it.

*Harry M. (for Mischievous) Miller is one of Australia's very few successful theatrical entrepreneurs and personal managers.*

# The Fruit Stand

## Warwick Jones

MARDI GRAS HAS ALWAYS been a family affair for me. My first few were shared with Stephen Fitzgerald, one of Sydney's leading dressmakers, who would start preparing our Mardi Gras costumes six months prior to the event. A group of people would meet up and together they would make the overall decision of the theme. I was too young to influence this important decision. I would only know when I was called into his shop on Crown Street for a fitting three weeks before the big day. Stephen's family and the girls who worked in the shop would be there with support, the odd needle and thread and, of course, a comment of approval. The fitting also kicked off the month of parties ahead.

The family theme continued with Rainee – my neighbour, friend and soulmate – who would insist on digging out the family Singer sewing machine to whip up something wonderful for me to wear, always offering to cut or trim one of her fab frocks from her wilder days. Another friend's mum would make a point of being in town prior to the event to assist with any last minute alterations, or to help if something from Aussie Boys needed repair. Jackie just couldn't help herself. 'Let me take your shorts up another inch, go on you've got great legs!'

And there will always be one special person who *really* knew how to have a good time, Stuart Bennett, who has gone on to Mardi Gras heaven, and who was one of the most inspiring people I have ever met.

Watching the Parade used to be a necessary hassle. In the last few years, however, my partner, Garry, came up with the 'Grandest Standest Maximas' also known as the 'fruit stand'. I am not sure what inspired Garry to do this, but maybe it was the rising price of milk crates ($5–$25). A trained backyard shed carpenter, he would always start with a detailed plan, resembling your very first tech drawings, smudges and all. A quick trip to Carol's hardware and away you go.

The stand has varied from two-tier to three-tier affairs. (Word of mouth about it has spread, and people are now prepared to pay for a spot.) A quick splash of paint and it is ready to be loaded into the back of the neighbour's 4WD, which we park in a back street until Saturday afternoon at about 4 p.m. for the annual unveiling.

Recently, the 'fruit stand' has become truly international, with madly dressed people from Italy, America and the UK. And for those who miss the Mardi Gras, Garry now tapes a commentary along the way, interviewing people and Parade entries alike.

Initially, Mardi Gras was only a party, a time to let go for a few days. However, over the years, having lost friends, experienced wonderful theatre, music and art, I believe that my life is enriched by my sexuality and the friendships that I have had and continue to share. The tireless efforts of people within my community continues to inspire my desire to want to give back something in return.

*Warwick Jones is a hospitality guru.*

# Two Dykes and a Private Dick

## Robyn Laverack

IN JANUARY 1990, Cath Phillips and I went to meet with Area Commander Alf Peate of the NSW Police Force. Cath was President of Mardi Gras and I was the Parade Co-ordinator. There were always doubts about the future of the Parade. Every year the crowds would get bigger, the fear of a major accident more real and Fred Nile's threats to disrupt the Parade more vocal. Anyone who'd watched video footage of the 1989 Parade was horrified at the sight of the awnings over the shops of Oxford Street straining under the weight of spectators.

Alf Peate had watched the video and his solution was simple. No more Parade unless we could convince him that we could bring the crowd under control. That's what our meeting was about.

Alf greeted us and sat us in two chairs facing his desk, which he sat behind. Along one wall sat several uniformed officers, including Inspector Kerrie Beggs who'd worked closely with Mardi Gras and who'd done much to enhance the relationships between the Surry Hills police and our community. Alf said he was unsure what to call us. Ladies didn't seem right, but nor did lesbians. I think we settled on 'mate'. I found it difficult to ignore the many qualifications, merit awards, honours and recognitions that hung in frames on the wall behind him. One which kept drawing my eye was a Certificate in Criminal Hypnotism. I was convinced that he could read my mind, that I would fall under a spell and agree to some foolish, impossible-to-meet condition.

Agree, however, we did. We promised that no spectator would be allowed on the awnings. We knew we had no option about this, we too could sense the potential danger. But it was an enormous undertaking and we had no idea how we were going to fulfil it.

Supported by the committee, Cath and I decided to engage a private security firm to assist us. Where do you find such people? In the phone book of course! Someone knew somebody who had worked for Business Risks International (BRI) and so we called them and arranged to meet for coffee. How would we recognise one another? We'd be the two dykes, they'd be the two private eyes. Let me tell you we had no trouble spotting one another! Nor did we have any difficulty understanding one another.

Thus began a long relationship between BRI and Mardi Gras – especially with Mytch Jeffrey, the Director of BRI, who was to become a friend, as we worked not only on that Parade but also future parties, parades, liquor licence applications, security for international performers and training for the Mardi Gras Rangers.

I was determined that not only was I going to run the safest Parade ever, but that it would also run on time! My public service mentality came to the fore – more detail than anybody would ever need to know! We put signs up on awnings, warning 'danger – keep off'. We ran training sessions for marshals on how to keep a crowd entertained for three hours while they waited for the Parade, and how to stop a crowd from surging (simple, put the children at the front). We organised the Parade into areas with co-ordinators, team leaders, marshals and medical teams in colour co-ordinated t-shirts. We allocated marshals to every light pole, bus stop and tree – anything that could give access to the awnings. We set up a control centre for the night in a bus on Oxford Street with radio control links to the police, ambulance, fire brigades and team leaders. The one thing we didn't predict was rain. It never rained on a Mardi Gras Parade but that night it did. Lots!

My proudest memories of my involvement with Mardi Gras are associated with that Parade. We had record crowds but there were no spectators on the awnings and no major incidents. Fred didn't stop the Parade nor did the rain.

The Parade not only ran on time, it was ahead of schedule. By the time we got to the party, we were drenched, exhausted but ecstatic. I was greeted by David Wilkins who in his best Dot Dingle voice asked me how *dare* I finish the Parade on time! Didn't I realise that because of the rain they'd had all sorts of problems at the Showground and had only just managed to turn the power on before the crowds came pouring through the gates!

At the party there was another storm – one of Dot and Peter Macdonnell's magnificent snowstorms on the dance floor to the music of 'Stormy Weather'. During the last number of the party I was lifted off my feet and passed from friend to friend, all of us in tears of joy, celebration and triumph!

*Robyn Laverack currently works for Pinpoint Marketing Consultants.*

# Girls on Duty

## Christina Mclean and Robyn Fraser

A PERFECT VANTAGE POINT to see the Parade and a cheap ticket to the Party were the only incentives we needed to volunteer as marshals. Yet the thought of standing on our feet for six hours, coupled with the prospect of an aggressive and unappreciative crowd to deal with, was daunting. Mentally preparing ourselves for the worst, we warned ourselves that it would be not a question how much homophobia would be present, but instead how it would manifest itself. However, we had underestimated both the crowd and the emotional impact of the whole experience on us all.

Once we took up our positions as marshals, we suddenly found that we had become the MCs for our very own stretch of Oxford Street. With enormous pride we were able to introduce our community to the huge crowd that had come to celebrate with us. Being there inside the barriers, amid the lights, music, fabulous frocks and floats, we were in awe of the sheer enormity of it all. The effortlessness with which the Parade seemed to flow by defied the extent of organisation and hard work we knew was involved in its preparation.

Thousands of participants and spectators celebrated our sexuality in all our diversity. It was twenty Christmases rolled into one. Our anxieties about crowd control proved unfounded. Nevertheless, we promised ourselves that next year, we wouldn't be marshalling, we'd be too busy marching.

*Robyn Fraser is a banker, studying Law. Christina Mclean is a ceramic artist. They live in Newtown with their dog, Ruben.*

# No Rain on My Parade

## Jacki Weaver

MY GOD, the sight and the sound!

An enormous thrilling explosion of colour and noise in a slow motion blur; a huge billowing cloud of roaring voices, waving arms, swaying bodies, stamping feet, cascading streamers, flowers, balloons, whistling, screaming, chanting, cheering; a spontaneous eruption of delirious mass pleasure.

That's what happens the moment the lead float first comes into view, when it turns the corner out of College Street into Oxford Strasse.

Half a million people, crammed all the way to Taylor Square, greet ecstatically the beginning of the Parade after hours, weeks, months of excited anticipation.

I've had some great opening nights in 35 years onstage, but nothing prepared me for this welcome.

A Krakatoa of sheer joy.

I wept.

A place on the first float is a genuine privilege and that was my good fortune at Mardi Gras, 1990. Lucky indeed for me, a mere Straight Sex Thimble from West Pymble – albeit The Smallest Fag Hag in Australia.

The committee had invited me to join the Mardi Gras Collection Float with Ignatius Jones and Richard Wherrett. This preceded the Parade by a few minutes, accompanied by a gang of money collectors walking alongside carrying buckets for donations to AIDS relief. The previous year, the same float with Maggie Kirkpatrick presiding had raised thousands so I was keen to help.

I was supposed to be the Queen of the Fairies, wearing a Titania costume with gossamer wings, my foot-high teased hair sprayed pink. Instead I more closely resembled, in miniature, the famous drag star, Divine. (God rest her dear soul.) When the rain teemed down, as it did that year, the pink hair dye trickled onto my face like a hundred rivulets of broken capillaries.

Richard made a far more convincing and glamorous Oberon, King of the Fairies, and Ignatius proved to be a brilliant spruiker on the microphone hustling money from the crowd. His powers of persuasion and his passionate Latin fervour made Richard and me seem painfully reserved and Anglo-Saxon – indeed, we were *pale*, by comparison. Nonetheless, the collection went well, despite the occasional coin hitting my head. And the torrential downpour did nothing to dampen the universal enthusiasm.

Neither was the mood spoiled by the disapproving presence of Fred Nile's contingent, standing in protest beside, appropriately, the Australian Museum, full of dinosaurs. There stood the wowsers, praying for a cloud to rain on my Parade.

They misname themselves the 'Festival of Light' – they're more like the 'Grudge Bearers of Gloom'!

'Judge not, lest ye be judged.'

At least ... that's what I *thought* I called out to them in my sternest voice. However, my family report seeing me on the TV news coverage, pathetically squeaking, 'Jesus loves everyone, sir!'

My other vivid memory is of Jude Kuring's fiendish glove puppet following me some of the way taunting, 'I knew you were a dyke, why else would you marry Hinch!'

One of the ubiquitous Dykes on Bikes assured me that I'd be 'under their watchful protection all night against any menacing blokes, there being a significant hetero-infiltration problem'. I've never felt safer in my life.

I lost count of the happy families I saw watching the Parade, kids of all ages sitting on dads' shoulders, many solitary elderly people smiling under their umbrellas, probably proud parents of participants. I've watched many Mardi Gras Parades but participated only once, in 1990. It's an honour I'll treasure always. Thank you.

*Jacki Weaver is one of Australia's foremost actresses.*

# Rain Cocktail

## Dorothy Porter

Rain spiked with diesel.
My first Mardi Gras
cocktail.

Behind a farting float
leaden-legged
in sodden jeans
holding a skimpy brolley
over a skinny queen's
wilting beehive
I waved to the crowd.

But
        what a night.

The night
so many of us
dropped
our mouse masks
and cruised
the tomcat rain, the oil slick
        streets.

*Dorothy Porter's published works*
*include the verse novel*
What a Piece of Work.

# Pat Gently

## The Show Must Go On

## Tony Cooper

ONE OF THE more spectacular entries in the 1990 Parade was designed by and centred around the infinitely talented Pat Gently. As a larger than life 'Southern Belle' who towered some 10 metres tall, she gracefully cut a majestic swathe between the throngs lining the Parade route. Like a perfect magnolia blossom, she was totally resplendent in a magnificent fluoro orange polka-dotted crinoline and matching picture hat with trailing bows. As this 'showboat' regally rolled along, she was escorted by a flotilla of glamorous showgirls and adoring beaus (myself included) all decked out in similar polka-dotted fashion.

This whole ensemble was destined to be the centrepiece of the opening show at the party following the Parade. This destiny was fulfilled after a narrowly averted disaster that has since become one of the many legendary tales of drama and triumph that is Mardi Gras.

That year it rained on our Parade – the whole bloody way! Thus it was a very sorry and soggy show troupe that arrived at the party in costumes that were by then impossible to perform in. And we had just 1¼ hours till showtime.

After some urgent consultation I commandeered the production manager's car and some security passes, and, at breakneck pace, headed for home and my tumble drier with the pile of soggy costumes. All was proceeding to plan and time schedule, when disaster suddenly struck. An overwhelming feeling of dread gripped my entire being the instant I opened the drier to behold a twisted and mangled mass of costumes – literally knotted into small, dry balls.

Trust me on this: if you ever end up with wet rope (in your hemline or anywhere else) *never* – I repeat, NEVER! – pop it into your tumble drier.

In a state of sheer desperation and barely controlled panic, I grabbed the nearest pair of scissors and began hacking off the first hemline. Given the degree of difficulty and the short time left me, I immediately realised that I could not win this battle alone. So, gathering every pair of scissors I could find (including nail scissors) I scraped up my mangled bundle and beat a hasty (even maniacal) retreat back to get reinforcements. To this day, I still wonder how the four cylinders of my borrowed car ever achieved what they did that night.

Arriving back, remarkably in one piece, and with just 15 minutes till curtain, I now found myself at the wrong end of a very packed pavilion with no way of getting through the crowd to the stage entrance on time. My only option was to scale a perimeter security fence and hope to break through a wall of the backstage tent. With a tenacious grip on my bag of costumes and a remarkable agility born of desperation, over I went, only to be confronted half-way by a security guard. All these years later, he is probably still reeling in shock from my screaming at him to 'GET OUT OF MY WAY, FOLLOW ME, AND GRAB A PAIR OF SCISSORS'. Then I dived towards the dirt, forcing my way under the nearest tent wall.

Popping up inside, still on all fours and with the guard now clutching my ankle, I bellowed for every available hand to grab a pair of scissors and hack off those hemlines. The girls struggled into their costumes and made chaotic final adjustments at the same time.

The last piece of twisted rope hit the floor at the top of the backstage steps as the overture ended and the curtain parted. Needless to say, yet another triumphant Mardi Gras show extravaganza unfolded to rapturous applause from 10 000 revellers who were none the wiser to any preceding drama.

# Whither Mardi Gras?

## (But hey, thanks for the memories ... )

### Ignatius Jones

I MISSED THE FIRST MARDI GRAS, because I'd been arrested a few hours before on the grimy stage of a rock venue called the Rex Hotel. The charges included, amongst other things, advocating same-sex fellatio, asking the audience to sodomise me and saying the 'F' word through a PA system while eating out my transvestite keyboard player, Joylene Hairmouth. All this was pretty par for the course in those heady days of punk rock/gay rights/music theatre. But I was pretty pissed off that I'd missed the riot.

It was the last time I'd miss the riot that was Mardi Gras for the next seventeen years. Jimmy and the Boys, the strange transvestite punk band that Joylene and I fronted, went on to achieve a few gold records and top ten hits, making us, I suppose, Australia's first completely 'out' pop stars. It says something about the infectious craziness of the times that we never thought of it in those terms, and that our predominantly straight audience happily accepted the drag-bondage we habitually sported. Nightly they joined in chanting the lyrics of our anthem 'Butchy Boys'. It began, 'Fuck me! Suck me!' and did not get better ...

It's almost impossible to describe how I felt the first time I stood beside Oxford Street with my boyfriend and girlfriends, and watched the glory that was Mardi Gras come marching, mincing, sashaying past. I knew this had never been done before. Here we were, the sodomite scum, the transgender filth, the dirty, hairy, man-eating dykes, the mentally and physically diseased (and our friends), the people normally despised by society because we were different, chose to be different, were born different or had had difference thrust upon us – here we were shaking our beads, in public, while hundreds of thousands of people, gay and straight, joined in to cheer us on.

We didn't need to make a political statement. Mardi Gras *was* a political statement. Our very survival was a political statement, and the fact that such a large chunk of the straight world would regularly join us in celebrating *us*, was a great *social* statement. That this young society, drawn from every corner of a tired old world, could come together to celebrate difference and tolerance was amazing. Amazing and wonderful and revolutionary, and long before Vaclav Havel could proclaim his Velvet Revolution, we knew that we had one of our own: the Sequinned Revolution.

The eighties certainly weren't a great decade for a lot of things, but they were Mardi Gras' Golden Age. The genius behind those parades, Peter Tully, understood something very fundamental about street theatre, and political street theatre in particular. Namely, that the worst way to make a point to a hostile audience, or for that matter to an indifferent or even a friendly audience, was to write that point on a placard and wave it in their faces. Fred Nile's head on a platter, Miss 3D in King Kong's hand, the giant Ronald McDonald buggering the giant Gumby, the colossal Imelda and her parade of shoes, the dykes on bikes, the marching boys, the gorgeous mums and dads and grandmums of PFLAG – all these things said, 'Hey, we may be oppressed to hell and threatened with death, jail and disease, but, shit, *we know how to party*!'

And what's more, you were all invited to that party . . .

But, alas, no more. Something sad and unfortunate has happened in the last few years. Quality, wit, intelligence, the incredibly wry, smart take on Camp that was Peter Tully – the very things that had made Mardi Gras so special and which differentiated it from any number of dreary gay rights' marches the world over – all seem to be disappearing. The thrill may not be gone yet, but it's certainly going. I don't know why anyone watches the parade now. With a few sparse exceptions it's become a cavalcade of tacky placards and poofs and dykes dancing on the backs of trucks. Mardi Gras seems to be slipping into an ugly abyss between amateur and awful, between the tackiest aspects of 'community' involvement and crass commercialism.

I don't blame the parade organisers, they do their best, but, apparently, their hands are tied. (As for the unspeakably awful television coverage, the less said the better.) I do blame the seemingly talentless, humourless apparatchiks who took a wonderful thing and shook it by its metaphorical neck till it lost the ability to laugh at itself. Who shackled it to indescribably petty 'community' politics and the demented spectre of political correctness gone mad.

The rot may have set in earlier, but I first noticed it in 1990, under the presidency of Cath Philips. It was a particularly bittersweet experience, because that Mardi Gras had started so well for me – up on a float with the editor of this book and the wonderful Jacki Weaver. We certainly hadn't planned it, but this is how it happened.

In the late eighties, a close friend and former lover called Adrian Gough started working for Mardi Gras, on the Party and the Parade. Adrian was the cutest of contradictions: deliriously decadent but completely organised, the brightest of bright young things despite an almost constant hangover of Biblical proportions. He'd joined the organisation full of fabulous ideas and plans, only to see them dashed on the particularly pointy rocks of gay bureaucracy. Every day he'd bring home tales of bitchery and back-stabbery, of lurid politicking and internecine machinations of Byzantine complexity. Well, darling, it's Mardi Gras, we'd say. When you've got that many queens and dykes all jammed together, each trying to push their own trolley, what do you expect? *Playschool?*

Besides, no matter what was going on down at MG HQ, it was still Mardi Gras and to us it was sacred. We'd do anything to make it work.

Take the charity float. Since 1988 this float had led the parade with some gay or gay-friendly celebrities exhorting the crowd to drop money in the buckets of the volunteers who swarmed around it. In 1990, Adrian was determined that the celebrity should be Kylie. He knew that her then-boyfriend, Michael Hutchence, was an old mate of mine from the rock'n'roll days, and asked me if I could pass along the suggestion. Michael called back and said sure. Actually, she'd *love* to do it. It was all on.

Then a week before the parade I get a call from Hutchence. Apparently his management had called Mardi Gras and asked for a few tickets so Michael and Kylie's minders could meet her at the party after she'd done her thing on the float. They'd been told – allegedly, in a less than soothing tone of voice – that Michael was a millionaire and he could jolly well pay for tickets if he wanted to come to the party. Michael was understandably miffed. 'You can all get fucked,' he suggested. And that was the end of Kylie on the charity float. (It would be another five years before Kylie made it to Mardi Gras.)

But that was in the future. What the fuck were we going to do about the charity float in *five days time*? Now you have to remember that this was before every man and his budgie wanted to march along with the biggest event in the southern hemisphere. There was still a risqué element to associating yourself so openly with all that screaming queendom in full panoply assembled. And besides it couldn't just be any celebrity, either. They had to be gay-friendly or gay-related or even better, openly *gay*.

Adrian racked what was left of his mind. As his less than perfect conduit to 'celebrity', he racked what was left of mine. No one swam into view, or at a few days notice, was available. Finally he fixed me with his big, almost lizard-like eyes, and said, 'It'll have to be you.'

'Me??!?'

'Yeah. Some people will remember who you are . . . You'll have to do.' He was right. At this stage in the proceedings, I was about as good as it was going to get. 'Well, I'm not doing it alone. Um . . . uh . . . I know! I'll ask Richard! And perhaps Jacki might do it too . . . We'll have to fly her up from Melbourne, but she might just do it . . .'

Richard had just mounted an acclaimed production of *Midsummer Night's Dream*, set at a dance party, for the Sydney Theatre Company, and was without doubt a gay luminary. Jacki Weaver had played Titania in the *Dream* and was also one of the most gay-friendly celebrities I knew. The two of them seemed strangely appropriate. I rang Richard. I begged him. Richard is not the world's most public person, and here I was asking him to drop all his plans for the evening and stand on the back of a truck begging hundreds of thousands of people to throw money. It was a big ask.

I could *hear* him roll his eyes heavenward on the other end of the phone. 'Yes, yes, of course I'll do it. But . . .' – I could see him pursing his lips the way he does and looking skywards again – '. . . why *me*? No one will know who I *am*. They'll probably think I'm my *brother* . . . Oh, dear . . .' (Pause) . . . 'I'll call Jacki.'

The night of Mardi Gras 1990 it pissed down with rain. Richard, Jacki and myself were huddled on the back of our truck, trying to find what cover we could beneath a flimsy plastic canopy that somebody had thoughtfully painted bright blue. Richard was wearing Oberon's costume from the *Dream*, which consisted mainly of a magnificently muscled leather breastplate and a short skirt. Jackie had come as Titania, and her Queen of the Fairies outfit was a dazzling confection of gauze and wings and sequins that even Ron Muncaster would have envied. Having put away the bondage gear of my youth, the most appropriate outfit I could think of for high-powered panhandling was the set of Cab Calloway white tails I wore in my jazz act *Pardon Me Boys*. We made a very eccentric trio.

We snaked our way down Oxford Street, taking turns to exhort the gathered throngs to give, give, give. Jackie was by far the best spruiker, fluttering about the float like the Good Fairy, while Richard and I fortified ourselves from several flasks of vodka secreted about our persons. (Richard, who is a laconic public speaker at the best of times, had managed to create himself a kind of chaise longue arrangement on top of the truck's cab. There he languished imperiously, dispensing the odd royal wave to the crowd.)

The rain hadn't dented the crowd's size or enthusiasm (it never does, Reverend Fred), but it had started to do strange things to us. Jacki, for instance, had started to melt. Our bright blue canopy leaked spectacularly, and its blue paint had splashed all over my white tails, until I resembled an Yves Klein study of Fred Astaire. Richard was undergoing an even more interesting experience. The rain wasn't constant; it would bucket down in great gusts and then be followed by spells of intense heat and humidity. When this happened the sodden leather of Richard's breastplate would begin to dry and contract, squeezing the breath out of him like some mediaeval torture device. Then it would piss down again, soaking the leather, and he'd be able to breathe freely once more. This went on and on until finally, when we reached the Showground, we literally had to cut him out of his boa constrictor breastplate.

Later, Adrian informed me that I was in deep doo-doo with the Mardi Gras powers that be because, when greeting the throngs from who I was trying to squeeze donations, I'd said 'Welcome to Mardi Gras!'

I had not said 'Welcome to *Gay and Lesbian* Mardi Gras!'

I was gobsmacked. Apart from the sheer pettiness of it all, this kind of gulag mentality worried me. I thought Mardi Gras was for all of us: fags, dykes, bis, blacks, whites, frocks, clones, fats, thins, trannies, drags, Muscle Mary's, Hairy Bearies, etc, etc. Wasn't that the message of our gorgeous Rainbow Flag? That *everyone* was invited to the party?

Now it seemed there was a big ugly bouncer at the door.

It didn't go all to hell immediately. But slowly, surely, the parades started to lose their charm. The parties were still fabulous, but the shows now could only manage a fifty-fifty success rate. The whole 'straights at the Party' situation got completely out of hand. (So I'm told. I've never noticed it. I never notice much at the parties but the shows, the wall-to-wall gorgeousness and everyone having a fabulous time. And haven't there always been straights at the parties? What's happened?)

I just hope the 'straights at the Party' anxiety isn't another symptom of that dumb 'reverse discrimination' which is one of the silliest concerns of the nattering nabobs of political correctness. I must confess I was really distressed when Richard mentioned to me that some Mardi Gras poobahs had tried to stop him using Jacki Weaver to open the first

*Stars Come Out* concert on the grounds that Jackie *was not gay*. Hello? And the next year, when I heard that John O'Connell, the man who choreographed *Strictly Ballroom* and *Romeo and Juliet*, had been prevented from using Bette Midler's 'Chapel of Love' for the lead float – you know, the wedding cake thingie – because Bette Midler *was not gay*.

Bette Midler!!??!!!

What next? Parade floats on which we burn books written by straight authors? Outing booths? Grey triangles for the straights at the Party?

Where are we going? What the fuck are we doing? I still love Mardi Gras, for what it was and what it could be, and I don't think all is yet lost. Perhaps I'm just getting old. I have millions of Mardi Gras memories, but the ones I treasure the most are of those who have left us, like Adrian and Peter Tully, laughing and swishing and sashaying, and marvelling at the magic they had wrought on Oxford Street and on the dance floors of the biggest gay party in the world.

I can't help feeling we have a responsibility to them. Because if things keep going the way they have, then memories is all we'll have left of the incredible event that was the One Night of the Year . . .

*Ignatius Jones' cv is longer than most Mardi Gras parades. Author – his book about the Australian tabloid sex industry is due out in mid-1999; musician – he leads swing conglomerate Pardon Me Boys; major event director – he works for Olympic impresario Ric Burch, etc, etc, etc. He is currently Creative Director of the only party bigger than Mardi Gras, the City of Sydney Millennium Celebrations.*

# Singing Up a Storm

## Paul Capsis

I GOT MY FIRST MARDI GRAS BREAK IN 1990. I had sent Gillian Miner-vini a tape of me singing 'Proud Mary' after answering an ad in the *Star Observer* calling for performers who were interested in performing for Mardi Gras to make contact. Up until that point I had only performed in talent quests around Sydney pubs, RSLs and Hell Angels' Clubs. I had a meeting with Gillian and I remember I had to do a lot of convincing for her to give me the gig. My first own cabaret act.

I shaved my legs for the first and last time in honour of the occasion, and made a huge bloody mess in my bathroom. Being of Greek/Maltese extract meant I went through about four razors. My legs felt weird. Numb. But I was ready for my Mardi Gras debut. It was the 17th of February and it rained that night. But we still partied hard. I danced on a truck with my shaved legs, Lycra shorts and newly purchased gold Lycra top that got ruined in the rain. But I didn't care.

I went on at 3.40 a.m. on a tiny stage far away from anything at the Showgrounds. The rain didn't help. All the seats were wet. I remember the audience being far away from me. There must have been one hundred people, all gathered around the edge of the seating. A bunch of my friends had remembered the time and had turned up. They screamed and cheered for me as I belted out Aretha Franklin, Tina Turner, Prince and Janis Joplin numbers. I wore a gold lamé halter-neck mini outfit with beads and gold-specked belt. My hair was bob-length and frizzy from the wet. The group of people who gathered got larger during the course of the set. I recall it was the first time ever that I managed to do more than one character on a single night. The reaction and feedback were wonderful.

I remember being backstage and feeling really pleased that I got to perform at Mardi Gras. Next thing, the dancer/choreographer Kim Walker and a bunch of drag queens burst into the dressing room, all laughing and smiling because the big show, *I Am What I Am*, in the main hall had gone off with a bang. They were all ecstatic with the response. It was like one big happy family. Little did I know at that time that in a few years I would be part of that family.

For the next two years, I performed around Sydney's clubs. I worked at the Albury Hotel and at Ian Jopson and Brett Chamberlain's Club Sugar Shack at Kinselas on Tuesday nights. One thing led to another and in 1992, I was invited to perform my first ever one-person show at the Downstairs Belvoir Street Theatre during the Mardi Gras Festival. I recall Penelope Wells asking me to do this show in a theatre context and Mardi Gras would produce. I would have to devise a way of pulling all my characters together for a one-hour show. I went with the schizophrenic approach. The two-week season went very well. But it wasn't until 1995 that I got asked to perform at the launch of Mardi Gras outside the Museum of Contemporary Art (MCA). I stayed in the men's toilet during vocal warm-ups with the lovely reverberation from 8000 people outside, feeling so nervous and yet determined to do well. I heard my introduction by the brilliant Julie McCrossin and then a cheer. When I came out onto the stage, a sea of people covered every square inch of ground space. I took a deep breath, conjured up the great opera divas and opened my mouth . . . Summertime . . . I heard people gasp and others laugh. I used every inch of energy to get across to such a large gathering and the most remarkable thing was this huge blanket of love came up and covered me. I felt extremely proud and moved and loved.

*Paul Capsis is to 1990s Sydney what Yma Sumac was to 1940s Manhattan.*

# The Power Song

## Rob Davis

THE 1990 MARDI GRAS PARTY was memorable for me in more ways than one. It was the last year that the party was held in a single venue – the Government Pavilion. It was also the year they had the spectacular pyrotechnics display, set to the accompaniment of Carl Orff's *Carmina Burana*. This impressed the Americans at the party, because the law in the USA does not permit indoor fireworks. Most people will remember 1990 as the one and only year that the Party has ever been evacuated, due to an over-enthusiastic punter scaling the arched girders of the pavilion, reaching the very top, and hanging from the beams above the heads of the party-goers.

No reason was given for the evacuation during the announcement, and the majority of the crowd on the dance floor had not seen the acrobatics above, so were oblivious to the purpose of the evacuation. This was also the first time I had been invited to DJ at a Mardi Gras Party. My set was yet to come and, like everyone else, I thought that it might be a bomb scare, so complied quickly with the request to leave.

Thousands of people stood outside, their anxiety profoundly enhanced by confusion and chemicals. It occurred to me only then that I might not even get to play the music at all! Could the party be over? It was now only 45 minutes before I was due to start DJing the third set of the night.

However, my fears were allayed when the next announcement informed everyone that the party was resuming, and as quickly as they had left, the crowd was back and partying hard again within minutes. Then it was my turn. I'd never played to a crowd that big before. Imagine the RHI, the Hordern and Dome crowds, all in one single pavilion.

Only days earlier, the big story in the news around the world had been about the release of Nelson Mandela from prison in South Africa. On the afternoon before the party I dragged out of my record collection the 12" remix of 'Free Nelson Mandela' by the Special AKA. This was already an oldie, having been released in 1985, but had an a cappella intro of a chorus chanting 'Free-ee Nelson Man-de-la'. I thought it was a timely statement to make, and it was a pretty good song, too. So I played it as my first song.

The roar that erupted from the crowd on the dance floor will be etched in my mind forever. The place literally went wild with cheering, applause and whistles. Everyone's hands were in the air. A sea of people. A sentiment shared by everyone. Freedom and celebration. The roar seemed to go on forever and I was overwhelmed with emotion at being able to create such a tumultuous response with a single song. After that, I was REALLY looking forward to playing the next four hours.

*Rob Davis, DJ extraordinaire, is clearly not afraid, when appropriate, to play 'golden oldies'.*

The beginning of the nineties is seen by many as a key juncture in Mardi Gras' history. Many local residents began complaining, understandably, about their noise-polluted Saturday nights as a consequence of the constant sequence of parties at the Showground. In the case of Mardi Gras, the demand for Party tickets had definitely outgrown supply. The Party's spiralling popularity resulted in the venue being enlarged to encompass three separate spaces – the Royal Hall of Industries, the Dome and the Hordern Pavilion. Its growing mainstream appeal also contributed to the 'too many straights at the Party!' issue. All of this led to the introduction of the controversial 'tickets for members only' policy. Meanwhile the Parade and Party's popularity has continued to grow unabated.

# Tapdancing My Way Through Mardi Gras

## Robyn Laverack

FLUSH WITH MY SUCCESS as Mardi Gras' first female Parade Co-ordinator, I put myself forward for the position of Party Co-ordinator in 1991. I would become the first female to hold the position – a major challenge to the party queens! Moreover, the Mardi Gras staff member responsible for the party this year was also a lesbian, Katrina Marton. We were a formidable team – scary some would say!

The plan was that I would bring to the Party the same organisational skills that I had brought to the Parade, and that, with Katrina, we would bring it in on budget – another first. What none of us counted on was that I would be like every other Party Co-ordinator and get thoroughly caught up in the choice of DJs, lighting design, and entertainment.

My research included doing the bars, night after night, listening to DJs, meeting drag queens, watching their shows, learning about dance music and rpms. I learnt to tell between the different sorts of lights, to know how much weight there could be in the RHI's lighting rig, and how to do a glitter drop in the Hordern. I learnt that none of the people

I worked with on the Party had any problem working with a dyke, although some of the punters saw this as yet more evidence of the lesbian takeover.

I also learnt that as Party Co-ordinator I had considerable power. I had spent my childhood watching Mickey Rooney and Judy Garland in the Andy Hardy films and had a burning ambition to one day put on a show. The problem was, I didn't want a drag queen-disco inferno-gym bodies pumping-kind of number. I wanted something more Busby Berkeley, more Broadway, something out of the dance party mode. I managed to talk the committee around, but they agreed only on the condition that the music had a dance party beat. What they don't know won't hurt them, I thought.

And so the opening show commenced with 40 tapdancing dykes in silver top hats and canes dancing to Glenn Miller's 'In the Mood' – the original recording! The crowd went wild and I knew I was right.

And yes, organisation for the Party was improved with changes to ticketing policies, with gay and lesbian Mardi Gras rangers patrolling inside the halls, with better perimeter fencing to keep out the gate-crashers, with procedures for tendering designs, with a much greater participation of women on the Party committee.

And yes, the party came in under budget – but next time, I'll have a hundred tapdancing dykes in gold sequins!

# RING RING RINoughort...Hello

## Portia Turbo

IT'S ABOUT 9 A.M. after the usual night working as an entertainer on Sydney's world famous drag circuit. People, even in the industry, still can't – or won't – understand that a night in heels is actually a gruelling day's work. There's half an inch of carefully applied, multi-coloured, jewel bright cement on your face. Your waist has been cinched in by no less rigid and cunningly engineered a construction than the Sydney Harbour Bridge. And you've downed the inevitable few drinks afterward. (You know the saying, 'One quiet drink and fifteen loud ones!') All to make sure your fans don't lose touch and the powers that be don't forget who you are.

As it is I've been asleep for maybe three hours and am feeling less like the glamorous sylph-like figure I was the night before and more like the wreck of the *Hesperus*. Left-over mascara and eyelash glue have combined in a black cloggy swathe across both my eyes. They have conspired in those few short hours to glue my left eyelid closed. An inner monologue insists quietly that I pull them apart. Suddenly, my eye springs open. The phone is ringing! I will remember everything that happens in the next few minutes as if it took a year.

The man of my dreams lies kind of crumpled in a heap beside me. No matter how late we've been out or what sort of devilry we've been up to, he still manages to look like a movie star and Prince Charming rolled into one. The bed smells faintly of disco fever and last night's rather frenzied bout of lovemaking. Clothes are strewn liberally about, giving off their musky perfume, which clashes with the scent of gerberas that I have bought to brighten our love-life and the room, in that order.

The sun is battling its way through the beige Holland blind in our small beige room. Situated on the east side of our rented, two-bedroom, circa 1972 terrace house in Annandale, the heat of a February morning is stifling to say the least. Anyway, let's get back to the phone call in question as it is this phone call that is my most memorable Mardi Gras experience.

'Hello?'

'Yeah . . . Hello.'

'I'm looking for Paul, er, Portia.'

'Yeah, that's me. Who's this?'

At this point, there's movement from the other side of the bed. Sleeping Beauty is rumbling unpleasantly as he throws off the sheets. A gurgle of disjointed and apparently random sounds lifts in a questioning tone, then he subsides back into sleep, unanswered and uncaring.

'It's Gary Leeson here.'

'Who?'

This was Gary's first year as Entertainment Director, so you can understand my ignorance.

'Gary Leeson, the Entertainment Co-ordinator at Mardi Gras!'

It's funny how those two words, at that particular time of year, can transform you from a grouchy, just woken up mass of confusion to an instantly quivering, wide awake, adrenalin pumping ball of chaos. Suddenly the only thing in the world for me was that soft tenor voice at the other end of the phoneline.

'Oh . . . er . . . yes, Gary?'

'Um. Well I'd like you to lead the opening show at Mardi Gras.'

I think you could only attribute what I did next to shock. I started waking up Sleeping Beauty. I had to share what was going on. I had to see if it was real; you know, a 'pinch me' thing.

'Hang on a sec, Gary.'

'Uh, okay.'

Turning, I thump the prone man next to me.

'WHAAAHT?' Sleeping Beauty opens an eye.

'Gary Leeson from Mardi Gras is on the phone and he wants me to lead the opening number.' I am speaking in a furious whisper.

'What?' Both eyes open now.

'They want me to lead the opening number at Mardi Gras. Isn't that great!'

'What? NO!'

'WHAT?'

'NO?'

'Why?'

'Last time you were in a Mardi Gras number I didn't see you for half the night and you might as well have fucked the guy you were partnering. And it's going to be our first Mardi Gras together, and I want to spend it with you.'

(THIS WAS HIS FINAL AND BEST DRAWCARD, IT HAD NEVER FAILED BEFORE AND HE KNEW IT WASN'T GOING TO FAIL NOW.)

However, a gleam of hope was at hand: 'Uh, Gary, listen, I can only do it if my boyfriend can do it too, is that okay?'

'Can he dance?'

'Yeah.'

'Well, we've got to have a meeting about the number anyway, but I think it will be alright.'

'Gary? What's the number?'

'"This is it" by Ruth Campbell.'

'Okay, I'd love to.'

'I'll call you back about the meeting.'

'Thanks, Gary.'

'Bye, Portia.'

That phone call in 1991 was something I'll never forget.

*Portia Turbo (aka Paul Thwaite) has worked extensively throughout the world. He currently resides in Pymble with his mum, is still doing drag, and sees no end in sight.*

# Mardi Gras – What's That?

## Tina Arena

MANY YEARS AGO I remember people would mention the word 'Mardi Gras' and everyone would say 'oh, what's that?' or 'oh, you mean the big party in Rio de Janeiro?' At the time I remember thinking how naive people were. Mardi Gras is a celebration of the gay community and their amazing open-minded, free spirit.

I got my first taste of Mardi Gras in March 1991 and at the time I wasn't quite sure what to expect. The very fact that I was scheduled to go on stage at 2 a.m. was unheard of at the time! I was terrified. I could hardly speak and the fact that I was sober made it even more frightening. I was automatically on another level to everyone else at the party. I wasn't shit-faced but looking back I think it would have been better if I was!

When the lights dimmed and the music started to the sound of the remixed version of 'I Need Your Body' the room began to shake and roar. The audience reaction nearly blew me off the stage. I finally felt like I was openly and honestly showing a real dimension of my personality to people who don't discriminate and who unconditionally support and love. It was amazing but, boy, was it hot on stage! Thankfully, I only had to do one song. I think I would have passed out if I'd had to do a whole set . . .

The gay community have been loyal supporters of everything I have chosen to artistically enter into and for that I will forever remain indebted to them. Mardi Gras was and will remain a highlight in my life.

*Tina Arena is Australia's highest selling female recording artist.*

# Berocca Bar

## George Prats

IT BEGAN A MONTH BEFORE Mardi Gras at a conversation in a house in Surry Hills where Andrea Szamek lived with Justin Donoghue, as lovers. We came up with the notion of making a few bucks at the Mardi Gras. After throwing some ideas in the air, Justin suggested that we sell Beroccas at the end of the party. We all agreed.

Putting it all together was very simple. I had a 1950s card table with collapsible legs, someone bought a large quantity of Beroccas wholesale as well as plastic cups, and we had a large, army-style, square water container with a built-in handle. We also had some vanilla ice cream. We made a large cardboard sign saying *Berocca Bar*.

We left the party at 4.30 a.m. to collect our goods. We got back at about five a.m. and set our bar up on the sidewalk outside the Hordern. By 5.30 a.m. the hot-dog Mafia (the guys who always sell hot-dogs outside the Party in the morning) were furious at us for taking the best spot. We were getting some filthy looks and comments, but we were having such a good time, we simply ignored them.

Shortly after 6 a.m. one of us came up with the great idea of moving the whole thing inside the gates, which we did. The hot-dog men became even more furious but, under the influence of certain elements – the Party, alcohol, dancing, making money – who cared? We didn't!

We set up our table under a tree, our sign roped to its trunk. Here we had the added benefit of being close to a water faucet.

|  |  |  |
|---|---|---|
| Our sign read: | Plain Beroccas | $2.00 |
|  | Berocca Spider (one scoop of ice-cream) | $2.50 |

We had just set up shop when Drag Diva Carlotta passed by. She adored the idea. She found herself a chair and sat with us till the end of the Party. Well, she was a great help because she became our announcer, shouting: 'Come on, everybody, come and get your Beroccas!'

The first Berocca Spider was purchased by Simon Reptile. To watch the joy on people's faces as they drank their Beroccas after such a party was very rewarding to us. I must add: we didn't have permission to set up the bar, but we had no hassles whatsoever – those were the days, my friend. Enough Beroccas were left to be consumed by us, and our friends, over the following two years of partying.

*George Prats lives in Surry Hills and is a great collector of objects.*

# Greyhounds

## Peter Bridges

RICHARD WHERRETT lived near the Showgrounds and it had become our habit to gather there after Mardi Gras and Sleaze Ball Parties for so-called recovery drinks. On this occasion I remember arriving a little late with Richard to find a bedraggled group already languishing on the house's stoop like the survivors of some aquatic discotheque. They were wearing a bizarre assortment of party gear and uniformly shielded their eyes from the fierce mid-morning sun with the latest in tinted eyewear.

After much peeling-off of uncomfortable outfits and many rejuvenating showers, everyone settled down to the serious post-party business of dishing and piecing together blurred recollections of what had been a long and eventful night for all. Tumblers of 'greyhounds' (vodka, ice and grapefruit juice), Berocca and, for the faint-hearted, tea lubricated the proceedings, amidst the tinkling of appropriately vague new-age CDs. Eventually, thoughts turned to the daunting prospect of venturing back onto the streets to participate in the serious public ritual that was 'Recovery'.

'Recoveries' involve standing in or outside various bars and cafés all day, like punch-drunk boxers refusing to lie down and take the count. The compulsion to do it is part stubborn refusal to let go of what has been a magical weekend, part heroic competition to not be seen to give up before anyone else, and part perverse fascination with the parade of walking-dead that passes by.

On this morning, Richard's flatmate, Corby, remained stubbornly ensconced on the sofa. Clad head to toe in towelling and lovingly nursing a fierce concoction of citrus and alcohol, he remained steadfastly prone. Despite much cajoling and incentives, nothing would convince this soldier to make another sortie over the top of the party trench. 'No really, I'm just going to take a couple of Valium and lie down.'

In due course, the house slowly emptied and we left our recalcitrant friend to the quiet comforts of Sunday at home as we girded our already tested loins for the final stretch of celebrations.

We found a comfortable gutterside to roost in in the lane adjoining two inner-city pubs. This was commonly known as 'The Gutter' or 'The Alley' – as in 'See you in the Gutter' – and it has become, over the years, a well and truly institutionalised part of any Mardi Gras weekend. So much so, in fact, that on this occasion a makeshift dance floor and tent had been erected in the middle of the lane, as well as barricades that closed the area off to all vehicular traffic.

After less than an hour I noticed a striking Gypsy-like drag queen picking her way through the empty cans and paper cups. There was something spookily familiar about her, but I couldn't put my finger on it. In any case, in moments like these it's best to pretend to know all drags – they could be anyone.

This one, however, seemed to be making a beeline towards our sleepy little group. Suddenly, as he came within squealing distance, I recognised the gapped teeth between those excessively glittered lips. It was the homebody whom we had reluctantly given up on less than an hour ago!

'You?' I screamed. 'What are *you* doing here? I thought you said you'd had enough?'

I couldn't quite believe it, but then again, when I thought about it, I could. In fact, I should have known better!

'Ah, well, you know how it is,' Corby chirped as he sipped on his schooner through a dainty plastic straw, 'After a couple of greyhounds and a Valium I thought, Fuck it, the weekend is but a pup anyway! It's Mardi Gras, isn't it?'

*Peter Bridges is co-owner of Bridges O'Neill Management in Melbourne.*

To call the events that follow the Mardi Gras parties 'Recoveries' must be the greatest euphemism in the English language. Effectively, every gay and lesbian venue in Sydney – pub, bar, nightclub – will be open for more partying for some, if not all, of the Sunday following and indeed on into Monday, and beyond. This is not necessarily just hedonistic indulgence: it is a perfectly normal part of tribal rituals as argued in my introduction, be it Aboriginal corroboree, Brazilian carnival, Hawaiian luau, and so on.

The 'gutter' has been the site of some of the earliest Recoveries and consequent remarkable happenings. Once an ambulance drew up to extract a passed-out patient and someone yelled, 'There's my taxi!' and climbed in. Another time, an amateur drag queen fell out of the Beresford to mime an impromptu performance of the disco-version of Ethel Merman's 'There's No Business Like Show Business'.

And so on and on . . .

# Two for the Road

## Craig Hassall

EVERYONE WILL HAVE a story about the lane (or the gutter, as it is sometimes more affectionately known). It's curious that such an unattractive location has now entered Mardi Gras folklore as one of the quintessential recovery hangouts. The area between the back of both the Beresford Hotel and the Flinders Hotel is now infamous. Anybody you missed seeing at the Party will no doubt be there. A visit to the lane is also a practical way to see how the people you arrived at the Party with, some ten or eleven hours earlier, have fared. The outfits are usually much the worse for wear, but people are generally still bright, chatty. And frantically chewing gum.

The more shady side of the street is soon filled with bodies, sitting, standing or lying in the gutter. Both bars are pumping out music and smoke. People tend to move off the mineral water by this stage and onto a schooner or two – the best way to cope with the strong morning sun.

The civic minded council has begun to erect barricades next to Bourke Street in recent years, to prevent the swelling crowd of partygoers from spilling into the path of the traffic racing towards the airport.

There are two ways to get to the lane. You can follow the sometimes solemn, sometimes revelling stream of people directly from the party, passing en route early morning horse riders and, on one bizarre occasion, hundreds of volunteers for Ian Kiernan's Clean Up Australia Day! This stream traces a path directly from the Showground over Moore Park, up Flinders Street and behind the pub. By doing this you can be guaranteed of having a beer in your hand within about 30 minutes of leaving the Party (nobody leaves the Showgrounds in a crashing hurry).

The more organised but slightly devious route is to get straight into a taxi outside the Showground and go home. You then leap in the shower, choose a new outfit, clean your teeth and arrive at the lane looking as though you have walked straight from the pages of *Vanity Fair*.

The latter is certainly the preferred option if you want to stay at the lane for any length of time. Coming straight from the party does turn into a bit of an endurance test and the sun really beats down on that concrete. Having said that, once somebody sets up speakers on the back of a truck and you've had a few more beers and a chat, it's easy to settle in for the duration.

Coming straight from the Party also gives you the feeling of a stayer – you wear your limp costume and glitter-covered face as a sort of battle scar of the night before, and that will often give you a lot of credibility with the crowd. I think for next year's Mardi Gras I will still head home first. I plan to construct an outfit that gives the impression of having been worn all night but still seems surprisingly fresh somehow.

In the sequence of events, a usual element in the ritual of Mardi Gras is a hearty breakfast on the morning after the party, before beginning the day of recovery celebrations. Café 191 is one of the more obvious locations for a debrief, being on the route home from the Showground and a great vantage point from which to view the bedraggled and sorry procession of hobbling drag queens, limp costumes and red-faced muscle boys, weaving back from the party.

One particular morning after, probably in 1992, David and I sat in front of the café tenderly chewing on plates of scrambled eggs as the last of the revellers dragged their aching carcasses down Flinders Street. From the bottom of Oxford Street, another procession had commenced. The major difference was that this group was the first wave of the cricket crowd, making their way *to* the SCG for the one-day match between Australia and Pakistan.

The closest analogy I can find to this situation is an image of two mighty rivers in South America meeting, their sources thousands of miles apart, and yet their waters still blending effortlessly together.

The crowd became, for a moment, a confused maze of glitter and zinc cream, leather harnesses and eskies. As easily as they came together, the two then separated and continued on their way.

Being Sydney, each group seemed merely to acknowledge the other and meander on its route, oblivious to the hyperbole of the situation.

*Craig Hassall is the General Manager of the Olympic Games Arts Festival.*

# Mardi Gras Myth 4

*In the early days, before Recovery Parties became the norm, groups of friends would gather at someone's place for a few hours, reluctant to call it a day. Showers, foot massages, another vodka, a cup of tea, a protein shake, fruit (cereal or toast inevitably tasted like sawdust) – and games. One of our favourites, and silliest, was called 'Mitzi'. Song or film titles would be suggested where the word 'mitzi' would replace the key word of the title, and points awarded for the degree of hilarity induced. So you might get* The Bridge on the River Mitzi, Mitzi Prefers Blondes, 2001: A Space Mitzi, *'Goodbye Yellow Brick Mitzi' and 'I Don't Know How to Mitzi Him'.*

*One year after the final stragglers had left I put glasses and cups into the dishwasher, pulled down the blinds and climbed into bed, trying to calm twitching muscles. The phone rang. Reluctantly, I answered. A low, soft female voice, slightly menacing, whispered, 'Play Mitzi for Me', and hung up.*

# Belonging

## Michael Freundt

I'VE ALWAYS HATED large crowds and it doesn't get any larger than a Sydney Gay and Lesbian Mardi Gras (SGLMG) Party. But this was my first.

'Hi Darl'.'

'Hi Hun'.'

Kiss to the right, kiss to the left, unless you (or they) are Dutch or you know them *really* well, then it's kiss to the right, kiss to the left, kiss to the right again. More is more.

'What are you doin' here? I thought you hated crowds?'

'I do.'

'So why the change of heart?'

'Drugs.'

It's true. When you're approaching middle age surrounded by eternal youth; when you're an 18-year-old surrounded by 18-minute stands; when you're a washing machine surrounded by washboards, you need a little confidence, and a little help, to go the distance. Joining the drug culture at 42 hadn't been on my life's little list but it was certainly becoming obvious that that was what I had to do. My partner and I were *expected* to attend the party because over the previous few years we had become EPs (Eminent Persons according to some street rag wit). In previous years we had avoided the party with excuses like 'We hate crowds' or 'No thanks, we have to work', but the real reason was we didn't think it was for us. (I thought . . . Let the young ones enjoy themselves . . . I sounded like my mother!)

But I was willing to give it a try.

I was ready for my first dance party.

In true Christmas-shopping style I raced into Aussie Boys on the afternoon of the party and bought a pair of light, tight, black jeans covered in glitter; a light, not-so-tight (thank God for the *blouson* look), black T-shirt and a silver chain on which to hang my VIP pass. Another essential for an ageing queen and another reason to make me go. I was now, apparently, a SGLMGVIEP.

We didn't see the parade – we really had to work – but at about 11 p.m. we climbed into our party pants, punched a hole in our VIP passes, slipped the chain through and over our heads, rolled a joint, and walked and puffed our way to the Showground.

So did a lot of other people.

'Hi Sweets.'

'Hi Gorge.'

'Didn't see you at Tamarama today.'

'No, I was expecting a phone call.'

'What?'

'I was expecting a phone call. I'm with Optus. No signal. Had to get to Bronte.'

'Bummer.'

Several friends of ours – same age but in denial: smaller waists but fruitier relationships – had done the gym *twice* in the week prior to the party. I knew that was futile and I think they did too. You just can't obliterate 45 years of not paying attention with two hours of doing so. But it was all part of the culture: part of . . . Belonging. When, for most of our lives, our cultural feeling was NOT belonging, this is a heady feeling.

So is walking hand-in-hand with your boyfriend.

Feeling comfortable about doing something so normal is what liberation is all about.

The party was huge. Bigger than I expected. The dance floors were packed. Everywhere was packed. A lot of flesh. Not a lot of fabric. The VIP bar, on the side wall of the RHI, became our base, despite the brightness of the room. Sunglasses were essential. It was somewhere you could meet friends *and* sit down. But most importantly there were little-known and well-lit toilets downstairs.

The bar – a crowd, noise, distractions, the necessity to stand very close together – was a perfect place to take our Es. Accuracy wasn't that important. Discretion was still advisable. One half at a time. We didn't want to overdo it.

A beer, a chat, admire a costume, admire no costume, admire no clothes, a water, a wee, a chat, a snort, a bit of bop, a fight to the bar, a toke, a beer . . .

Time had, by now, slipped to the bottom of Life's Little Regulators and the measuring of it . . . well, forget it! It was somewhere in the *middle* of the night and the E had kicked in. Actually the E had kicked much earlier, but it hadn't registered with us. It had, however, registered with everybody else. We innocently went up to friends and said, no, what a shame, but we don't think it's having any effect.

We saw stunned and hysterical faces gawking back at us.

They saw two overweight queens with exploding irises, tongues down each other's throats and hands down each other's pants.

We were informed: The Es had *definitely* kicked in. Phew!

And the beer kept flowing. Beer is good not just because of the bubbles but also the bitterness, like roasted sandpaper, which itches the back of the throat and lubricates what feels like irrigation ditches. Wow!

And that's another thing. For some inexplicable reason words like 'wow' had suddenly creep into our rapidly diminishing vocabulary. Words like 'groovy' and phrases like 'Yeah, wow' and 'Wow, look at that!' And then sometimes words became redundant altogether and you simply spotted someone you knew (or didn't) and a simple flare of the eyeballs was all that was 'said'. And then you seemed to be aware of a sudden drop in extremely short memory retention because, just minutes ago, you were . . .

(And what about that gum? The TV ads for chewing gum should warn you about the shredding effect your teeth have on the inside of your mouth. Chewing Inaccuracy *is* Collateral Damage.)

At regular intervals throughout the night, a spectacular show would happen. Spectacular for the number of performers involved or for the simplicity of the thing. A stage full of energetic and precise dancers, with or without a Boy George or Kylie Minogue; fireworks, explosions, colour and movement; or a single drag queen suspended high above our heads, resplendent in peacock blue, miming an anthem to 'free, gay, happy'.

But the prelude to each show was a precise stratagem. Word got to you (God knows how) that a show was imminent. A grab of a bottle of water from the bar, a grab of your boyfriend's hand, a few kisses goodbye.

'See you back here in an hour, Sweetie?'

'Okay, Darls.'

A rush to the toilet – a real wee this time – a launch out the bottom door into the madding crowd. A plan was very important. Head away from this side of the stage and rush around the back to the other and squeeze yourself onto the dance floor. Clever. However, this strategy involved the unlikely scenario that you were the only two of 16 000 people who had come up with that brilliant idea. Oh well, if you can't glimpse the stage you can at least hear it and soak up the ambience.

That particular show was 87 drag queens doing a disco version of 'Luck Be a Lady Tonight'.

At some time we went for a stroll. Definitely not a walk. A stroll. A languid, meandering, hand-in-hand, 'Hi Darl' stroll to the Dome.

The Dome was built as an exhibition hall for the presentation and judging of meat. Some things never change.

Around its dimly lit walls, away from the throbbing core, stands a long line of men. Usually with heads back against the wall, staring into the middle distance making out that they were listening to the music. They wear only skimpy underwear, or jeans with the fly-flaps peeled back like banana skins. And they are usually hairy.

I went up to one such being: head back, no expression, a slight, oh so slight, hip throb to the music but really looking like there was no one home. Just this shell, this warm passive, hairy shell, just leaning there. I wiped the palm of my right had over his furry chest. Bingo! Like flicking a switch. The eyes came on, a smile came out and expectation gushed out of every pore. This subsided a bit when the eyes focused on who had touched him. My boyfriend yanked my arm and I walked on but I looked back to see the smile go back inside, the eyes go out, the throb start up again with head held back staring into the middle distance.

Jonestown was a delight. Officially called the Chill-Out Bar, Jonestown was a smaller venue with less techno music, a small dance floor and a large sea of pillows and bodies. Some asleep, some on top of others, some on top of several, some between several . . . all moving j-u-s-t a little bit. It was very sexy. I wondered what the chance was that just-a-little-bit-of-moving might turn into something more serious. I shouldn't've bothered as I found out later in the safety of our own bed: the drugs of today completely obliterate the sex of the moment.

I wonder if Fred Nile knows that?

Back in the VIP bar it was a bit of a shock to see daylight around the edges of the blacked-out windows. Sunlight!

Suddenly I wanted to be horizontal.

We wavered into Oxford Street. I needed a pie. With sauce. We turned down Bourke Street. Our party gear was not living up to expectations. We didn't care anymore. Someone in a small Austin stopped in the middle of Bourke Street, wound down the passenger window and called out to us. He wanted to know how the party went. Did we have a good time?

I think he was taking his kids to Sunday School.

I think it was the Lord Mayor.

*Michael Freundt, with his partner Geoffrey Williams, ran the Tilbury pub for many years, creating a whole new demand for cabaret theatre in Sydney.*

# The Night of His Life

## David Franklin

'WHAT ARE YOU WEARING?' Brad had been asking everyone this question since October. I was naive enough to think that the chances of him
actually having to make a wardrobe decision for Mardi Gras were
Buckley's. But Brad wasn't going to let CMV, MAC, toxoplasmosis and
a little case of dementia stop him. Oh, no! He was going to party, big,
one last time.

To be perfectly frank, at first glance, he looked pretty cool. He was
wearing a cut-off western shirt and black jeans, teamed with a Balinese
straw hat that he'd cleverly transformed into a red cowboy hat. (He'd
made two more, for Mark and I. The three amigos.) But physically, he
looked shocking. His body was ready to pack it in, but tonight was a
time for celebrating.

If you've ever taken a seven-year-old with attention deficit disorder
to the Royal Easter Show, then you'll have some idea of what it was like
going with Brad to the Party. He wanted everything and everybody –
now! It was wonderful to see his excitement and pleasure, but the bottom
line was that he was out of control. Mark and I became more and more
concerned for his safety. I began to wish that Brad had been into leather
so he could have been harnessed. By 4.30 a.m. Mark and I could cope
no longer. Brad informed us that he was peaking and couldn't possibly
leave. He'd 'forgot' to tell us that as part of his party preparations he'd
organised some ecstasy for himself. I didn't want to rain on his parade
but if we didn't get him home now we were sure to lose him and in his
state that was definitely dangerous. Our half-truth that Mark and I were
tired (and we were – of looking after him!) was equally unsuccessful in
getting him to leave. It was time to fight fire with fire. I mentioned that
I had more eccies at home and why didn't we go back to take them?
My fiendishly simple plan worked like a charm.

Once back in the relative safety of home I gave Brad two more 'eccies'.
These were in fact Normison which should have calmed him down. I
turned my back and he was out the door staggering down the street,
heading back to the Party. Out came the big guns. One Rohypnol should

have knocked him out for a good 12 hours. It could have been a saccharin pill for all the sedating qualities it invoked.

By 9.00 a.m. the tally was 5 Normison and 1 Rohypnol. Mark and I needed reinforcements and called Richard, who conceded perhaps another half a Rohypnol. The effect was negligible. Brad was as restless as ever, desperate now to get out to the recovery parties. So we decided to visit Richard and Brett. That would get him out of the house and give us some respite. We arrived, supporting a now legless Brad between us. His first words to our hosts were, 'Hi! Got any eccies?'

We all waited for Brad to slow down. We rang a community nurse for advice on what more we could give him and finally resorted to a Mogodon, telling him it would make him sleazy. He downed it with alacrity. Still no effect. It was now past noon. We were all lying around the living room, beginning to unwind. Brad, after a 10-minute struggle to raise himself up on one elbow, declared, 'I'm off now.' Without missing a beat, or interrupting my conversation, I knocked his elbow out from under him.

Brad collapsed back onto the bed, from whence he immediately began his quest to rise again.

Richard tried reason. 'We're just relaxing here for a while to calm down and be together before we tackle the heat and crowds of the recovery parties, okay?'

'I'm sorry, Richard, but that's just not me,' Brad replied.

At one point I took a break, smoking by the window, and Brad confided to Richard loudly enough for us all to hear, 'I think David and I will be together forever, don't you?' All of us, Brad oblivious, dissolved into tears.

At around 2.30 that afternoon, Brad agreed, surprisingly, to return home for a bath – someone's inane suggestion. Events would later argue that this was an elaborate hoax on Brad's part. At home I bathed him and returned him to his bedroom. We lived in hope that the Mogodon was working. Half an hour later he emerged resplendent in a new outfit, pink singlet and rust velvet shorts, clutching the door for support.

'See you guys, I'm off,' he declared.

By now, Richard had decided that truth was Best. 'Brad, you're not going anywhere: a) because you can't walk by yourself; and b) because none of us are going to help you.'

Brad looked mildly hurt. 'But I'm an invalid, Richard.' He retired to the living room. By now Mark and I had been coping with him for fifteen hours and were falling asleep in the kitchen. The community nurse had okayed another Rohypnol. We were waiting for it to work. Fat chance!

Feeling guilty, Richard went to find Brad. He was sifting through photographs and Richard asked him to show his favourites.

At around 4 p.m. Mark and I joined the boys. Richard was sitting on the sofa with Brad, his arm around his shoulders. Suddenly, or perhaps gradually, Brad's muscles began to relax. His head began to nod on Richard's chest. Stillness. Silence.

'I think he's off,' Richard announced.

SHHHH! I admonished, desperate we didn't disturb him. We carried him to bed. He was out to it.

Brad died a few weeks later.

*David Franklin is an actor who is currently co-producing a movie of the hit play* Dags, *in which he excelled as head nerd. Brad Levido was a highly regarded artist who frequently exhibited at the Coventry Gallery in Sydney.*

# Bright Blue Light

## Mark Nicholas

IT'S EIGHT O'CLOCK in the morning and I'm lost in the music in the left hand corner of the RHI. The incessant rhythm that has been pounding out of these speakers for the past few hours has become my heartbeat. Besides me, someone has dozed off in a small mountain of plastic mineral water bottles. The air is thick with a humidity of sweat, smoke and amyl, and I'm taking in dizzy gulps of this as I dance.

There is an urgency now. This is Mardi Gras, the night is almost over. Rushes of pleasure course through my body. There is a fan blowing and we are bathed in patterns of bright blue light as the beat takes over. I'm slithering around enjoying what seems to be talcum powder or dust. It's making the floor great to dance on. Thus music slides into an old disco track, 'The love, the love I lost, was the deepest', and I notice men crying beside the dance floor.

Later that morning, my friend explains that we'd been dancing on the ashes of a man who'd recently died and had asked that they be sprinkled on the dance floor at Mardi Gras.

*Mark Nicholas divides his time between the UK and Australia but is always in Sydney for summer and Mardi Gras.*

# What Are You Wearing?

## Wendy Harmer

WHEN I WAS ASKED to be a special guest on the lead float in the 1993 Mardi Gras, I was, of course, overcome with pleasure. I remember that moment very clearly, because it came a split second before I was plunged into the greatest existential style crisis of my life.

*Ohmigod! What will I wear?*

Now I have had style crises before. Anyone who remembers *The Big Gig* will recall a tragic parade of earrings bigger than my head, merino perms, jackets with shoulderpads you could land an F1-11 on, tulle fairy skirts, daisy tights and all manner of unfortunate garb.

But this was bigger. A *lot* bigger.

This was not merely a matter of 'fashion'. 'Fashion' is for amateurs – a superficial consideration of hem length, necklines, cut, colour and other mere trivialities. However, what one wears to the Mardi Gras is an expression of self on the deepest level. I realised that the question was not 'what will I wear?' but rather, 'Who am I?'

And then came the final body blow. I would be standing next to Julian Clary. The answer to 'who am I?' now came to me with blinding clarity. An utter dag.

This was like being invited to be the guest of honour at Truman Capote's Black and White Ball, Princess Di's wedding, the *Dynasty* wrap party and a taping of *Oz Aerobics* all rolled into one. For weeks, I agonised over the possibilities.

A big meringue wedding dress thingy? No irony there, I'd just look like a desperate single straight in a gay, gay world. Nude with body paint? No, think of the rear view angle. Leather and studs? Done, done, *done*! Flashing fairy lights? So last year. Etc, etc.

Well come on . . . You think of something that will make you stand out in a sea of heaving flesh, feathers, glitter, bottletops and crêpe paper daisies! In the end I gave up and wore a black trouser suit. I added a beret, a big cigar, dog tags and pretended I was Fidel Castro . . . without the beard . . . and . . . er . . . the uniform and stuff.

On the big night Julian Clary turned up in a white Lycra full body suit encrusted with big fake rubies . . . and a plaster cast. Of course! How could I have missed it? Darling, it was so obvious!

Needless to say the night was extraordinary. An evening never to be forgotten. But even now, years later, I still run into people who say, 'Oh yes, I remember you on that float. You were in a beret and you had a cigar. What were you supposed to be?'

I can only answer, 'I'm sorry, I have absolutely no idea.'

*Wendy Harmer – comedienne, performer, writer, broadcaster – is also a mum and is quite clear about who she is.*

# When We Were Slightly Younger

## Stephen Dunne

SOMETIME AROUND 1993, we witness the last sputter of public in-yer-face Sydney AIDS activism. ACT UP are geniuses at the inexpensive fashion statement, so it's stylish black T-shirts for all (except for Kirsty, who paints 'Silence=Death' across her tits in body paint. Later at a family gathering, a cousin announces 'I was at the Mardi Gras. And I saw *everything*!') The T-shirts are emblazoned with a slogan in bold white on black: 'Fight for the living!' As we turn the corner into Liverpool Street, people cheer. For reasons I'll never know (apart from the fact that it felt right), I spend much of the night doing odd Black Power salutes.

The following year, you and I decide not to go. We are minding a flat for Frank and Geoff, so we tuck ourselves up at their end of Potts Point, still marvelling about a building with a swimming pool. (Frank and Geoff's block is modern and ugly with a pool; ours is old and classy with no amenities whatsoever.) We go up on the roof for a whisky and a chat, and are rudely, but fascinatingly, distracted by the sight of a Classic Sydney Gay Boy trying on his party costume in a nearby apartment. From the rooftop, all the big lounge room windows of the next building are visible, like a video wall, with each screen obsessed by its own pro-gramme. Two windows down, a leather queen slowly stitches himself in. One floor above, a bloke wanks on the phone.

But our attention is held by the kid with the 'what to wear?' dilemma. Our classic Sydney gay boy has a ritual. First he emerges from the bedroom in a costume, then he has a practice boogie in front of the mirror, just to check it out, just to see how it looks, and finally he returns to the bedroom (out of sight) to change.

It is over half an hour (and half a dozen costumes) before we realise there are in fact two of them, identical in all respects. Two Classic Sydney Gay Boys in a Classic Sydney Gay Boy Relationship trying to find the Classic Sydney Gay Boy Outfit to wear to the Classic Sydney Gay Boy Party. After what seems forever – and while you and I col-lapsed into giggles on the rooftop, next to the pool and under the mean, struggling stars of a Potts Point night – they settle on: white T-shirt, cut-off jeans and black boots.

What else could we have reasonably expected?

*Stephen Dunne is a journalist and theatre critic with the* Sydney Morning Herald.

# Black Cockatoo

## Anthony Babicci

I SPENT TWO WEEKS before the Parade, in what little spare time I had, making a big floppy-eyed mask on a stick and a chandelier hat for myself to wear to Mardi Gras, to wobble and twinkle at people. I wasn't happy about either of them. The chandelier, which was wired to the top of an old crash helmet, proved to be a real pain in the neck.

An hour earlier, I'd been nervously dressing for the night, wondering whether my handiwork was good enough to wear amongst the creative competitors of this extremely critical city. I couldn't make up my mind. I had been promising myself for months that I would be part of the Parade, but I was running late. I tried to calm my nerves before presenting my lunatic self to the public.

Suddenly, there was a serious knocking at the front door of the warehouse. Annoyed, I took the chandelier off my head again, and went to see who the unwanted visitor was. It was like opening a surreal cupboard door on a TV show. There stood Malcolm, our black sister, totally freaked out. He was wearing an odd array of huge pink-and-yellow handmade feathers, which were so big that their papery surface reminded me of palm leaves. There was still enough of his velvety skin showing to make a girl blush. Squawking like a parrot, Malcolm said he wanted to see my partner desperately. I explained that Panos, who had helped Mal with his float the previous year, had already gone out to watch the Parade. Malcolm looked crushed so I invited him in.

Apparently there were twenty other people, attired in the same costume as Malcolm's, somewhere out in the street that night. They were supposed to be on a float together as this year's Aboriginal entry. Malcolm, who was part Torres Strait Islander, had gathered and co-ordinated his mob for it, as he had the year before. In that Parade, he and his mate, Eric, had sailed up Oxford Street in a long canoe on wheels, flying the Aboriginal flag on a mast. They'd been magnificent together: a camp blackfella's send up of Captain Cook and Sir Joseph Banks, wearing tinsel instead of braid on their outlandish cartoon frock coats, their hats bigger than the Ascot scene from *My Fair Lady*.

Disdainfully surveying the sea of mostly white faces, they'd flicked their cheap, oversized lace handkerchiefs in a pantomime of white attitude.

This year, they had prepared a bigger float, but then disaster had struck. The driver of their float failed to materialise. When the time came for the Parade to start, Malcolm's feathered friends had dispersed on foot and, disappointed, he'd found his way to our place.

Trying to resolve both our dilemmas at once, I said, 'Let's go together, I'm ready.' Malcolm was still so upset that Panos wasn't there that I had to try and be cheery, even though by now I was absolutely convinced that my outfit was completely tragic. Moreover, Malcolm's strength through what could only be called a major disaster made me see how pathetic my costume insecurities were. I decided to stop critiquing my cossie and get out there regardless. The moment had arrived. I also knew that the Parade wasn't going to wait for us.

We scuttled down the stairs and into the street together. By now Oxford Street was over-crowded and impassable, and so we decided to take a short cut to the starting point. Striding through the back lanes of Darlinghurst with Malcolm, I realised how colonial my chandelier helmet and mask were next to this blackfella in his pink-and-yellow palm-like feathers. Together, our disparate visions made a strange kind of sense, and the electric energy in the air dissipated both our misgivings. I had met Malcolm a number of times over ten years, in theatres and bars, but it wasn't until that night that we started to become friends.

We climbed the hill at the beginning of Stanley Street, but when we got to the Parade route, the street seemed almost empty. It was eerie. Something else had gone wrong. We looked to the left and saw a couple of floats disappear around the corner into Oxford Street and then move down to the right, where William Street crosses College Street. The rest of the parade had been stopped by police.

In a strange antithesis to this reconciliation story, I went back to the part of the Parade that had been held up to see what had gone wrong, and Malcolm went the other way because he wanted to be at the beginning. We kissed and hugged, wished each other happy Mardi Gras, and split in opposite directions. By the time I got down to where the police were, they had let a whole lot of clogged traffic through to William Street and the Parade continued. I don't know where I got the energy from but that night I danced with the ghosts of my childhood; no longer scary in the pink lights of the Parade, they had transformed themselves into seductive fairies.

I remembered how queer Malcolm had looked as he stood in my

doorway, like a cockatoo that had been hit by a truck. Much later that night I saw him again on the dance floor at the Party. He was holding another black sister, who was crying on his shoulder. Later, Malcolm told me that this man was their missing driver. Swallowing his disappointment, Malcolm had forgiven all, even though their beautiful float was still back at the Mardi Gras workshop collecting dust, unseen by the crowd. As the time of the Parade had drawn nearer the man had grown afraid that his family would see him on television and find out about him. Like many of us, that fear had stopped him from showing up.

*Anthony Babicci is a set and costume designer of theatre and film, and was a Mardi Gras board member for a number of years.*

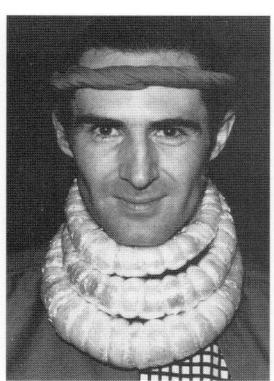

*Clockwise from top:* Ron Muncaster and Jacques Straetmans out of costume and in leather; William Yang and Allan Booth; Dennis Altman and Craig Johnston at an early gay rights rally; Lex Watson; Peter Tully, who brought urban tribal wear to Sydney, in one of his necklaces.

*Clockwise from top:* Mardi Gras
creative powerhouses, David
McDiarmid and Peter Tully; Brian
McGahen declares himself a pansy;
Nell Schofield and Fran Moore;
Peter Tully in parade.

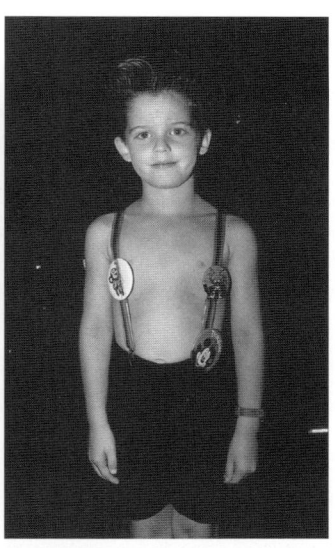

*Clockwise from top:* The incomparable
Doris Fish; Adam Cahill at Mardi Gras,
age 6; another member of the Ritchie
family, Cindy Pastel; from left to right:
Robyn Botelle, Monique Kelly, Dawn
O'Donnell and Simone Troy.

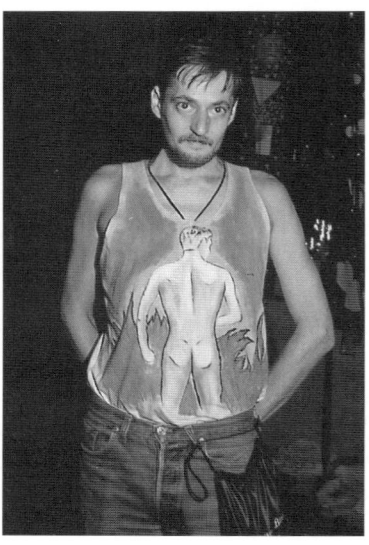

*Clockwise from top:* Phil Scott; Colin
Fawcett and Bruce Pollack; DJ Bill
Morley; Brad Levido at a 1988 Mardi
Gras event; Murray McLachlan, Robert
Lake and Anthony Babicci.

*Facing page. Clockwise from top:* MPs Clover Moore
and Elisabeth Kirkby march under umbrella; Wendy
Harmer in her favourite Fidel Castro number with
Mardi Gras girl scouts; one of the wet years; Maggie
Kirkpatrick (far right) is joined by Geraldine Turner
and Fanny Farquar on the donations float.

*Clockwise from top:* From left to right,
Twistie, Miss 3D, Doris Fish and Cindy
Pastel at a Mardi Gras event; the eternal
figure of Miss New Zealand; Torrie
Finlayson and Ian Jopson (on left);
Lance Leopard with Victoria Bitter.

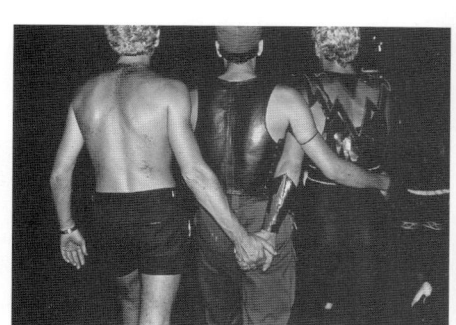

*Clockwise from top:* Menage á trois; bears on parade;
members of the tap-dancing lesbian group.

*Clockwise from top:* Revellers; Aboriginal marchers Stephen, Russell and David from the Bangarra Dance company float; marching boys do their thing; one of Mardi Gras' most popular entries, PFlag.

# Mother and Child

## Sue Frankham

WE MET WHEN WE WERE TWELVE YEARS OLD. That was in 1959, when we were in our first year of high school, sitting next to each other in English. We remained friends for years, drifting apart when she and her family moved to Canberra after her children were born, and only seeing each other spasmodically over the next few years.

About four years ago, my children and I were the subject of an article in the newspaper. My friend told me some time later that she was shocked to read that both my children were gay.

That was before her son came out.

For the last four years I have been part of the PFLAG (Parents and Friends of Lesbians and Gays) group in the Parade, and for the last three years my friend and I have marched together. As she said to me one night while we wended our way down Oxford Street: 'Whoever would have guessed, when we were at school, that we would be here tonight?'

We are both immensely proud of our children, and we can't wait for each Mardi Gras Parade to say to the world, we are the proud parents of gay children.

During one Parade, my friend had words with the Reverend Fred Nile as we passed his contingent. I recall some of them as being 'judge not lest ye be judged'. I hope he was listening.

My friend and her husband are moving to Queensland, but she'll be coming back every year for the Parade.

Some of the parents at PFLAG have lost their children to AIDS, and march to honour their memory. One couple comes each year from interstate, they wear T-shirts with their son's likeness in the Parade.

There is another wonderful woman who comes from New Zealand each year to be in the Parade. She spends the weekend with her son, marches in the Parade, and goes to the Party with him afterwards. Her son delivered her to the PFLAG group the first year I marched (he was a marching drag queen). Now she carries a small bag in the Parade. It contains her son's handbag and stilettos for the party.

*Sue Frankham is a solicitor who lives with her German Shepherd, Lily, in Lilyfield.*

Letters to the Editor
*Sydney Morning Herald*

3 March

Dear Sir,

Last Saturday I had one of the best experiences of my life.
Together with a lovely friend, I marched with my gay son in the
Mardi Gras parade.
The three of us held hands and marched under the family banner of
PFLAG (Parents and Friends of Lesbians and Gays) with other
supporters, friends and family (mostly mums, not too many dads)
and we were completely overwhelmed by the support and love shown
to us by that wonderful capacity crowd.
We wanted to make some sort of statement, so on our arms we boldly
wrote 'Proud Friend' and 'Mum' and this seemed to say it all, for
us and the crowd. Cheers and cries of 'Good on you, Mum' followed
us all the way. People shook my hand, congratulated me and
expressed their wishes that their parents could do the same. Come
on, you folk out there. You encourage and support your children
through school achievements, sporting events and the like, so
trot yourselves out to next year's Mardi Gras and share a
fabulous warm feeling with your beloved child.
Many issues concern parents of gay children not the least of them
being the prejudice and loathing our child will experience from a
mostly ignorant public and if our united display of love and
support will help to mellow the attitudes of at least one hostile
person, then perhaps some of our parental fears will be lessened
for the future.
Thank you PFLAG, for inviting us to march with you. We will be
back again next year with a bit more tinsel and glitter. Thank
you, Sydney Mardi Gras.

Coral Lester, Summer Hill

# The Induction of
# Sister Carmen Get It

## Peter McCallum

I WAS A TEENAGER IN 1978 when I heard about the militant Sydney (gasp) '. . . *homosexuals* . . .' (gasp) marching defiantly up the main street. Knowing that Melbourne would never stand for such nonsense, I became determined to get to Sydney, one way or the other. It took fourteen years before I finally walked in my first Parade, but it was worth the wait.

My 1993 Parade saw me walking with my newly acquired boyf in the 'Clean and Sober' contingent, mainly made up of gays and lesbians from AA. That was 'special'. The roar of the glitter and the smell of the crowd is something I will never forget, and I suppose that I can be thankful that my Parade virginity was lost at a moment when I had all my faculties. I still have my cut-off shirt and obscenely tiny denim shorts – a bit like a bride keeps her wedding dress, really.

With boyf and his non-indulgent habits replaced, the 1994 Parade was decidedly different. Sister Carmen Getit, OPI, made her Mardi Gras debut – as a driver. This was a year that the Sisters of Perpetual Indulgence decided to put in a float, and so for the second time in history, the urinal we had commandeered from the demolished Green Park loo was put on public display. It was lashed to the Popemobile (a mini moke) with a big sign saying 'The Most Holy Relic', and a lovely but ageing transgender, Father Izzie-Over-Done, from the Adelaide house stood waving from the platform atop. No one realised beforehand, but it soon became obvious that Father Izzie was thought to be the Most Holy Relic, rather than the large bit of metallic history underneath!

We had two vehicles in this Parade, the second being a rented 'ute' of which I was the driver. It was a simple but effective float, adorned with little more than a chair. Nothing more was needed really, because on that chair was enthroned the regal majesty of Sister Mary Daisy Chain, who for the reasons unknown to almost everyone, had decided to come out of the RSL (Retired Sisters' Lounge) and be part of the Parade.

'Driving Miss Daisy' (as I like to remember it) was an experience. I recall desperately trying not to run over Sister Iona Ducati who kept flying in front of me on roller blades at the most inopportune moments. At the same time, I had to make sure that the ride was smooth enough so Daisy didn't go lurching off the back in any unseemly and un-nunly manner. All was well in the end and no grief came to either sister.

It wasn't until my 1995 Parade that I actually interacted with the crowd myself. Only weeks before, I'd returned from a work trip to Tokyo. I decided to turn my bandeau (a nun's headband) into a 'hachimaki'. I painted a big red spot in the middle of it and put the characters 'ka' and 'ma' on either side. (I had learned that 'kama' is colloquial Japanese for 'poofter'.) Adorned with this multicultural adaptation, I took great and evil delight in racing up to every group of Japanese tourists available, and greeting them in their own language! My retinas still haven't recovered from the camera flashes, but it was worth the gasps and shrieks of horror, surprise and delight that I received from my victims.

1996 and one of my great dreams was realised. I had always admired Mardi Gras' Marching Boys not only because of their acres of collective flesh, but because of the wonderful energy that they had. After long debate and much encouragement, I went to the cattle call, and passed the audition! I was in the LAST EVER official Mardi Gras Marching Boys entry! Rehearsals were appropriately gruelling, and although I thought that I would never remember the routine, come the night everything was faaaabulous! We wore Lycra shorts with the bum cut out in the shape of a heart (waxing was essential of course). That was the first year we were televised, and my heart shaped bum had its 2.5 seconds of international fame. I think it was the enthusiasm from the crowd that kept up the endorphins which enabled us to get to the end of the march.

The 1997 Parade was entirely different. Being an accredited security officer, I was working as a Ranger (Mardi Gras Security). Having to start work at 9 p.m. I was able at 5 p.m. to help the Redfern G & L Social Group prepare their float. I then had a quick look at the other entries, and walked up the middle of the route to get to work (my own little parade of one!) From 9 p.m. to 4 a.m., I was on the VIP gate at President Avenue, letting in the 'VIPs' – that term is rather fluid and indeterminate if you ask me! – as well as the larger frocks that couldn't fit in through the turnstiles. I was fascinated at the number of girlfriends that Mardi Gras President Bev Lange had apparently acquired, especially ones without tickets! Needless to say, in the nicest possible way of course, their efforts at entry were not altogether successful. After receiving unreasonable flack and rudeness from the disorganised new girl in charge of security (which is another story in itself) I vowed and declared never to do it again. Despite the mixed feelings, it was yet another aspect of the Parade, and I am thankful I experienced it.

1998 and I was ready to Party hard. This all came to a grinding halt when I was rung up and asked if I would come back as a Marching Boy in the 'Retro' entry. It was not difficult to say 'Yes'. I was being considered veteran enough to be 'Retro'! We rehearsed down at Technology Park in the abandoned train sheds doing one of Sammy Shalom's brilliant routines.

For me, having performed a new function at every Mardi Gras, each Parade has always been very different. One thing I've noticed is that every time I've done one, a new aspect of my personality has been on display. I can't wait to see what I'll be up to next! Once, I thought I was an outsider to this city, but being part of the Parade is one contribution I can make to the community, and one that has made me feel I do belong.

*If you don't know Sr Carmen Get It (aka Peter McCallum) by now, you must have been hiding under a rock!*

# The Rehearsal

## William Forsythe

MY STORY STARTS mid-week February 1994 and I'm rehearsing *Go West* with 170 performers. It's the first time I have had this many volunteers on such a large stage with too many entrances and way too many stairs. Also this year I'm choreographing Kylie, the pressure's on, and I'm my usual unpleasant, super-stressed, tyrannical, smart-mouthed, arsehole self that everyone has come to know and love.

Anyway I'm at about my tenth hour of rehearsal, around 10.30 Thursday night. I'm standing with a mike in my hand, feeling very tired. I turn to the stage manager, who I notice is new. Every time I turn right or left I bump into her. So I ask ever so sweetly if she could get me a chair to sit on and I go back to work.

Ten minutes go by and I look behind me and the stage manager is STILL standing there and with no chair. Our eyes meet. I say 'the chair, I'd like it – NOW!' – Please remember, I'm very tired and *very* stressed. Off runs the stage manager, looking back at me like a deer seeing headlights in front of her. She returns very apologetically with my chair.

An hour or so goes by. Gary Leeson, Party Co-ordinator, my mentor, friend and god arrives. Seeing my stress, which is now being bestowed on anyone within a metre of me, he tries to calm me down to no avail. So he goes off to find the new president to see if they can help.

Meanwhile back at rehearsal – there's sweat, there's tears and a tad of yelling, followed by more sweat, more tears and definitely more yelling. Gary returns with the president. I turn around and to my horror, the president standing in front of me is my deer-eyed stage manager!

That's when I first met Susan Harben, whom I now love, adore, worship, and would die for.

*William Forsythe is a choreographer.*

# A Night with Kylie

## Duncan McGregor

SUDDENLY APPOINTED to the board of Mardi Gras when a casual vacancy arose towards the end of 1993, I didn't have any particular job to do on the night of the 1994 Party until the opportunity arose to look after Kylie Minogue. Kylie had agreed to do the 3 a.m. show at the Royal Hall of Industries. Kylie's performance was to be 'What Do I Have to Do?', choreographed by William Forsythe and produced by Gary Leeson.

It should have been the best and most exciting volunteer job that a board member could undertake on the night. Certainly it should have been glamorous. Following years of failed attempts to secure Kylie for either Mardi Gras or Sleaze Ball, Gary Leeson, Mardi Gras' entertainment co-ordinator, had received a call from Kylie's manager. He'd told Gary that Kylie was interested in performing at Mardi Gras. It was only a week or so before the end of January.

One of the most important considerations from the Mardi Gras Board's point of view was secrecy. Each of us had to swear not to tell a soul. For me, this meant not telling Richard Wherrett and Brett Sheehy, my flatmates. I managed to be fairly discreet, but Brett had overheard a telephone conversation in which I was making arrangements to pick up Kylie at a particular time for rehearsals. I didn't confirm to Brett that it *was* her, but did say he and Richard should be in the RHI between 2.30 and 3 a.m. to see an unnamed performer. Much rolling of eyes evidenced my failure to convince!

Friday morning, less than 48 hours before the Party, and Kylie flew into Sydney from Melbourne. Susan Harben, President of Mardi Gras, and I met her on the flight bridge leading from the plane. Unfortunately, as we introduced ourselves, half of gay and lesbian Melbourne filed past, looking wide-eyed at the diminutive icon, ready to confirm to their friends the already existing rumours about Kylie performing at the Party.

Of course, there's no such thing as a secret amongst queens, so by the time the Party started, the gossip about Kylie was pretty strong – even though the Mardi Gras Board had tried to encourage an alternative rumour by pretending to prepare for an M People show in the Hordern at 3 a.m.

Kylie had picked up the choreography for the show in about two seconds flat, the male dancers were firing, and so the show was looking pretty good by the end of the last rehearsal. She seemed relaxed but incredibly excited at the prospect of performing at the Party. She was certainly more relaxed than the board members who were working that night. Kylie was one of the biggest acts to perform at a Mardi Gras Party, and it was hugely important that the show go smoothly.

It almost didn't.

Something had gone disastrously wrong earlier in the evening with the varilights used to light the stage. As we got closer and closer to Kylie's performance, no one was sure whether the varilights would be working again. Video footage of the night shows members of Mardi Gras' fantastic production and lighting team frantically changing the whole of the lighting desk twice, and anxiously waiting to see whether the lighting programme for the 3 a.m. show would re-boot.

In the meantime, the rumour that Kylie was to perform had continued to spread, and the RHI had turned into a can of very sweaty sardines. This situation became such a concern to those running the party that at about 2 a.m., two decisions were made. The first was to bring Kylie's show forward as much as possible. The second was to close the doors to the RHI shortly before the show.

I was responsible for communicating the change in show time to Kylie, to the dancers and to the stage management. But at about this time, my walkie-talkie packed it in and there was no time to get another. This meant I had to run messages between party control – some 150 metres from the RHI – to Kylie and the dancers who were waiting at the entrance. By then, the area around the RHI was chock-a-block with people trying to get in, so 'running' was more a matter of dodging and pushing my way through the crowd.

Finally, at about 2.30 a.m., it was determined that the lighting situation wasn't going to be fixed and that the show should go on with the stage lighting largely being manually manipulated. At that point, Richard Cobden, Mardi Gras' Honorary Secretary, and I ran from Party Control towards the RHI and through the crowds now hanging around the closed entrances to the hall. People were milling around everywhere, frustrated in their attempts to get inside by the security guards at each door. We gave the message to go on to Kylie, the dancers and stage management. Kylie and the dancers were then escorted backstage by a pack of burly uniforms, leaving Richard and myself stranded outside the doors of the RHI.

Desperate to get in, we raced to the Hordern end of the RHI. One of the doors had been closed for such a long time by that point that no crowds were near it. Richard began scraping his fingernails against the locked door to no avail, other than to establish the need for a good manicure. We raced around to another door where the crowd was about 40 deep, but at least there was a security guard who was letting people out. Realising this was our last chance, Richard and I bolted for the door. To this day, I don't know how we got through the crowd. The only image I can recall is one of sheep dogs running across the backs of sheep in the yards.

Eventually, we got to the door and, with a lot of shouting and waving of security passes, managed to convince the guard to let us through.

Once inside, we raced to the DJ and lighting box at the end of the dance floor. The last song before the show was just coming to an end as we sprinted up the stairs to get into the box. The lighting still hadn't been fixed. Would the show work with only manual operation of most of the stage lighting? The tension was palpable.

To make matters worse, Susan Harben had her arm around my neck and, in the excitement, was apparently trying to strangle me.

Suddenly, from beneath the stage, Kylie let out an excited scream which the crowd immediately recognised as hers. The 8000 people or so in the RHI went wild. And Susan's arm around my neck tightened with nerves.

In a second, it was all over. The crowd had gone berserk and the show had been an unquestionable triumph.

Susan relaxed her arm and I was able to breathe again.

*Duncan McGregor is an environmental lawyer and was a Mardi Gras board member during 1994 and 1995.*

# Magic and Other Celebrities

## Johnny Dawson

I WAS 24 AND IT WAS SUMMER. We were all giddy with excitement because the day had finally arrived. It was 1994 and it was Mardi Gras.

The way I remember it is like this: Matthew Westwood and I were sitting in a café that no longer exists in Oxford Street, Paddington. Butterflies worked on our tummies as we forced down some food we really didn't want to eat. Our words, always clever, flew over the table at high speed, gossip, shrill laughter. We didn't think we could get any more excited.

Suddenly an electric current burst into the room like St Elmo's fire. It was our buddy, Eric, who was hysterical. In his overwrought condition he explained that he had just been told by a friend of his that his friend, so and so, who has been friends with Kylie since he did her hair on *Neighbours*, just saw Kylie Minogue at Five Ways, and, you'll never believe, oh my God, I can't believe it, Kylie is doing the 3 o'clock show in the RHI.

Three shrieking queens jumped up and down in a quiet little Paddington café on the most important day of their lives. It was, and still is, the most electrifying moment of rumour and desire that I have ever experienced. The extreme sensation of soaring high on a possibility is the most potent magic I know of.

Magic is an illusion, unfortunately, and after a while, the wily observer can see the trick.

In December 1995, Judith Fletcher, who was the Executive Officer of Mardi Gras at the time, picked me to be her assistant. I didn't know anything about the organisation. I didn't know any of the people, but in a very short time I was about to meet a lot of them. My days as the bright-eyed party boy whose only knowledge of Mardi Gras was the mirror ball over the dance floor and my treasured memory of Kylie (who actually did perform) were over.

I got cynical fairly quickly and I lost that innocent edge somewhere between the internal politics of the place and the next party. I enjoyed the pace and I liked being in the know about who the acts were and what times they were on, but somehow I lost out on the magic. I heard the rumours but I knew they weren't true. I missed shrieking with my friends at the prospect of a possibility.

Summer of 1998 was one of the hottest for years. It was Thursday night and I was sitting in my living room when an electric current burst into the room like St Elmo's fire. My flatmate, Grant, came bounding into the house. He was shrieking of course, 'Have you heard? Is it true?' Mardi Gras gossip, ask Johnny.

Usually, I prepare myself to either deny what is true or be bored by rumours that are so off the mark that they are ridiculous. Like Madonna.

'Have you heard, it is true? I rang my friend at Warner's and she said Madonna has checked into the Ritz-Carlton at Double Bay! Do you think it could be true?'

The phone rang at that moment and the rumour was alive. This was the telephone transcript:

'Grant?'

'Hi Nathan.'

'Guess what – a friend of a friend just saw, oh my God, you are going to die, he just saw Madonna, at the Showground, getting into a limo. Can you believe it?'

The wave of energy passing through our house that warm summer night was almost unbearable. We stayed up and played her albums for hours, hoping, believing.

The point where a rumour swallows you whole is not definable. It could be because you want to believe it or it could be because the facts stand up for themselves. Or it could be that sometimes cynicism is so unrelentlessly boring that your psyche gives it the shove. I don't know really, and I don't care, because on that Thursday night, with two more sleeps, I, who should have known better, believed that Madonna was performing at Mardi Gras. The rainbow high possibility had me hooked and I was taken over once more by the sensation of possibility.

By now everyone knows that Madonna didn't play the Party. But for me it happened again. I gained something I thought I had lost forever and it reminded me of innocence in a way. Once more I was at that café squealing gleefully, clutching my friends and being inspired by the feeling of Mardi Gras I used to know before I got too close to the flame.

I will cherish that moment of delusion. It is summer, it is memory, it is possibility and it has refreshed me. But who could it be next? I hear Dusty Springfield is doing the closing show. Nah, it's Martina Navratilova, alone on stage hitting tennis balls into the crowded hall. Magic!

*Johnny Dawson, also known as Jack, performs, writes and does bon vivant on Sydney's seedy side. During the day, you'll find him 'taking a letter' at Mardi Gras.*

# Rumours on the Net

**Newsflash:** Kym Mazelle to sing 'Young Hearts Run Free' in the RHI.

*Sister Sioux*

**Hot tip!** RuPaul and Diana Ross will be performing 'I Will Survive' at the Party, believe it or not!

*Coco*

**Sister Sioux and Coco**, really, where do you get your information from? It has to be Kylie or Madonna. See you PD and AF under the Mirror Ball – oops! That's getting pretty tacky. Have a good one darls.

*Ms Lou*

**Yes!** I've heard this Donna Summer rumour too – I'd be happy just to see Kim or RuPaul. Parade tip: For perfect vision, stand on *two* milk crates – it's quite safe – tested and tried last Mardi Gras.

*Dom*

**Rumour No 69:** Jason Donovan.

# Mardi Comes Home

## Robyn Laverack

IN 1995 MY MARDI GRAS swan song was to run the pub in a tent in the Bobby Goldsmith seating area during the Parade. Judith Fletcher, my partner, and I started work at the site early in the morning. By 2 p.m. we were up to our fifth change of clothes because it had rained non-stop since we arrived. Sitting on the park rail beside the tent was a very wet, bedraggled bright yellow love bird. Either too tired or too wet to fly, he sat watching us. When I put my hand out he hopped on and up on to my shoulder. I put him in the cabin of the truck where he stayed for the day, sharing a cup of tea and a meat pie for lunch. As I drove around Sydney picking up supplies and more dry clothes, he balanced on the steering wheel. Clearly this bird was trained and talented.

It was also clear that he would be coming home with us after the Party. We named him Mardi.

He settled in well, adjusting to the cat and dog, and they to him. He would fly around the house, join us in the shower, help with the washing up and amuse the dinner guests tearing up paper while we were in the kitchen.

It was a few weeks before he showed us his best party trick. Whenever he wasn't eating he would hump his perch for what seemed like hours and then he would throw up. The vet confirmed that it wasn't some weird disease, he really was masturbating. Our dinner guests started suggesting we should eat out.

We realised Mardi hadn't escaped, he'd obviously been thrown out of his previous house. One day we would like to meet the Darlinghurst queen (it would have to be) who taught poor Mardi such dreadful habits – and give him back!

*Robyn Laverack still works as a volunteer for Mardi Gras, and enjoys a Mardi Gras party or two.*

# Bob and Blanche

## An extract from Peter Blazey's diary

GOD SO MUCH HAS HAPPENED. We went to the Mardi Gras. Tim and I dressed as Bob and Blanche. Sensational fun and a huge hit all the way up Oxford Street. Greeted with 'Hi Blanche! Gidday Bob!' It might have rained on our Parade but we had cheers for an hour and a half. If this is the popularity of a politician or a star then we both love it! Very addictive. People afterwards coming up, hoons in flannelette shirts, gap-toothed drunks and eccied out queens roaring approval. 'We loved Bob and Blanche! Loved your Act!' Blake was right when he said, 'The strongest poison known to man came from Caesar's laurel crown.'

Tim liked it cos he was behind a mask – the eternal attraction for artists and thespians. I was behind the mask of caked-on foundation and blue eyeshadow, a $5 blonde wig, gold chunky jewellery and an Estée Lauder white bathrobe, occasionally touching Bob in his matching robe and cardboard mask, done for us by a cartoonist on the *Daily Telegraph*. I enjoyed grabbing him or even pretending to go down on him – which the crowd loved but the former Prime Minister hated! Too undignified.

So many other witty and relevant floats. Chinese women swimmers – men with enormous shoulders; Madam Lash dressed as Sister Mary MacKillop; the rural outreach from Albury/Wodonga and Wagga Wagga; the Tasmanian law reformers got the biggest cheer of all! Tim and I got on the SBS (lesBiEss) news, but not the Gay B C unfortunately. If they'd interviewed us, I would have told them we were on our way to the Ritz-Carlton! Much madness and mayhem. So many people seen. Edmund White in the VIP room with a pink feather boa and fluorescent false eyelashes holding court to gay scribblers and groupies. It makes you look forward wildly to the Mardi Gras next year. I've never felt like this before. Previously it had been a bit of a duty and it showed.

The TV commentary proved interesting. David Marr was horrified by Julian Clary's lubricious camp double entendres . . . but the ABC's coverage was bolder and sexier and more polished than the year before. As I said to William Yang today, 'If you and I had seen this at 6 or 16 our lives would have been different . . .' It's incredible that it should be on prime time TV, it makes Sydney unique in the world for gay power and gay friendliness, miles ahead of Amerika, which is clamping down again ... especially now NYC has got a Republican back in power. Of course we have plenty of detractors here too but as Tim's friend, Brett Davies, said to his CES workmates: 'If we have to put up with Christmas, you have to put up with Mardi Gras.'

*Peter Blazey was a political advisor, journalist and author of the memoir,* Screw Loose. *He died in 1997.*

# We Love Lucy

## Elisabeth Kirkby

I CAN'T REMEMBER the first Mardi Gras I attended. It was long before I became a Member of Parliament. I would stand in Oxford Street, trying to get a step up on a beer crate to get a better view. I was jostled and pushed by the good-natured crowd of parents with children on their shoulders, toddlers in strollers, giggling teenagers – a motley Sydney crowd intent on having a night out in a perfectly harmonious manner.

So when I went into Parliament and listened to Fred Nile rail against the Mardi Gras suggesting that the Mardi Gras Parade had introduced HIV/AIDS into Sydney; that the crowd was composed of voyeurs and perverts, I began to understand the level of homophobia that existed in 1981, when Fred and I were both elected.

I also realised that I had to get actively involved in the Parade, I had to take part – not just be a passive on-looker.

It wasn't difficult for me to be accepted by the community. My association with *No. 96* – the first soap opera in Australia (or perhaps the world) to portray gay men as human beings and not as stereotypes – meant that the gay community made me welcome.

I also can't remember the date of the first Parade I took part in. I think it was in 1983 when the bill to decriminalise homosexuality had been introduced by the Wran Government – the legislation that made it possible for gays to 'come out'.

In those days the march started on Elizabeth Street, went up Liverpool Street into Oxford Street, before turning right at Taylor Square to the Showground.

It was also in these early years that I was invited to judge the costumes at the party after the Parade was over. A difficult job even then, an impossible one now as the numbers of floats, individuals and groups has multiplied tenfold.

My gay friends told me months in advance of the preparations they were making personally. Designing and sewing elaborate costumes, building scenery for the floats and tableaux. Rehearsing the marching bands, choirs, dancers. Each year the presentation became more exotic, more elaborate and more exciting.

I remember the occasions when I walked with other Parliamentarians behind a group of dancers who literally kept up their routine for the entire distance from the City to the Showground. How many kilometres is it? The sweat poured off their bodies – and often the rain – but the dancers never faltered. An athletic feat to equal any City to Surfer, to better any 400 metre swimmer or long distance runner. The Mardi Gras dancers have the stamina of a Spartan phalanx or a platoon of US Marines. Something modern Army commanders might remember when pontificating about the unsuitability of homosexuals as fighting men.

I also remember the years when HIV sufferers were brought to the motel at the corner of College Street and Oxford Street, overlooking Whitlam Square, so they could enjoy the atmosphere, see the Parade and meet old friends.

It is the electric atmosphere of the Mardi Gras that is so intoxicating. The thousands of people lining the route are entranced by the spectacle and generous with their praise.

Originally, when I walked in the Parade, I was greeted affectionately and vociferously as Lucy Sutcliffe – my *No. 96* character – the character that gave me public recognition in Australia. She was a character the TV audience loved.

In 1996, after the Private Members Bill to end vilification on grounds of sexual orientation was introduced by Clover Moore in the Lower House and by me in the Upper House, Clover and I took part in the Parade in an open sports car. We were received with a warmth and enthusiasm that was overwhelming.

The bill was only passed when Ted Pickering, previously Minister for Police, crossed the floor to vote with the Opposition and crossbench members of the Legislative Council. In doing so, he kept an election promise made at Les Girls – Ted and I had stood on stage with Carlotta and other members of the cast as he promised his support. It was a move that cost him dearly in political terms, but proved he was one of a rare breed – a politician who keeps his word.

As I write this the Australian Democrats are preparing to enter a Float in the 1998 Parade – the twentieth anniversary of the most famous Mardi Gras in the world. I'll be on that float surrounded by friends and Democrats, both gay and straight. I'll enjoy the night as I always do – but I know the excitement, the warmth of the crowd, the carnival atmosphere – are at their best when you walk behind a group of marching dancers whose stamina and skill you can never equal.

After the Parade, I will walk back, as usual, across Oxford Street, past St Vincent's Hospital and through Kings Cross to Potts Point, knowing that on the night of Mardi Gras, I am safe and in the company of friendly strangers who have come to enjoy the carnival – our Mardi Gras – now a world event and one of which Sydney can be proud.

*Elisabeth Kirkby headed the Australian Democrats in the NSW parliament until her retirement in 1998.*

Political support for Mardi Gras has grown over the years from that of a few key progressives such as Elisabeth Kirkby and Clover Moore – who have expressed their commitment not only on the night but in their legislative efforts over the years – to wider expressions of support from the political mainstream. Of course, there has and perhaps always will be a vocal homophobic fringe. In the early 1980s there were fights with the Anglican church over the use of City Square for the start of the Mardi Gras parade, and there have been ongoing calls by conservative members of State Parliament, in particular the Reverend Fred Nile, that Mardi Gras be cancelled. But Mardi Gras has increasingly served as evidence that the economic and political might of the gay and lesbian community is best not ignored. Today, with economic impact studies confirming the many millions of dollars in economic activity that Mardi Gras brings to Sydney, and politicians from both sides of the House (in NSW at least) happily endorsing the event, it is worth remembering the efforts exerted in making these simple facts known.

This is evidenced in the following letter from Garry Wotherspoon to the *Sydney Morning Herald*, in reply to a statement by National Party MP, Peter Rowland-Smith, that the Mardi Gras parade be banned from Sydney's streets.

Dear Sir,

P.B. Rowland Smith's homophobic rantings (*Sydney Morning Herald* letter's page, 24 February) cannot be allowed to remain uncontested.

The reason that Metro (12 February) could claim that the Sydney Gay Mardi Gras Parade is one of Australia's biggest celebrations is simply because it probably is the largest parade unassociated with war and violence that ever passes through an Australian city. What it might lack in horses and cattle, sheep and dogs, pigs and other livestock (some country criteria for a parade?) is more than compensated by the visual splendour and variety of the floats and revellers.

It is hardly a condemnation of Australian society that such an event occurs. Since there are, by conservative estimates, at least 1.7 million lesbians and gay men in Australia, we represent a sizeable proportion of the population. Research from the Sydney Gay History Project and the Australian Gay History Project shows that those with homoerotic desires have been here since before the first days of the Anglo-European invasion. We have been represented in all walks of life, and have provided Australia with bushrangers, suffragettes, Attorneys-General, soldiers, a Premier or two, novelists and poets, at least one president of a State branch of the RSL, sundry Governors, painters, feminists – and one of our country's most distinguished Nobel Laureates. (I bet the National Party can't match that.)

But Mr Rowland-Smith ought also to note that lesbians and gay men are taxpayers and voters. As taxpayers, our money helps pay for the institutions of a society that is, at least nominally, committed to equality and non-discrimination. And as voters, often in marginal electorates such as that of Bligh, we will bear Mr Rowland-Smith's words in mind when we enter the polling booths on March 19.

Gary Wotherspoon
Department of Economic History, Sydney University

# Truck with a Driver

## Jan Burnswoods

FOR MANY YEARS NOW I have marched in the Gay and Lesbian Mardi Gras with fellow Labor MPs and a few ring-ins, had a magnificent time, flown the flag of the ALP and gone home. But really we were boring – not even a nice frock between us! So I thought, let's have a proper float, with costumes, music, the lot. Let's have a theme – My Age of Consent Bill – and a setting, the outrageously camp Legislative Council. The trouble was, this crazy idea of trying to organise an extravagant float and lots of people hit us about four weeks before the Parade.

Our first task was to find a truck and a driver. We hit bingo when we pulled in a few favours with a prominent trade union, though its rather macho image led to a few very odd conversations. A truck and a generator for our lights and sound system were organised. These would be driven up from Wollongong for the Parade – no problem. We also found a driver with the necessary licence. Then we lost him to a problem baby-sitter a week before the Parade.

So seven days to go. We had people, they all had their passes. We had a truck (well sort of, it was in Wollongong and we weren't going to see it until the day). We had many ideas about costumes and decorations (nothing was made yet, but you don't want to rush these things). And we didn't have a truck driver, music or lights – no problem! In the end it only took us a few days to find a driver, an unemployed worker who not only earned some extra money but also enjoyed himself immensely. John Howard would disapprove on both counts!

We rang up and booked lights, no problem. Then we attempted to book some hi-fi equipment. But we didn't know what kind of generator we had and whether it was likely to blow the whole lot up! Having costed everything and realised that we probably couldn't work the equipment anyway, we decided to hire a DJ. Have you ever called a DJ company and told them that you want a DJ for the back of a truck? Very interesting. We managed to get hold of one who agreed to do it and arranged to meet him and his music on the day.

It was the day before the Parade and everything was hired and ordered. We'd remembered the wheelchair for Fred Nile, the wig for Paul O'Grady, aka Franca Arena. The only thing we needed was to figure out how we were going to decorate the truck, buy it all and make it all. Not a problem, despite our total lack of creative flair. We bought everything we needed, spray-painted a few banners, made a few costumes, went to bed, and figured we would think about the rest tomorrow.

Mardi Gras day dawned. The DJ rang to complain about the rain, the truck arrived four hours early in the city with nowhere to park, my car full of stuff broke down, and we all began to have nervous breakdowns. But we finally found the truck, the DJ and the driver, and only got lost twice finding our designated position. We left them to set up and do whatever they wanted with the truck, and went to have a long hot shower and squeeze into the bondage and fairy costumes.

When we returned, the truck was looking good, the DJ had the generator going, the music was pumping, the lights were on and lots of people had arrived. The Parade was fantastic! The ALP signs and the Age of Consent banners got a lot of cheers. It was great!

Next year, I thought exhausted at the finish, perhaps we should take the easy way out and turn up, march, have a magnificent time, fly the flag of the ALP and go home. On the other hand, someone had a great idea for a float the other day . . .

*Jan Burnswoods is a Labor Member of the NSW Legislative Council, associated with the Sydney Gay and Lesbian Mardi Gras since Paul O'Grady started the Labor Parliamentarians Marching Group. When Paul resigned Jan took up the role of chief Mardi Gras organiser for the Labor float – with her sole member of staff, the long-suffering Emma.*

# I Walked Alone

## Greg Logan

IT WAS MARDI GRAS 1996 when I came out to my parents on national TV. I was 28 years of age and had been gay as long as I could remember. I knew my Mum and Dad knew, and they knew I knew, but it had got to the stage where we just couldn't verbalise it.

We are a close family, so I was frustrated that we couldn't talk about an important part of my life. Many, many times I had gone to dinner with the intention of telling them I was gay, but couldn't get the words to come out of mouth. It was time to do something.

I'd been in the Parade a few times before and knew what sort of exposure you could get. I thought if they saw me on the telecast, then we'd have to talk about my sexuality. To make sure they got the message, I marched alone, holding a sign that said, 'Mum . . . there's something I've got to tell you.'

Funnily enough, I was placed behind the PFLAG (Parents and Friends of Lesbians and Gays). They were lovely and gave me a lot of support. So did the crowd. One woman called me over and gave me a big hug.

It was one of the great experiences of my life. Six hundred thousand people cheering and waving as I walked by, waving back, holding my sign. I was proud, not only telling my parents, but the whole world, I was gay.

That year Mardi Gras was on the same night as the election, so the telecast didn't run until Wednesday night. I rang Mum and said I wanted her and Dad to watch it.

'Why?'

'Because I'm in it.'

'Oh no, I'm not going to see your bare bottom, am I?'

I assured her that I looked respectable. I must have, because that Wednesday night on television, I received quite some exposure. David Marr, the commentator, even said my name. I figured my parents must have a fair idea by now.

What I hadn't figured on was that my grandmother would be watching. And she wasn't happy that the family name was plastered all over the Sydney Gay and Lesbian Mardi Gras. She called my father straight away. 'Your son's on TV and he's a homosexual.'

She began to question all her grandchildren, and asked Dad to call my brother and sister to ask if they, too, were homosexuals.

My mother has a twin brother who has always been the 'theatrical' one in the family, if you know what I mean. Nan gave Mum a call the next day. 'Well we all know which side of the family those genes come from.'

'What do you mean, Nan?'

'We all know that Uncle Peter is a poofter.'

'How dare you call my brother a poofter!'

'I watched that telecast from beginning to end and I know what I'm talking about – they call them poofters!'

Mum and Dad didn't have quite the same reaction as my grandmother. Mum, bless her, said, 'You didn't need to go to all that trouble because I've known for a long time anyway.'

Dad simply asked, 'Why couldn't you have just told us like any normal person?'

And if you're wondering how Nan is these days, well you'll be pleased to know that I'm now the number one grandson again. You see, not one person at her bowls club mentioned that her grandson was seen parading at Mardi Gras. Her reputation was intact. That's all that mattered.

She's even invited me and my boyfriend over for morning tea. And she didn't once call us poofters.

*Greg Logan writes advertising copy, newspaper columns and film scripts.*

# Election Night

## Nic Frankham

1996 SUCKED. I flew in to Sydney on the Friday afternoon crumpled and exhausted, sickened by the prospect of the weekend to come – not because of the thrilling marathon of dancing, sex and sleep deprivation that lay ahead nor the intensely stressful organising that Mardi Gras requires. I had been working in Canberra as a hack for one of the ministers in the Keating Labor Government and the federal election was polling the same day as the Parade and Party.

The month long window prior to the climactic Parade and Party is a lot like an election campaign: attending countless functions, launches and openings; meeting hundreds of people you'll never see again; thrusting many topics into the public arena for debate so the community can be at least exposed to the issues.

I wasn't looking forward to the poll – throughout the campaign, it had been impossible to gauge the mood of the electorate. I had worked every day for six weeks in five different states, missing all of the Festival except for an opportune stopover in Sydney on Fair Day. I would have missed that too if I hadn't had a tantrum decorated with expletives and melodrama.

The campaign had been long, hot and frustrating. The Coalition had revealed none of its plans – using instead massive debt figures to convince voters that we had blown the budget big time. That the overwhelming proportion of the debt was private debt didn't matter. They weren't plugging up the shitty, racist spray of their candidates either (except the malignant Pauline Hanson who got dumped at the last minute). The electoral impact of the bigot factor was unquantifiable – probably because no one thought it possible for a mainstream political party to run a campaign characterised by a lack of commitment to indigenous people, multiculturalism or women.

By the time Mardi Gras was nearing its spectacular finish with a celebration that is living proof that a once-reviled minority can flourish in a climate of acceptance – my blithe faith in Australians' tolerance was fast coming undone. And, catastrophically, I had nothing but a Classified Waste bag and a wig made of shredded Cabinet documents to wear to the Party. Things weren't looking good.

Oblivious to the siren-esque lure of the Parade, I sat at home and watched forty Labor seats and my job go down a televised toilet, flushed reluctantly by Graham Richardson. It was all over by 7 p.m. – from desperation to despair in less than an hour. John Howard was our new Prime Minister, and my shredded wig had irreparably fallen apart.

A hideous insurance queen lived where I was staying. He had a Queensland homo liberal staffer over to watch the coverage. 'Love, you'll get that job now,' the bitch croaked to his mate between puffs of a cheap menthol cigarette. Miss Insurance was about to move to Brisbane to 'further' his career. I decided, then and there, that I wouldn't speak to him until he moved out.

I retreated upstairs with a bad taste in my mouth and put on the paper dress (conveniently obscuring my Canberra-enhanced arse). My darling best friend, Rueben, arrived to save me from the trolls downstairs and we went to the Party. I immediately banned the election defeat from all conversation, avoiding people where necessary, staring at suspiciously smug revellers. I found myself estimating how many of the 20 000 or so people at the party had voted for the Coalition. No one I met confessed.

Several colleagues and other True Believers were in attendance. My dear Canberra flatmates were there: one of them still wearing his polling booth uniform – an ALP T-shirt splashed with cheap red wine and cigarette ash. He was utterly drunk and devastated, repeating over and over '40 seats, 40 seats'. I ran.

My boyfriend, Corby Beard, was running the Drag Bar, and the marquee assigned to them was unsuitable. Attempts to maintain a reasonable sound level were repeatedly thwarted. Eventually, they gave up and shut it down early. Nothing seemed to be going right.

Tragically, I started to cry on the dance floor in the Royal Hall of Industries when I saw another best friend, Kane, and his boyfriend, Eddie. They consoled me briefly.

By sun up, my dress had endured a hundred stupid questions and a severe rip. Opting instead for a stretch gold lamé halter neck, I staggered over to a sunny gutter, only to discover another colleague – Keating's political adviser – sitting down wearing a boiler suit with 'Dependence Day' emblazoned across the back. Judging by our appearance, he remarked, we should be photographed with the caption reading: 'and they wonder why they lost the election . . .'

I still wonder.

*Nic Frankham is a writer who lives in Redfern, and this is one of several stories he has written on Mardi Gras.*

# Little Boxes

## Bill Bowtell

I'VE ALWAYS LIKED BOXES. Boxes are for keeping things in – precious jewels, private papers, deep secrets. Boxes keep separate things that shouldn't be mixed and shared. A place for everything and everything in its place.

Children love boxes, because putting things in them is a way of trying to bring order to their world. By sorting and categorising and naming, by choosing what is in and what is out, children enjoy the calming illusion that they might control their lives and their destinies. Of course, as we grow up, we leave childish things behind.

But I never left behind my deep attraction to boxes, my classification fascination.

I became very successful in putting bits of my life into the appropriate box. Indeed, through my various careers as a diplomat, then as chief string-puller for the Minister for Health, then internationally, I never tired of sorting, organising and labelling my life.

Friends, causes, sexual identities, political allegiances, lovers and families were stacked neatly into the correct receptacle, to be drawn upon as and when required. Provided you sort and classify your problems faster than life throws them at you, calmness and serenity prevail. But the essential requirement is to make sure that the things that live in one box never introduce themselves to the things that live in an adjacent box. That way, you can have a peaceful, stable and ordered existence.

I chose two very big boxes that on first inspection seemed well-made and sturdy, but simply didn't last the distance: one labelled gay man, and the other, political idealist.

The gay man box I took off the shelf at about age five. The political box I squeezed into about 1981 – first as an adviser to the Wran Government, then hitting the big time as apparatchik first class to the Commonwealth Health Minister in 1983. After 15 years, the label on the political box had been painted out and scrawled over many times. By 1994, the political box said 'Senior Political Adviser to Prime Minister Paul Keating'. The sexual identity box still said 'gay man'.

Over the years, I threw a lot of stuff into these two boxes. As it turned out, rather too much to be safely stored. They might as well have been labelled 'nitro' and 'glycerine' – safe apart, but dangerous together. Boxes can only take so much before the weight of their contents starts bursting through the joinery. The bonfire of my world of boxes took place on Mardi Gras night 1996.

As I whirled and blurred my way through 1995, I'd accumulated many new things for both my boxes. Some good things – the overthrow of the Tasmanian anti-gay laws, the birth of the Republican movement, Mabo – representing verve, excitement and movement. And some bad – the fear of the new, the quiet desperation of the newly poor, the decline of our institutions and the adulation of the mediocre. All these streams were represented by a cast of characters as flamboyant in their own way as a revue of Oxford Street drag queens. Australian politics is like *The Addams Family* meeting *Camelot*.

By early 1996, the poor old boxes were beginning to crack under the strain. The nitro started to leak into the glycerine. Logic and reason were overtaken by drama and romanticism. Loggers blockaded our offices for a week. Students, unionists, greens and most of the ALP head office seemingly defected to the Liberals. Parliament was consumed with the Penny Easton/Carmen Lawrence story direct from *Melrose Place*, while the media moguls placed and hedged their bets. Slowly at first, then with increasing clarity, our doomed destiny came into focus. By January 1996, I had begun to feel like a conscript in the charge of the Light Brigade, or a volunteer coming ashore at Gallipoli. But given the chance to bail out, I decided to stay to the bitter end, and so answered the question about why soldiers go over the trench wall to certain death.

My growing feeling that my tea had been spiked with acid came when Paul Keating told me that he had called the election for the same day as Mardi Gras in 1996. The last remnants of my box collection dissolved into dust. My lover had been awarded the contract to do the 1996 Mardi Gras poster – the one with the silhouettes. I couldn't tell which character had come from which box. The last month of the Labor government was a spectacular collision of all my lives. Who was more real – political commentator Laurie Oakes, or drag artist Maude Boaté? Politics became show business, and show business became politics. On election night, the curtain fell on one long-running show.

Between Labor's wake at the Bankstown Sports Club, the Liberals' celebration at the Intercontinental Hotel, the several thousand election night parties and the Mardi Gras, can there ever have been a night in

Sydney's history when more people got so totally trashed?

My life fell apart that night, but it was worth it. I learnt some valuable lessons from Paul Keating, and from the spirit of the Mardi Gras Party. Passion and truth and beauty belong together. Their enemies are mediocrity and fear.

Fear makes us build boxes and shut out life. But living is not about classifying and sorting your past, or trying to squeeze into boxes that other people build for you, or, even worse, the boxes that we build ourselves. We can only be defeated if we give into fear, and crawl back into the false security of the cell. On Election Day and Mardi Gras night 1996, I realised finally that boxes are only good for one thing – to be buried in.

*Bill Bowtell was political advisor to Prime Minister Paul Keating from 1994 to 1996 and an architect of Australia's HIV/AIDS policies. He is currently Managing Director of Pacific Applied Consulting P/L, specialising in internet applications.*

# A Little Miss Adventure

## A bedtime story

## Little Miss Drug-Fucked

THERE WERE FIVE Little Misses in all, boys and girls.

Little Miss Putrid lived far away in the land of The Queen. Little Miss Cocksucker had befriended her on a recent 'R & R' (Rooting and Rooting) holiday. Little Miss Lost The Plot lived not quite as far away in a town named Perthetic, where hardly anyone has any perthonality. Little Miss Butt-Fucked lived very close in Surry Hills. Little Miss Butt-Fucked so wanted to be a Marching Drag but failed the audition, as well as that of the Marching Boys, Marching Dogs, the Lead Float and all the shows for the Big Party. So Little Miss Butt-Fucked had no choice but to be true to her nature and join her Little Miss sisters, including me.

The Little Misses needed some help to become as big and round and flat as they should be for the Big Parade. So they visited their friend Little Miss Mindless. Little Miss Mindless worked at the Big Toy Shop at Erskineville, where she played with power tools and the minds of the young and impressionable.

The Little Misses worked tirelessly for days and days and days. They hammered and glued, and painted and varnished, and sliced and grated, and julienned and spack-filled until they finished their frocks.

On seeing them, Little Miss Mindless enthused, 'Wow ... great,' which was about as animated as she could be while she was inhaling her Therapeutic Cigarettes.

Little Miss Putrid arrived, after a flight from London in which she consumed more alcohol in 24 hours than a drag queen from the Albury would in a month of DIVA awards nights. She loved her new outfit, but wasn't sure if she should wear it in public.

'I'm having severe second thoughts about this, darl,' said a worried Little Miss Putrid.

'Piker, piker, piker!' screamed Little Miss Cocksucker. 'We've made your costume bitch, now you're gonna wear it.'

'I'll look tragic.'

'No, you're Putrid. Little Miss Tragic is leading the Marching Boys. Get here and I'll put you over my knee, girl. You're gonna wear it!'

Little Miss Putrid was convinced.

Little Miss Lost the Plot had no such qualms. When she saw her new costume she got so excited she flapped and flapped and flapped until she was practically airborne.

The day of the Big Parade had arrived. However, before the Little Misses could don their lovely new costumes, they had to perform their democratic duty.

'An election on Mardi Gras? What gives?' queried Little Miss Putrid.

Little Miss Drug-Fucked thought it was one extra thing she didn't need in her day, as she laboriously numbered her ballot to put Little Miss Creant from the Circus of God last, since he was again praying for hell, fire and brimstone to rain down on their Parade. 'This is definitely not my type of cubicle,' she thought.

The Little Misses were vaguely worried, because the incumbent government of Little Miss Arrogant was under threat from Little Miss Lazarus with a Triple Bypass. But still, the Big Parade was more important.

Little Miss Drug-Fucked was driving Fifi, a Big Orange F100 utility truck borrowed from Mr Muscles, to the Big Parade with all the beautiful costumes on it when, 'Bang Fut FUT p FUT!' The ute stopped.

The ute would not start. 'Fuckin' Fords!' cursed Little Miss Drug-Fucked.

So Little Miss Drug-Fucked ran as fast as her long, muscular legs would carry her, all the way back to the Big Toy Shop where she consulted one of the hairy-legged ones wearing comfortable shoes, whilst Little Misses Putrid and Lost The Plot guarded the costumes at the truck.

'F100, ey mate? By the way that you described those "Bang Fut FUT p FUT!" noises it sounds as if Fifi is out of juice. You'll need diesel,' advised Little Miss Diesel.

Gerry-can in hand, Little Miss Drug-Fucked ran back to Fifi. GLUG-GLUG went the diesel. FUT p FUT NOTHING went the truck.

'Fuck shit cunt bitch gonads,' wailed Little Miss Drug-Fucked. 'We are not going to make it to the Parade on time.' So she called Little Miss H..E..L..P..

VROOM VROOM went the van from the NRMA depot. Out stepped Mr Jumper Lead. 'It's not a diesel mate. It will have to be towed.'

'Fuck shit cunt bitch gonads perineum prostate!' she railed at the vehicle.

Mr Jumper Lead radioed for Mr Tow Rope to take the ute to the garage next to the Big Toyshop. It looked as if after all their hard work, toil and preparation, the Little Misses were going to miss the Big Parade. Just then, a Big Expensive Truck belonging to the Australian Council of Nepotism drove past on the way to the Big Parade.

'Stop! Stop! Help us!' they cried.

'What's in it for me?' demanded ACON menacingly.

Little Miss Cocksucker offered her body. Little Miss Drug-Fucked offered her mind. Little Miss Butt-Fucked offered her first born, which ACON foolishly accepted.

The Little Misses jumped for joy as the Big Expensive Truck delivered Little Miss Butt-Fucked and their beautiful costumes to the Big Parade Assembly point. Little Miss Butt-Fucked tended the costumes at the designated Assembly Point as she watched all the glamour pass by.

'They are so late. How will the other Little Misses find me in this chaos?' pondered a vexed Little Miss Butt-Fucked.

The other Little Miss's searched high and low, dodging tacky drags and news crews, and overdosing on sequins. They were almost swallowed by the Cronulla Outdoors group when, what do you know, there was a panicked Little Miss Butt-Fucked amongst the pandemonium.

'Hurry, it's starting!' screamed Little Miss Butt-Fucked.

Pausing only to swallow their cotton-coloured candy and touch up their make-up, the Little Misses began their march into Mardi Gras legend.

On the Big Parade route, the happy children shrieked, 'Look at the Little Misses!' in amazement at the wonder of it all.

'Don't look at them!' screamed the parents.

'Mummy, what's . . . butt-fucked?' asked one.

'Ask your father,' replied Mummy.

Following Little Miss New Zealand up the road, the Little Misses drank in the appreciation of their adoring fans. At the end of the Parade, the Little Misses were exhausted and worn out from all the adulation, so they escaped back to Little Miss Cocksucker's house to prepare for the Big Party.

Five Little Misses needing rejuvenation. Five Little Misses wanting care and affection. Five Little Misses changing out of their sweaty costumes.

Five Little Misses all showering together and washing each other squeaky clean. Little Miss Butt-Fucked dropped the soap repeatedly. 'No, don't go there!' warned Little Miss Putrid from experience.

So after the Five Little Misses pampered and preened each other like sisters do, they were transformed into big fluffy clouds of relaxation. But just as they were about to float off into Nirvana, Little Miss Drug-Fucked exclaimed, 'Shit girls! The Big Party!'

So they changed, imbibed some more and made their merry way back to the Big Party. But that is another story.

The next day the Little Misses looked at their dishevelled costumes with pride. But sadly their joy was short-lived when they realised that Little Johnny Howard was the new Big Little Miss.

'Fuck!' they screamed. 'How could this have happened?'

'I'm so depressed,' said a teary Little Miss Drug-Fucked. 'What day is it?'

'It is Sunday,' replied Little Miss Lost the Plot most emphatically.

'Are you sure? I don't understand then. I don't usually feel like this until the Tuesday after a party.'

They were soon to rename him Little Miss Governed. And that story, boys and girls, is yet to have a happy ending.

*Little Miss Drug-Fucked (aka eddie torre) is print media liaison officer for ethel yarwood enterprises <http://www.yarwood.com.au>.*

# Handy Hints from Miss New Zealand

AS I FLOAT UP THE STREET, folk always ask me how I appear so fresh, year after year, and pose other more pertinent questions, and queries.

I have reached into the windmills of my mind and come up with a mish-mangle of ideas, tried and true. Ideas and hints for the now-girl and the young man about the house and town. Hints and ideas to get you through the busy festival season, beauty and accessories, decor and the home, cuisine and a few more.

- It's a wise idea to paint the metal frame of a new handbag with colourless nail varnish to prevent the frame from tarnishing.

- Regular oiling is essential if you want a smoothly running sewing machine. Before starting to sew after oiling, run a piece of blotting paper through the machine several times to absorb the excess oil.

- You can produce a salad in record time by serving the contents of a tin of mixed vegetables tossed in mayonnaise.

- A dab of transparent nail varnish on the centre of buttons to seal the thread makes them stay longer.

- Give width to small or closely set eyes by applying eyeshadow to skin above the eyelid; not the eyelid itself; smoothing across and outwards. The deeper the colour the more effective this trick will be.

- 'Good humour is one of the best articles of dress one can wear in society.' Thackeray

- Prefer the paler lip colours? They're easier to wear if the outline on the mouth is first defined with a deeper shade then fill in with the paler shade.

- Ironing is a chore that is tough on tired feet. Next time try standing on a cushion while you iron.

- For a face that looks blue in the cold weather try a warmer toned make-up. Honey-toned foundation and a coral lipstick will give you a glow.

- Perhaps your problem is too much colour? It can be subdued with a dusting of green, yes green, face powder over your normal make-up.

- A small splinter in the finger is painlessly extracted if a piece of sticking plaster is placed over the area overnight. Next morning the skin will be soft and the splinter is easily removed.

- A warm dry towel around your head will speed up the setting process if you want your hair to set quickly.

- And one I personally use everyday (for general beauty and confidence): 'Stand tall, Smile and Breathe.'

*Miss New Zealand (aka Brent Beadle) is a Mardi Gras Hall of Famer who has for many years dignified the Parade with quiet elegance and good taste.*

# Our Love is Here to Stay

## Simon Burke

AT THE BEGINNING OF 1997, I returned to Australia after five years in London. I was in the middle of rehearsing my first ever one-man show for the Mardi Gras Festival when I got a call from the Festival's Director, Jonathan Parsons, asking me to perform at the Mardi Gras launch on the steps of the Opera House. After a great deal of thought I decided to do 'Our Love is Here to Stay' and my musical director Ron Creager and I came up with a version that started with the beautiful but little-known verse from 'As Time Goes By'. This is the entry from my diary the day after we did it.

**Saturday, 1 February 1997:**

I've just woken up and still feel it. I've never been so shit-scared but also never before been able to walk out there and suddenly master and harness it and step back from it at the same time.

It had poured down non-stop for five days and I had already written the whole thing off. Indeed I was almost glad as it had been such a nightmare getting it organised, and I felt tired and nervous and had talked myself out of the resonance of the song that had first jumped at me. But suddenly no rain yesterday morning and its threat seemed to subside inch by inch throughout the day until 7.30 when God produced the pinkest, poofiest most beautiful sunset and Sydney evening you could ever hope for.

And there I was, back after five years in the city I was born in and missed and love so much, flatteringly introduced by MC Glenn Butcher as a 'huge spunk'. Shouting, 'It's so good to be back in Sydney!' like some dreadful old Billy Joel clone. Then I launched into 'Our Love is Here to Stay' at which point my audience broke into spontaneous applause. During the last chorus, however, I slipped in my own verse, singing:

'In time Fred Nile may tumble,

Pauline Hanson may crumble . . .' The fireworks went off and everyone went apeshit. I'm so glad I did it – one of the most important nights of my life.

**A postscript:** I was desperate for a nervous pee just before I had to go on so Duncan (my minder for the evening) against his better judgement, rushed me to the wheelchair access loos near the Stage Door. As I was about to go into the Gents an old digger hobbled in before me. Bladder bursting, with two minutes to spare, I decided I had no choice but to fling open the door to the Ladies, only to find Margaret Whitlam powdering her nose.

'Can I help you?' she enquired absolutely à la Margaret Rutherford.

'I'm terribly sorry, Mrs Whitlam, but I have to sing onstage in a second and a gentleman is already using the gentleman's and I really need to go,' I simpered rather pathetically.

She looked me up and down, in haughty amusement, and said 'Carry on.' And I did.

Well they say everyone has a Mardi Gras toilets story.

*Simon Burke got his first acting role from Richard Wherrett when he was 12 and wore braces. He has gone on to star in musicals and* Playschool, *amongst much else. His teeth are now straight.*

# Broadcast News

## Tottie Goldsmith

AFTER HAVING HOSTED *Sex/Life* for a year it was indeed an honour to be asked to host the 1997 Gay and Lesbian Mardi Gras Channel 10 broadcast. Having never been to the Mardi Gras before, it sure came as a wonderful surprise to see first-hand how much effort, colour and passion is put into this event.

I would say I'd been chosen to act as a kind of conduit between mainstream heterosexuality and more wide-ranging sexual lifestyles. We did the broadcast from above Café 191 in Taylor Square. There were hundreds of people crammed into this tiny room. I had been to dinner the night before with the producers and felt fairly confident that with the auto-cue, prompter and a list of the floats in order, I could keep track of things. In the afternoon I had noticed people already lining the route and started to sense how big this thing was going to be.

I did my opening piece to camera from a cherry-picker raised 40 feet above the ground, which looked right down Oxford Street from Taylor Square. It was the closest I've ever felt to being a rock star. There were tens of thousands of people screaming 'Tottie, Tottie' and I was trying to remember my lines and there was this unbelievable energy everywhere. I've never experienced anything quite like it.

I was reassured to be working with Mark Trevorrow (aka Bob Downe) as we had gone to acting school together. As the heat and noise grew, we began the broadcast. I soon realised that the list I had been given of the Parade entrants was wrong. What was supposed to be 'Dykes on Bikes' looked more like 'Alice in Wonderland'. A voice in my earphone was telling me one thing and the auto-cue another, while Mark pointed at the correct information on the sheet. Thank God for Mark! His assistance was invaluable.

I was swept away by the energy of the night. I remember checking with my producer that my lipstick was still on. He assured me that it had only just been touched up by the make-up artist. I stopped for a breather and checked how much longer we had to go with the crew.

I felt we'd been going for about an hour. 'No, that's it,' someone yelled. 'That's the three hours. Parade's over.'

I didn't go to the Party. I was just worn out. I just wanted someone to give me some water and put me to bed. It was all too much – in the best possible way – but my brain was sizzled and the Party would have to wait for another day.

Looking at the thousands of people in the streets, the rainbow flags hanging from the hotel balconies, I couldn't help but think what an extraordinary city Sydney really is. I wondered if gay men and lesbians were attracted and drawn to all that is beautiful in Sydney or whether they were, in fact, a part of what makes Sydney so beautiful and vibrant.

I came away reminded of what my heterosexual girlfriends in Sydney had told me about the lack of eligible, straight men. I really don't think your average heterosexual could ever create something as colourful, alive and camp. Just as well I do love a bit of glitz and glam!

*Tottie Goldsmith is an actor and television performer.*

# Not My Aisle

## Frank Rutherford

ONE OF THE HIGHLIGHTS OF 1997 was marching in a first-time float called *Gayviation*. This came about after a small get together of 50 flight attendants and friends, at the Newtown Hotel in September 1996.

I know each one of us in this group experienced a wonderful camaraderie. I believe most of us had never partaken in a Mardi Gras Parade before, so we were not sure what to expect. We had up to fifteen rehearsals. We had to visualise marching between the forward entrance and the rear tail of a 747. We marched and danced the airline safety demonstration, we mimed pushing trolleys, we closed overhead lockers, we buckled up seat belts and we calmed hysterical passengers – all to a disco version of Peter Allen's 'I Still Call Australia Home'. What's more, we did this behind a huge and very real 747 fuselage.

On the evening before the Parade began, it was fabulous to walk amongst the floats parked in the street, all of us waiting and anticipating the beginning of the Parade. The buzz and excitement was electric! Then the big moment came. Hearts in our mouths, we swung into our routine and into Oxford Street. Nothing had prepared us for the reception that the crowd gave us from start to finish. The chant from the crowd, 'The airline float is coming,' was at first frightening, then awesome.

One of the great moments came when we hit Taylor Square. The vibe from the crowd was unbelievable. We stopped under the enormous mirror ball. I could not believe the sights or sounds, especially looking up and seeing drag diva Mogadonna doing *Evita* from the Courthouse balcony. Then the Channel Ten camera came swishing down on us, on a large arm, filming us. One of the marchers said to me that he felt like a movie star – he was American, of course!

The march came to an end at the Football Ground. We all gathered for a glass of champagne. We laughed, cheered and promised each other that, as the Peter Allen song says, 'One day we'll all be together again'. But first things first.

IT WAS TIME TO DANCE!

*Frank Rutherford is currently a flight attendant with an Australian airline.*

# Ain't No Man

## Janey Lewis

I WAS INTRODUCED to Mardi Gras through my good friend Dean Essing, who was one of the most popular Mardi Gras DJs. Dean and I both worked as flight attendants and first hooked up through our love of music, even though he was the DJ Diva and I was the rock chick from hell.

The 1997 Mardi Gras was Dean's final DJing performance. Probably suspecting that this might be his last Mardi Gras gig, nothing would stop this brave and spirited talent from fulfilling his commitment.

Dean was to play the first set of the evening in the RHI – from 10 p.m. till 2 a.m. Special guests of Dean's – Les McDonald, Richard Wherrett, three other close friends and myself – were invited to the VIP bar for drinks in Dean's honour prior to the party's start. The extraordinary complicated and circuitous route we were required to take into the Showground and the array of security passes needed was like getting into Fort Knox. As we walked from the car park to the RHI at 9.00 p.m., the vast area was eerily empty and quiet. I had always assumed the gates opened sometime prior to the music beginning, but the gates would open, and the sound and lights would begin simultaneously, on the stroke of 10 p.m. I was usually only just getting up by 10 p.m.!

Around 9.45 p.m. Dean gave us a kiss and a hug. Waving goodbye, he commanded, 'See you on the floor at ten.' He threw a special look at his boyfriend, Les. Clearly, he intended to kick off with something special to them.

At 9.55 p.m., we duly made our way on to the dance floor – the vast RHI was empty and dimly lit with working lights only. It was strange yet exciting. And then, as promised, on the stroke of ten, a blistering dance beat rocked the air waves and a staggering blaze of light turned the space into a fantasy world. The song was Dina Carroll's 'Ain't No Man (Like You).'

These days the crush on the dance floor persists until the final moment of 10 a.m., twelve long hours away. But for fifteen minutes or so, the six of us had this fabulous space all to ourselves – an unforgettable treat. And then, of course, we were quickly swallowed up by thousands of others all groovin' to the beat of Dean's magic.

Dean ended his set to the thunderous applause of thousands of sweaty, exhilarated fans. For the rest of the night, he was congratulated and patted on the back by many hands.

It's a tribute to Dean and the phenomenon that is Mardi Gras that this old rock chick could be turned on to the disco beat.

*Janey Lewis is a rock/disco chick from hell headed straight to heaven.*

# Your Loving Arms

## Les McDonald

THE LYRICS TO disco music usually escape me. Of course, the great 'anthems' of gay and lesbian culture will eventually stick – an 'I Am What I Am' or 'I Will Survive' – but the words of hundreds of other great tracks, I only catch snatches of at best.

At least that was the case, until I met Dean Essing in 1990. Dean was a flight attendant by profession, but his great love was music and he gradually built up a reputation as one of Sydney's leading DJs – gigs at nightclubs and pubs which he'd squeeze in between flights to Perth or Cairns or wherever. And, of course, he played for Mardi Gras. By the end of 1997, in fact, he had played more Mardi Gras and Sleaze Parties in the RHI than any other (male) DJ.

Dean was my lover and my soul mate. When we moved in together he needed a whole room for his music – his vast collection of discs and his equipment with which he'd experiment with mixes, overlays and underlays and the rest of it. Inevitably, as I heard a particular song six or eight times as he played with it, the lyrics would get into my head. A particularly favourite track was 'Your Loving Arms':

> Put your loving arms around me
> And you whisper to me
> Then you
> Put your loving arms around me
> Inside this love I'm burning . . .

At the 1995 Mardi Gras, Dean was particularly happy. He had played a great middle set in the Hordern and then had the rest of the night to party on. We'd lost each other, however, as so often happens amongst 20 000 people. I didn't fret about this – I knew we'd always find each other again. At about 7 a.m. I was dancing with a group of friends when I suddenly discerned a mix leading into the unmistakable intro to 'Your Loving Arms'. I shut my eyes and let the moment take me over, wanting only one thing more.

Suddenly, I felt a pair of loving arms around me and warm lips caress my neck. He'd found me – right on cue. At that moment nothing else mattered. It was our moment – full of life and love, intensely joyous yet private, in the middle of 8000 people.

Dean was the love of my life. He died on 7 October 1997. I still close my eyes when I hear that song, but, oh, how I missing those loving arms.

*Les McDonald is the owner of The Bookshop, Darlinghurst, and co-producer of the Locker Room and Summer parties.*

# The Hum

## Campion Decent

MY FIRST MARDI GRAS. Year uncertain. Me: Too-thin-by-half, anti-surfing, opera-loving kid from the northern beaches suddenly living in a Paddington terrace. Upstairs is the sweetest homosexual from Amsterdam one could ever hope to meet: a real life Mrs Madrigal dispensing tea, sympathy and a love of gay life in healthy dollops. I wander up to Oxford Street on Mardi Gras night as instructed. I remember a hum, the hum of a crowd. When the hum has died down, I feel different. The aftertaste of the hum is ripe with possibility.

Memories. It is impossible to give priority. Why bother. Mardi Gras is not a simple grab, nor an easy relationship. It comes to me in snatches, so I'll tell it in snatches. Giving priority robs it of its complexity; editing the cavalcade of 'moments' implies somehow that one or two don't work. It's the *this* and *that* of Mardi Gras that makes it what it is. Whatever that is. One certainty: without it, life would be different.

On Mardi Gras night a year later, the hum is louder. Maybe I am closer.

With a friend at my side I am freed. He's a straight boy built like an Adonis-in-waiting; a straight boy who in-between girl bonks, gets a buzz out of befriending young queers; a straight boy built like an Adonis-in-waiting who has been my weekly wank-fantasy. Freed in front of a quarter of a million people.

We last three floats before our tongues are entwined. (This lip-smacker is attempting to claim first kiss status in my memory. Not true. But it's the first public kiss, the first I-don't-give-a-flying-fuck-what-THEY-think kiss. The first kiss to tie my wrapped-up lust in a ribbon of celebration). We last two more floats before being pointed homeward by our obstinate erections. The simplest Mardi Gras? Yes. Five floats and the fuck of my dreams.

The next day my Dutch Mrs Madrigal hands me my 'Life's a Banquet' diploma and sets me free.

Part of the freedom package includes confidence. With the hum in my ears, I leave behind my northern beaches lethargy, my mind-numbing day jobs (videos, insurance, market-research) and lodge myself in the academy (the geek rather than the jock variety). As an undergraduate, I discover politics, mainly gay politics. As a postgraduate, I discover under- graduates, mainly ripe-for-the-plucking undergraduates. During this period the hum is somewhere in the background. I am too busy to answer its call, gathering degrees and establishing a modest – yet successful – franchise of Mrs Madrigal's 'Life's a Banquet' course for promising young men.

I have no idea that my very private relationship with Mardi Gras is about to be supplanted by a more public connection; first, as editor of the gay and lesbian community newspaper, the *Sydney Star Observer*, and later, as festival director on the board of Sydney Gay and Lesbian Mardi Gras.

At the *Star Observer* we are paid (poorly by today's standards) to be intensely interested in everything that Mardi Gras does or doesn't do. If we catch the whiff of a fart at the Mardi Gras bunker, we do our best to turn it into a front-page turd by the time it has travelled two blocks.

I write so many stories about Mardi Gras during my editorship that the words 'fabulous' and 'crisis' are interchangeable and keyed in via macros. But it is those dreadful letters to the editor post-Mardi Gras that I am sure will live long in my memory: endless drug-fucked queens com- plaining about the music, the shows, the lesbians, the crowds, the 'straights', the bag search, the drag queens, and the door policy, party after party. (I wish I'd had the guts to run a blank letters page in one issue with *Get a Life – the Editor* set in 8-point, smack in the middle of the nothingness.)

Mardi Gras president Susan Harben woos me onto the Mardi Gras Board when I leave the editor's seat at the *Star Observer*. She rings me up and says, 'Darling, can you do something with the Festival? I know it can work but I'm just a lesbian who likes a painting and doesn't know why.' Or words to that effect.

Against my better judgement, I agree. The festival portfolio involves everything bar Fair Day, the Parade and Party. We're talking dozens of art exhibitions, performing arts events, community one-offs, so on and so forth.

I direct two festivals while on the board. My pick: the very first opening of the late-night feral cabaret, cLUB bENT (it's been in every festival since 1995) where a healthy mix of vaginas, leather, dicks and sequins share the limelight. Playtime for polite young queers.

My pan: being stuck for two hours with Boy George's manager the year the Boy plays the Party. (I've tried to wipe the manager from my memory so I'll call him the Annoying One.) After the Parade, I have to escort this man from the viewing room out to the Showground. It is raining. The Annoying One whinges all the way, threatening full-tilt through exasperating lungs to pull the Boy out of the party. (Everything about Sydney was fucked; everything about Mardi Gras was the most fucked.) To top it all off we have trouble getting through the security gates at the Showground. Finally, we arrive at the Boy's caravan. The Annoying One ushers me in and declares to the Boy that everything is off because everything is fucked. The Boy, with a glance of sympathy towards me, says calmly to the Annoying One: 'Shut the fook up you stupid little queen.' God bless the Boy!

Nowadays, I return to the Festival, Parade and Party to rediscover my private relationship with the Gras. Visits are enriched by my more public connections but I am relieved to discover the hum that got me there in the first place still resonates deep within.

My latest Mardi Gras memory. Me: dancing as the daddy of 8-month old twins (thanks to an olive tapenade jar, a turkey baster, a lesbian and two supportive partners). Amid a sea of bodies, I ponder dress options for the twins' inevitable future Mardi Gras debut. The hum is warm, wrapping me in tight, snug as a bugger in a rugger.

The aftertaste of the hum? Still ripe with possibility.

*Campion Decent is artistic director of the Next Wave festival, showcasing contemporary arts practice for young and emerging.*

# Fifteen Footsteps of Fame

## Philippa Playford

EVERY YEAR AROUND JANUARY – for the past nine years at least – I seem to go through a bit of a panic. Actually, it's a serious fashion crisis. I start to feel the hype, not only from my friends and community but also the mainstream media. Pressure is building within my body. My ego is demanding. It wants to flaunt a new creation up the Mardi Gras Parade route. It needs to be fed.

I set myself a standard, a personal brief if you like. The costume should have a lesbian sensibility, a political message, be inventive, utilise a variety of different materials, be lightweight, waterproof, bright, loud, unique and fun. Usually the title or the idea behind the costume comes first. Then the hard bit, how the hell do I put it all together, so that all the above can be worn on my body? And every time I say, 'I'll start earlier next year.'

Well, it was October 1997 and in the process of making a 'Barrier Reef' inspired head-dress for the *Atlantis* Sleaze Ball I had a flash of brilliance for my 1998 Parade costume. Even more brilliant, I was ahead of schedule. I was so thrilled and bursting with excitement that I had to call a few friends straight away. Consequently, construction of the Coral Reef headdress was now running behind schedule, but I didn't care: I was on a high.

I went to bed that night dreaming and developing my outfit. I could see it all so clearly. It was made from raincoats and umbrellas, all colour themed in yellow and blue. I'd be surrounded by dancing lezzies dressed in yellow raincoats and boots, each holding a banner which proudly proclaimed, 'Lesbians Commemorate the Wet Years!' Oh, it was all too good to be true. I was inspired!

It was late February when I woke from this dream to reality. The bubble burst the moment I tried on the massive sculptural structure which I casually called a head-dress. I stood in front of my fellow costume makers with a look of sheer determination on my face, trying to steady and control my neck as it buckled under the weight. 'Oh, it's quite heavy. I hope it's not windy on the night!' I said.

My friends shook their heads in disbelief and refused to let me even entertain the idea that I might be able to wear this contraption for more than two minutes, without causing serious and permanent damage to my neck and spine. I sat down, deflated, and a little voice in my head suggested that we just watch the Parade this year. 'Yeah, right, as if!' said a louder voice, deep within.

Emergency costume re-design and reconstruction began with the assistance of troubleshooter, Jane Murphy, and consultants, Luke Atkinson, Glen W. Johnson and André Bremer. We didn't have much time to waste, the sparks from the angle grinder lit up the dimly lit studio as we cut into the sculptural head-dress. We worked late into the night and I became quite delirious with laughter at the thought of gay costume-makers calmly sewing and gluing on sequins while the lesbians used power tools!

The original idea had changed but I prefer to say that it *evolved*. I did try to entice four dancing lezzies (one for each year that it had rained over the past twenty) to get hip with me in the Parade, but the thrill of leather and a machine purring between their legs was far more enticing than yellow wet weather gear. Why do DYKE and BIKE have to rhyme so well?

On the morning of the parade I feel calm, the costume is ready. The meeting spot with my other costumed friends has been organised and my parents have called to wish me a safe and happy night. My moment of fame has come.

It's very thrilling for me to walk up Oxford Street in front of a cheering crowd of 400 000 or more people, cameras and film crews, celebrating my sexuality through my creativity and spirit. My heart pumps hard against my chest with the excitement and my blood feels thick as it races through my veins. My body is noisy but my mind is peaceful.

Then the parade comes to an end and I feel like a lesbian entertainer finishing my shift for another year. I am exhausted and feeling kind of numb. There is a need to find my own tribe. My friends and I sit down under a tree outside the Showgrounds and talk about our experience. There is a lot of love for each other and a bond that has grown through our shared creativity and humour.

I guess that is what motivates me and why I'll do it all again next year. 'Mmm, I hope it doesn't rain!'

*Pip Playford is a visual artist. Her artworks include public art commissions and community and cultural development art projects.*

In the March 1989 post-Parade Party, the legendary Leggs Galore led sixty-eight drag queens topped by ten leather-clad dykes, in a spectacular version of *I Am What I Am*. This was new, and I guess something of a turning point in Mardi Gras entertainment, in that it was the first show to be mounted on a very large scale. There have been many since, as well as many great solos. I will never forget Jay Jay winding her way around the pavilion to end the 1988 Party with Shirley Bassey's 'Rhythm Divine'; or Miss 3D's amazing solo at 10 a.m. of the 11-minute mix of 'I Will Survive' to the delight of the 5000 remaining party-goers; or Mogadonna soaring above our heads, all glitter and feathers, to Diana's 'The Boss'. Gary Leeson invited me to remount *I Am What I Am* for the twentieth anniversary of Mardi Gras in 1998, this time with 125 drag queens and kings.

I had never taken a call after any of my shows, but on that occasion I thought – why not! As I insisted everyone had to do drag, I felt the least I could do was join the club. As each group or individual entered, they held a placard revealing who or what they were: a Melbourne contingent, the Albury Hotel, The Bookshop, Carlotta, and so on. Assuming I would not be recognised in my gorgeous drag, as I took my call with the choreographer Tony di Dio, my placard simply read 'Richard Wherrett'.

Sadly, as I made the descent down steps that even Talullah Bankhead would have balked at, I was holding my placard back to front.

I could hear 10 000 people wondering, 'What's that older woman got to do with it?'

# Letter to Steve

## Jim Anderson

15 March 1998

Dear Steve,

Thank you for your letter inquiring how Mardi Gras went this year. Yes, it would be better if it was called QUEER GRA and I agree that 'Gay and Lesbian Mardi Gras' is hopelessly clunky but it covers the bases and I think we are stuck with the title into the millennium. And yes, I was on a float for the first time. It was put together at the last minute by the Southern Cross Outdoors Group, my bushwalking group and it was a satirical comment on Sydney's new Star City Casino. GAYSINO cried our big signs. Behind us we hauled a CHILD CARE CENTRE, not a pedophile paradise, but a reference to local outrage when it was revealed that gamblers have been leaving their tiny tots locked in the family car in the parking lot while they play the pokies. You may seriously wonder why a bunch of dedicated walkers was dancing on the back of a truck rather than striding purposefully along in hiking boots and carrying alpenstocks, but please don't. Basically we were a bunch of well-preserved men in our second prime dressed up as croupiers in sequinned minishorts, lurid waistcoats and tennis eyeshades covered with glitter. We were probably tacky, but not as tacky as the décor of the casino we were mocking. We secured the attention of the onlooking throngs by throwing packets of chips, gyrating to old disco hits ('Go West', for example) and by framing ourselves with large playing cards each featuring the Queen of Hearts, large pink dildo in hand.

'Wayne (my nephew) *saw* you!' cried my sister in an accusing tone, as though I was *still*, at my age, a disgrace to the family name. I wonder what he *saw*? I was definitely modestly covered. Maybe he noticed me 'misbehaving' with the Sunboys (a nudist group) after the Parade. The Sunboys had shed the teensy posing pouches the organisers insisted they wear along Oxford Street and were relaxing *au naturel* with a few beers before going into the Party. Having attended the Sunboys' Nude Mardi Gras Barbecue earlier, I was on kiss and dick-holding greeting terms with some of them. So nice to be among men who welcome a firm hand, and don't see it as sexual harassment or a preliminary to a labour intensive hand job.

This amiable Moore Park encounter reminded me that the Party was not just about dancing and floor shows, socialising and solidarity against the hetero world, but about sex. I had already heard rumours of a Men Only space, DJed by one Buck Naked, and that could mean only one thing, couldn't it? I dashed back to where I was supposed to be helping dismantle our float. 'You still have that spare ticket?' I asked Fred, who had been drinking bubbly with me on the truck.

Once at the Party, I realised that I hadn't arranged liaisons with Fred or anyone else for that matter. Suddenly I was lonely in the crowd, adrift with only my sequins for company amid 20 000 revellers, all intent on their own pleasures. I had a beer, then another. I kept myself busy, wandering about, beverage in hand, fully orienting myself – the Cloak Room, the Hordern, the Costume Parade venue. That was all fun for about ten minutes. I mistook the Women Only Space for the Hall of Industries and was firmly refused admission. I found the Dome and managed to give myself to the truly sensational lightshow and the pumped-up dance music. Before long I was definitely feeling I was an integral part of a sea of waxed, tanned and perfectly primped and drugged bodies. All very nice, but now it was 2 a.m., I had not encountered a single person I knew. I began to get *really* lonely. I downed a Stoly and tonic. A triple.

Out on the open prairie between pavilions once more, I heard an angelic voice call my name. 'Jim!' A crocodile of spectacularly furbished drag queens was traipsing by. I caught an eye. After a full second I said, 'Wanda!' It was my oldest friend, Richard Wherrett, who never gets into drag, done up like a parody of a mature Double Bay matron on the way to the re-creation of his and Corby Beard's 1989 super-production, *I Am What I Am*. 'You must come and watch! Meet me backstage afterwards.'

The show was stunning, a rush and all too brief. Richard was the last to descend the broad stairs, his sign a simple 'RICHARD WHERRETT'. 'Well of course it said that. That was the whole point. I had no intention of getting done up and have no one know who I was.' It was an act of heroism in those fishnets, that wasp-waisted, laced leather bodice, that five-car pile-up of hair.

After the *I Am What I Am* extravaganza, I was taken up to the VIP room which was so jammed with nonentities like me I suspected there must be a VVIP room somewhere else. I mean, where were Dannii and Kylie and what about all those rumours of such mega-fauna as Keanu Reeves, Elton John, Samuel L. Jackson . . .

A couple of bourbon and Cokes, several inconsequential conversations struck up, and the night began ticking over very satisfactorily. It might have remained at that speed and I would have been safely home in bed well before the dawn's early light if I had not run into a large man whose shape I knew vaguely from one of my canyoning excursions. He was as desperately solitary as I was, in fact, and looking for someone to help him smoke a joint he had been saving for just such a moment. Although I am not a doper or even a smoker these days, I inhaled.

It turned out to be a highly resinous sensimilla, the sort of grass you only need one toke to get off on, but there I was sharing a whole fat joint of the stuff. We found ourselves out of our minds, tripping amid the now even more ecstatic and light fantastic wonders of the Dome where a lot of beautifully conformed young men seemed to have removed most of what little clothing they had on in the first place. I was soon locked in commune with my drug supplier. I liked his Canadian accent, his profile, the mutton chop whiskers, the Rocky Mountains grizzly bearness, the tightly stretched Tokyo Shock Boys T-shirt. Yes, yes, stoned at four in the morning, I liked everything about him. After all, he was going to rescue me from dancing the sunrise in alone, not Mr Right but the fabled Mr Right Now. One thing led to another and when I found myself with his rough paw inside my shorts and both my hands hauling down his black vinyl, I unglued my mouth and gasped, 'Let's go somewhere less crowded.'

I have to confess we wound up somewhere even more crowded – yes, the unofficial 'Men's Space', that is, downstairs in the fetid underground of the Hordern toilet. There was a minor incident as we arrived, with the Security man at the top of the steps most distressed at having failed to catch a dyke in a bow tie and braces who had slipped past him. 'I can't imagine why she would want to go down there,' he sighed. 'It's just men's business. I mean, it's seriously disgusting.'

What was 'down there' was wall to wall John Rechy's *City of Night*. What indeed could the dyke have been after? Surely not the aroma of Locker Room, hot metal and maleness, of sweat and other bodily fluids, of eau de toilette, mouthwash and Vaseline Intensive Care deodorant, of slowly corroding Jean-Paul Gaultier minimalist leather? Maybe she was a reporter from *Lesbians on the Loose* who just *had* to check out the quality of Buck's musical accompaniment to all this.

What was I reminded of? I guess that time in the woods in Marin County, California when in a shadowed glade I came upon millions of ladybirds crawling all over each other, accompanied by a low wattage happy buzzing, exuding moist secretions and an attractive odour of multitudinous insect fucking. If there was one thing in the world I could have been sure of at that moment, it was that there was no equivalent scene in the Women Only space.

Steve, you being you, I know the sound of this has turned you on, particularly the dungeon-like locale and the smell of expensive designer leather. I can hear you demanding to know if Sydney's infamous Trough Man was present. I did not see him but the word was that he had been lying on the floor somewhere, along with an apprentice Trough Boy. By the time we arrived, they had both gone off to a REAL toilet, for some REAL enjoyment, because no one was pissing where we were any more, just cruising.

God knows how long we were in that steamy twilight zone, but with standards continuing to drop even more rapidly than the Aussie Boys Lycra, and my glasses permanently fogged, we reluctantly decided to leave. Easier said than done. Against the in-rushing tide it proved to be an elemental struggle to get out and up those tragi-comic steps.

It was 6 a.m. with the softest of warm rains falling – there was exhaustion in the air, people passed out on chairs, on tables, commiserating in the gutters, others leaving, but the Dome was still the place and we stomped and smooched amid other never-say-die hedonists until we noticed the light of morning gathering. We went out into the pearl grey. My ever-attentive Rocky Mountains husband bought fresh lemonade from a stall thoughtfully located nearby. From a sheltered seat we watched the brilliant passing parade until it was time for the Hall of Industries with Jimmy Somerville. I felt utterly replete and happy.

Well Steve, it's all over for another year. Sorry you did not make it this time. As usual at this juncture I resolve to give myself more to the gay community, but again I find myself in retreat. I guess one has to take it easy after all the hyper-excitement. The cultural seductions of our dazzling Gay Festival month, not to mention all that schooner drinking at the Beauchamp and the Barracks, have taken their toll on me. And since the wildness of that climactic night, I have not wanted to have sex, take drugs, or even socialise. I have, in fact, avoided Oxford Street entirely. My Mr Right Now has telephoned from his distant western suburb more than once, but for the moment I am keeping him at bay. His name, by the way, is Dan.

Does ambivalence always exist, is commitment always a task for tomorrow? Is it because I am *still* running away from myself and from being queer that I can't develop a deep and meaningful relationship with anyone? I know that you feel that those are questions one does not ask at our age. But then again, you have Ben.

Love and best wishes. To Ben too.

Your friend,

Jim

*Jim Anderson is the author of two novels,* Billarooby *and* Pleasure Beach, *and was tried for obscenity with Richard Neville in London's Old Bailey in the 1971* Oz *Trial.*

# My Jewel Encrusted Fists
## Miss Information

MY JEWEL ENCRUSTED fists crash down across the concierge counter.

'Room 2001, the penthouse,' I bark at the well-upholstered clerk. His porky little fingers waddle across the keyboard.

'Your key, Miss Information. Enjoy your sleep.'

'Mind your own business!' I quip on a 180 degree turn, as my heels click-click across the lobby floor.

'Get out!' I snap at a group of fussing homosexuals already in the elevator.

I cram my jewels into the safe and pour myself a drink. I run a brush through my hair and dress for a late night assault. In the lobby, a group of Melbourne queens scurry for cover as I exit the elevator. I am en route for a late night cocktail the night before Mardi Gras with a group of my closest friends – their names temporarily slip my mind. Outside the street is a fussy flurry of Mardi Gras Eve posturing and posing.

We cross the road to the drably named Stonewall Bar and find ourselves upstairs surrounded by VIP Melbourne socialites. You know, the ones that work in shops. I force my lips apart and smile.

'Hi! How are you?' *Kiss, kiss.* 'When did you get here? . . . Where are you staying? . . . You look fabulous! . . . Talk to you later.'

The truth is, I love Mardi Gras and I love Sydney. But seriously, I love Mardi Gras and I love Sydney. Like 'please' and 'thank you', 'love' is not a word I concern myself with except when I find my pockets empty after my 18th vodka.

'Thank you, I love vodka, please.'

'Please, I love vodka, thank you.'

'Thank you vodka, please love.'

'Please, I love you. Buy me a fuckin' vodka . . . thank you.'

However, 'love' is a word I lavish upon Mardi Gras. I love to skip down Oxford Street surrounded by buff, fluff and puff, stuffed in crack-creeping Lycra. I love being halted in the street by cheesy white-bread Americans: 'Oh, hi guys! Happy Mardi Gras! Me and my buddy were looking for somewhere to eat . . .'

'Sure, there's a gorgeous little café in Cabramatta.'

I love it when I find myself saying 'hi' to that Melbourne queen I really hate and shall not acknowledge again until next Mardi Gras. I bid good night to all my friends, crawl in a cab back to the hotel.

Tap, tap, tap . . . 'Housekeeping!'

I crash across the room, removing from the inside handle the 'Do Not Disturb' sign. My naked claw creeps through the opening. Unable to speak, I hand it to the attendant and push the door closed. It's 3.15 Saturday afternoon. I am still drunk. I tiptoe to the bathroom and run myself a bath. Bash, bash, bash . . . 'Let me in!'

I answer the door to my associate, Hot Coco, who looks resplendently transsexual, dressed as a horse. 'Come on, it's 6.30,' she nags, as she clipclops her way to the minibar. 'We have to be at the Parade in ten minutes, and I'm not a horse I'm a fucken' unicorn.'

My counterpart, Miss Everywhere, hustles together our Parade costumes. 'Fuji Fags,' swathed in Fuji flags and multi-function-polis headdress, we leave for the Parade.

We plough our way through a Mardi Gras of waiting Mardi Gras floats and a conspiracy of Maude Boaté wigs. We applaud long and hard at the 'Melbourne Follies': a mummy's favourite of freckled redheads in sequinned hotpants, shirtless in bedazzled waistcoats, bow ties, glitter-bombed tilted bowler hats, black socks and school shoes. Of course, lesbians with whistles and balloons always go down a treat. And no Parade is complete without moustached hairy men in mothball-ridden Fairy Queen ballgowns. We swoon as a pageant of Asian exotica in full Princess regalia swan the asphalt with royal importance.

'Why do poofs take on the looks and mannerisms of old women, and dykes the personas of pre-pubescent schoolboys?' I ponder as we march up the street. And isn't it fabulous we get to parade up the world's longest catwalk in absurd, ridiculous outfits because we put our dicks up other men's arses? I wave to all my friends.

Pruned, pickled, plucked and preserved, a swirling sea of perky pectorals and packages patrol the parameters inside the Sydney Showground. Drag queens overwrought with excitement whip themselves into a frenzy, throwing shade at their own shadows.

Kylie and Dannii bubble and squeak across the stage like singing circus fleas, backed up by the now regulatory Mardi Gras dancercise routine. Fluffy bra'd, Chuppa-Chup sucking, bum-bag wearing girls litter our landscape.

'Can I try on your headdress?'

'I love you gays.'

'My cousin's gay. His name is Jason. Do you know him?'

'Yes, I shat on his face last night at Bodyline.'

Walls become doors become floors become walls as an old acquaintance approaches me in fours. We plough the early morning field of empty cans and bottles. The previous night's perfect complexions now resemble rancid week-old strawberries; those perfectly placed pectorals now pendulate in the morning breeze. Exiting the gates, I step on a leaflet-wielding Christian before crawling into a cab.

My jewel encrusted fists crash down across the toilet seat as I rummage amongst a refuse of powders, pills and pocket personals. Fingering the fluff off some Valium, I dry swallow before crashing through the buzz of mirror-hungry drag queens and associates. I herringbone my way through a cavern of jaw-gnashing discotheque debris. I perch myself at the bar between two moth-eaten drag queens, both in the later stages of decomposition. They jabber away at me in Polish and Portuguese, I slide off my stool and on to the floor, where I quietly slip into a coma. Septic and fly-blown, I am kicked and shuffled around the floor until the hand of benevolence thrusts refreshing smelling salts up my nostril.

With a festering spasticity, I tramp through the hotel lobby.

'Good afternoon, Miss Information, check out time was 11 a.m.'

'Thank you, Miss Primwhistle.' I swipe at the desk clerk before falling into the elevator in an odoursome flurry.

I drag my sad and sorry arse to Sydney Airport, ready to bounce the bitch behind the check-in counter if she asks me any questions. I return to Melbourne. Everything is over. I don't wish to speak to any of my friends for at least a month. I once again ignore that Melbourne queen I hate.

My jewel encrusted fists crash across the keyboard at work. Five numb toes, one having dislodged itself when removing my shoe at the airport; two collapsed nostrils, generously garnished in 'Shocking Red' blistering burns; a dislocated hip, furiously bound back in place with gaffer tape; half a dozen or so cigarette burns – two on my face, one perilously close to my eye; two smoker's fingers resembling a couple of large Twisties . . . Available balance $2.48.

Happy Mardi Gras!

*Chris Orr (aka Miss Information) is a fortnightly columnist for the* Melbourne Star Observer, *a competent graphic designer and a professional gymnast competing at international level.*

It has always fascinated me that some of the most feminine looking and behaving men I know are straight and that some of the most disturbingly aggressive macho men I know are gay, and that there is the vast range in the spectrum somewhere in between. And so it is with women. And it is worth noting that when it comes to getting into drag, that there are drag kings as well as drag queens. But a little definition is perhaps appropriate here, for men in frocks are and always have been a very prominent fixture of Mardi Gras, and they certainly aren't all drag queens.

Sydney has spawned the Diva awards – the Drag Industry Variety Awards – and a great night out it is too. But the awards are for those great numbers of performers and related artists who make their living via drag. On the other hand, the lawyer or builder who might 'frock up' for a one and only Mardi Gras is a very different thing. Getting into drag does not per se a drag queen make.

But it is fun.

Some of my favourite moments have been in rehearsals on fiercely hot summer days when the drag component will be strutting their stuff – shaved heads, hairy chests, cut off shorts, stubbled legs and high heeled shoes. It's a very special look.

# The Siege of Troy
## Garry Scale

THE LEGEND LOUNGE was set up for the duration of the Mardi Gras Festival by Geoffrey Williams and Michael Freundt, the boys who established the Tilbury Hotel, Sydney's one-time home of cabaret. The Legend Lounge was to provide cabaret for Queers, by Queers, with the occasional 'Legendary Fag Hag' thrown in. It was conceived as a place to adjourn to after a Mardi Gras event, to sit in comfort, slurp on a cocktail, snack, if you can find the time to between the 'Hello darlings' and the 'Look at hers', and mix with all shapes and persuasions from multipierced Lesbian packs to Cosy Old Cardie Queens.

I have had the distinction to compere it since its inception, a task I have relished, giving me a chance to drag out a lot of old routines and brush them up for a new, younger, and unsuspecting audience. At the Koala in 1997, the lounge was a huge hit, admirably supported by all and sundry with an eclectic array of talent. In 1998, at the Banana Bar, it was a dismal failure! Obviously folks are too scared to cross Gilligan's Island to this rather sweet bar. Some old fag curse I am yet to uncover. The talent was awesome but in the empty auditorium, one could hear the crickets. I shouldn't have been surprised as every cabaret venue to open, after the Tilbury's regrettable demise, has folded after short seasons, including our own production of *Titanic* at the Cambridge Inn.

In those two years, I have presented some remarkable talent: Hugh Monroe, Michael Cormick, Paul Capsis, Angela Toohey and Judi Connelli, to name several. To finish the first season, we had booked Simone Troy, that extraordinary performer with a mouth and wit to trade your pearls for. I had always worshipped the woman and was looking forward to that final night.

From the very start, however, things started to go wrong. Simone Troy hadn't seen the room before and was surprised by the mix of the crowd and by the evening's format. In the weeks before, I had developed the style of the room and given it its informal repartée. Simone was to follow me on. But her dancers were late, and we were running out of time. 'Fill,' she yelled at me.

I threw on my tired old 'Liz Taylor' frock, did my number and was received enthusiastically. I glanced to the wings to be confronted with a steaming drag queen and no male dancers. 'Fill!' she bellowed.

I moved into the audience, discovering a glittering crowd, just ripe for the picking. Dawn and Anek, Maggie Kirkpatrick, who'd just been outed as a hetero in the gay press, and gorgeous John Michael Howson, who coincidentally had just returned from Liz's 60th birthday in LA. He was a hoot, the room was buzzin'.

A scurry at the back: the boys had arrived.

From the wings: 'I'll deal with youse fuckin' arseholes later.'

From the stage: 'Ladies and gentlemen, Miss Simone Troy and her Boys.'

What followed was a slick, Oxford Street show but completely wrong for that night and that room. Lukewarm applause accompanied the diva to the wings as she proceeded to tower above two very meek and tardy dancers. I, in the meantime, came back to farewell the room, the season and do my thank-yous in song, dressed as Norma Desmond. Three feet away from me, during my big emotional moment, Simone's two dancers were being called every name under the sun as they were promptly, and in a very ladylike way, given their marching orders. So I held my mike and the audience was afforded one of the very best of all possible cabaret finales.

'Youse fuckin' cunts have just ruined my fuckin' career. Where the fuck were you? Fucking your dumb arses off in some sleazy backroom. You'll never work in this strip again. And if you think ya gonna get paid then think again. Now pick ya skimpy G-strings out of your cracks and fuck off.'

*Garry Scale does not swear, cried at his 40th birthday party, is modest in success and gracious in defeat (not uncommon in showbusiness). But betray him and you'll be cursed for life.*

# Mardi Gras Myth 5

*One of the great stars of Australian drag, Melbourne's Miss Candee, was driving home from the Party a little, shall we say, unsteadily as her car swerved from median strip to kerb and back again. A policeman pulled her over.*

*'What's your name, madam?'*

*'Candee.'*

*'What's your full name please?'*

*'Miss Candee.'*

*'Would you step out of the car please.'*

*'No.'*

*'Why not?' (with infinite patience).*

*'Because I'm too fuckin' pissed to stand, that's why.'*

# Lolita 2000

## Lance Leopard

WEEELLLL, I must have seen it all by now. Jaded – at the tender age of 30! But then again, I *have* been going to the Mardi Gras for half my lifetime it seems. Makes a girl think. Of course, being the automatic socialite that I seem to have become, when I think of the good old MG, I naturally cast my mind to the Party.

Guilty! As everyone knows, there also happens to be a month-long festival, swimming soirée, a Fair and that goddamned Parade to consider. But I shall (for the purposes of this waltz down memory lane) concentrate what remains of my memory on the Party.

The Party. Whacko! Sister! What is it *like*? *What are we like*? One immediately thinks of that lurid scene in *The Ten Commandments*, when the heathens are totally out of control and wallowing in the fleshpots. You know, the part just before Moses rains on their parade by marching down that backlot mountain and declaring his ten good reasons for being a crashing bore. Let me tell you confidentially that I have *never* seen Moses at the Party. I have, however, seen a complete slut there – year after year. And year after year, I've watched her go round and reap the whirlwind. You probably know her. Her name is . . . Lolita. Lolita, Lolita, Lolita. Lolita 2000!

At every party, just expect Lolita with the flicked-back hair. Lolita – gliding past you outside the RHI on her skateboard in tight-white-slacks, leaving a trail of Charlie's Angel Dust. How do you solve a problem like Lolita? What's the Lolita secret? Some would say Farrah Fawcett-Majors. Well. The hair, perhaps. But Farrah was pure LA. Lolita, of course, is pure Gold Coast. At the Showground.

I've gotten to know her quite well at the Party over the years. She hails from San Souci. The San Souci Siren as *Capital Q*'s astrologer, Stephen Devine, once dubbed her. She owns a nail shop out that way called The Nail Game – and her nails are *always* a talking point in the VIP Bar.

Lolita likes to talk to boys. But what everyone doesn't know is that she's changed her name. Several times. I once remember her name being

Angie Dildo. Well, that had to go. Bothered with black'n'blue pinch bruises all over her ass – she dyed her hair red and set off to the Party as Stacii Daggers. Do you remember Stacii? Could she moonwalk! She had that irritating little portable record player that only played 'Streetdance'. But she still wasn't content.

Then came Florida. Florida Turnpike. Florida was a Slut for Jesus. Jesus, Florida was a *slut*. Only one thing could come next: Lolita. Lolita Del Ray. But just as Dana, the Israeli tranny Eurovision winner, changed her last name to International, so Del Ray changed hers to 2000. 'I just felt it was a mark of respect to my city for winning the Olympics. And it's no secret that I'd like to open the ceremony,' Lolita confessed.

Asked about what appears to be a long, continuing running feud with fellow Party-gal Cora-Beth, Lolita looks pained. 'There are ugly things happening in this world we live in. And jealousy is one of them. Anyway, I thought this story was supposed to be about *me*. That woman simply gets on my nerves.'

Many people, on first seeing Lolita, are amazed by her deep, full suntan ... 'but I have no one to thank bar the San Souci sun and, of course, Mother Nature'. Modest. Not a trait I'd have confused with Lolita. Is that the same Lolita who, blond locks flying, fronted up to the urinal at the party and, how do I put this delicately, became quite *sensual* with herself to the delight of the chap standing next to her? The same chap who declined to help when her gold stiletto spike got stuck in the urinal gate? Probably. She's a pretty complex chick – and not one to let a good Mardi Gras opportunity slip from between her brown fingers.

Which is why she's launched her own signature perfume. Called, simply, 'Lolita'. It is the scent of 2000. In its distinctive pine-cone shaped bottle with a yellow plastic lid, the perfume smells ... well, *cheap*. If there's one thing Lolita is disappointed with, it's the Showground being turned into a movie studio.

'Well, yes. I'm angry with the entire motion picture industry. Why shouldn't I be?' she flashed. 'They took my name. My image. *Me*. And made it into a movie that's been banned in every country in the world. And that hurts. That girl doesn't even *look* like me.'

Oh well, Lolita. It seems you can't win 'em all. But I'm counting on one thing. At the Party next year, whatever I do, wherever I go, I know I'll see Lolita. Next year, I may even dance with her!

*Lance Leopard (aka Lounge Lizard) is a regular gossip columnist for* Capital Q Weekly. *Lance stresses that he is not Lolita 2000. But he knows who is!*

# Pete's Ridge

## Nell Schofield

I KEEP TRYING to write about Mardi Gras. My desk is a pathetic jumble of scrawled attempts – sad little sentences crossed out and rewritten with arrows directing them off onto some other piece of recycled paper and its convoluted stream of self-consciousness. Unsatisfactory efforts one and all.

Underneath them, the increasingly exasperated tone emanating from Richard Wherrett's letters. 'Girls, girls, PLEASE!' was the latest. It's tragic.

And Franny's no help. I sit her down and try to get her to remember something suitable about our friend Peter Tully's seminal contribution, or a memorable moment with our other pioneering pal David Mc-Diarmid to throw in. I want to honour these innovators whose ashes are scattered up at our country retreat on Dead Pete's Ridge. But nothing seems adequate.

I try to write about the time we marched, the year after Peter's death, when we overtook the marching boys in a desperate bid for freedom and had to pull ourselves up short of leading the entire Parade. Or the urge I had to mother my father during one particularly lively Party.

Ten years of impressions are, at this very moment, vying desperately for space on the laptop and the deadline expired months ago. There's our first Parade as spectators and that initial blast of hilariously delirious pride vibe. There's the first broadcast when I was on the streets with the Juggernaut trying to make my questions audible above the uproar as I reported for national television. And last year's guest appearance when I got a good look at Dannii's surgically reconstructed face.

But I think I should draw the line on the past right here and look towards the future. May Mardi Gras bring people laughter, provide a creative outlet for their talents and work towards establishing a space for old groovers like us amongst the thumping techno beat.

*Nell Schofield is a writer, broadcaster and TV presenter.*

# You Say Chimera, I Say Chameleon

## Craig Johnston

THE PARADE IS MARDI GRAS. So it was in the beginning.

The first Sydney Gay Mardi Gras was not the first gay political demonstration in Australia. That was in October 1971, in Sydney.

It was not a carnival, despite the organisers' attempt to distinguish between a street demo in the morning, Saturday 24 June 1978, and the 'festival' (as the poster called it) in the evening, Saturday 24 June 1978. The morning demo attracted a couple of hundred people. The evening parade attracted a thousand. I did not go to the morning demo, I did go to the evening parade.

There were quite a few people in costume. The most famous being Peter Tully as an American Indian. I am not sure whether this was a tribute to the Village People whose debut album had appeared in 1977, or to the kids' games and Anglo-American cultural imperialism of the 1950s. And there was a sound truck – which has the same holy status in 78ers' iconography that the urinal from the Green Park bog has in the Sisters of Perpetual Indulgence's history. It played that awful Tom Robinson 'Sing If You're Glad to be Gay' which is a paradoxical commentary on the oppression homosexuals experience, hence the funereal way in which he sings it. For some reason gay libbers of the time thought it was an affirming song and tried to sing along with it in an upbeat way that didn't work. The police, however, gave the parade some life by trying to end it a brutal way.

From then on, goodbye carnival, and hello new left street demo . . . linked arm phalanxes all the way, just like Epaminondas at Leuctra. Fifty-three casualties, a battle lost.

But how could there not be another Mardi Gras? In 1979, the bastard begot a bastard.

In the medium term, Mardi Gras brought in a sea change in the nature of the gay/lesbian movement in this city – from one based on critical social analyses of the intelligentsia to one based on the consumerist lifestyles of the queens. Same politics of dignity and rights, different style. Gay liberation's ideological sharpness was defused as it diffused into the pores of the scene queen's body.

And this signalled a warning to the gay left – change or wither. The gay left had been open to the possibilities of a carnival, they incubated the dowdy cocoon that was '78. But when the butterfly wanted to emerge and go its own way, they were petulant, critical of its sexism, hedonism and commercialism. 'Ideologically unsound' was the term used then, it means 'not politically correct'. Mardi Gras became the unimaginable, the inconceivable, because of the fantasies and creativities of the 78ers, 79ers, 80ers, 81ers . . . Mardi Gras also killed off socialist-feminist gay liberation politics as defined in 1978, and allowed gay radicalism to grow up.

You could do away with any other one single event. The Party, the Fair, the Festival, Sleaze Ball. And Mardi Gras would still be Mardi Gras. But leave all the others and take away the Parade, and there is no more Mardi Gras. And so it always will be.

Change. Continuity.

This is why I haven't given up on it, and it hasn't left me behind yawning.

I do not know these thousands of gays and lesbians and trannies and bisexuals and straights who march in the parade. ('March'. Now there's an old left word. It's how I described what the participants in the first parade in 1978 did, when I wrote about it then.) The TV docos produced by the ABC and Channel 10 have presented little vignettes, backgrounders, on some of them sewing clothes and nailing down signs and VO5ing wigs. But beyond those teasers I have no idea where the marchers live, if they have day jobs, if they grew up in Bowraville, if they've had voice elocution lessons to sound butch-er, how old they were when they came out, if they're out. Why some are into costume and some prefer dour Levis. Whether they abstain from sex the night before to conserve their energy to brazen their way through Windy Square. How their floats manage to play the same brackets of music from a pool of four tracks, without any co-ordination or directives, as if there is a predestined repertoire that spontaneously emerges from the hundred of disconnected, unknown planning meetings all over the eastern seaboard.

Mardi Gras is easy to criticise. Its harshest critics are to be found among the bitchy camp men of Sydney. It's commercial, yes. Too big, yes. Mainstream, yes. Vacuous, yes. Self-satisfied, yes. Tacky, yes. Up itself in that very Sydney way, yes. A spectator sport, yes.

It's changing. From a GAY AND LESBIAN Mardi Gras representing Sydney's distinctive place in homosexual subcultures to the Sydney Mardi Gras representing queers' place in Sydney society.

Mardi Gras is in your eye, homophobe. Disreputable, yes. Those tits and hairy bums give homos a bad image, and are not a good role model for children or closeted paedophiles, yes. Participatory to the max, yes. Shameless gay and lesbian militancy, yes. A civil rights march, yes.

And yet, it is also about commercialisation. Commodification. Normalisation. Voyeurism, mainstreaming. Virtual homosexuality. Gays and lesbians are fêted for (and no other reason) the dollars they bring to the heterosexual state's economy. (But the state's parliament cannot repeal discriminatory laws on age of sexual consent or on de facto relationships.)

The price for this fêting is the surrender of an aggressive gay and lesbian identity. An Oedipal reading of Mardi Gras casts it as a product of the baby boomers. The post-boomers with their creed of post-modernism decry 'gays and lesbians'.

I suspect that queer, the destructionist, will not be able to destroy the gay and lesbian activism and discourses that built the Mardi Gras completely, though they may well overtake them and recast Mardi Gras in their own fractured flickers. For we have seen these successful American invasions before. 'Gay' itself came here from the USA and overcame 'camp' which was what homosexual-identifying males and lesbians called themselves into the 1970s. We then young(er) gay liberationists insisted that the signs reading 'camp' be painted out from the names of homosexual student organisations. In the 1990s, 'queer' arrived from the USA and the new organisations called themselves queer and the signs reading 'gay and lesbian' were painted over.

But elements of camp have survived. Camp drag metamorphed into radical drag and fan-danced its way through Mardi Gras in the 1980s. Sylvia and the Synethics, Doris Fish, Peter Tully, the Planet Sluts, and David McDiarmid gave gay lib its glam. Camp style barebacked gay identity politics in the Mardi Gras Parade. Queer will likewise need to accommodate its progenitor. Queer triumphant and in power will need the gays and lesbians who are . . . homosexuals. If only because the intelligentsia needs audiences and legitimacy and front line troops jumping the barbed wire, because intellectual fashions do not propel social change.

A mainstreamed, queer, de-gayed Mardi Gras for Sydney, the global city, will need to engage, negotiate, struggle with the same contradictions that faced the gay/lesbian liberationists in 1978, when the Mardi Gras was conceived, and which faced them in 1980, when the vote was taken to move the Mardi Gras to summer, and again in 1985, when the forces of moral panic demanded that Mardi Gras be cancelled as a risk to public health . . .

How do you balance conflicting demands, make trade-offs? How do you represent that subjectivity, which is homosexual, as both natural and different, normal and transgressive? And how do you stay in front, retain integrity, be radical?

The 'cultural' content of the first phase of the 1978 Mardi Gras parade – from Taylor Square to Whitlam Square – and the 'political' nature of the second phase of the 1978 Mardi Gras march – from Whitlam Square to Kings Cross – are both necessary to understand the phenomena as consumer spectacle and as a civil rights march, today. Stories around the painful/militant/radical 'birth' of Mardi Gras in 1978 are an important part of what gays and lesbians want Mardi Gras to be, today. Mardi Gras is a contradiction (in the Marxist sense). and this contradiction is its continuing strength.

*Craig Johnston is a social policy analyst, and a 78er who has been at every Mardi Gras so far.*

# Then and Now

## Robert Johnston

THE ADRENALIN WAS STILL FLOWING. Both arms were growing weary from constant waving but the spine-tingling pride banished all thoughts of tiredness. For this 78er walking at the head of the 1998 Gay and Lesbian Mardi Gras Parade was liking living a fantasy and enjoying an honour that only seemed possible in my dreams.

Then we turned into Driver Avenue.

Before us were the long curved tiers of the Bobby Goldsmith Foundation stands, row after row of faces, dazzling lights, waves of chaotic sound. Our group of veterans suddenly seemed small, almost vulnerable before this spectacle, and for an instant we were humbled into a respectful silence. As we approached, the people in the stands on the western side, under the shadowy columns of Moreton Bay Figs, began rising to their feet. The cheering and waving became tumultuous. Each face was distinct, the excitement and exhilaration individual, but together they were expressing a common and collective spirit of affection and appreciation. Across the seats, across the barriers, and into the roadway, every one of us was embraced by that spirit and all of us, marching veterans and waving watchers, just soared. We soared together on the sense of occasion and the commemoration of what we all have become.

Above the incredible din I heard an announcer say: 'Thank you for giving us Mardi Gras.'

A double take. Hold on, I thought, is that what we were doing twenty years ago, giving the future its Mardi Gras? But as quickly as it came the question was swamped by the sheer magnificence of the moment. The emotional screws were turned to an irresistible level and the last stretch of stands passed by in a blur of tears.

Afterwards, though, when I had regained some sort of equilibrium, that question returned. Were we creating Mardi Gras twenty years ago on that cold and vicious night? At the end of it, when we were milling across the road from Darlinghurst Police Station, our backs against the old prison walls, I remember being scared, shocked and angry. That night had not been miraculous like this one just past. There was no pride, no joy, no soaring spirit that night.

We had started out innocent in our naiveté and the earnestness of our purpose. We were showing solidarity with all gays and lesbians everywhere in the world. It was to commemorate the date of Stonewall, that trigger for the gay liberation movement, a strand in the broader movement of sexual liberation. We wanted to change perceptions, to change feelings, to break images, to break constraints and find new and finer ways to relate physically and emotionally to one another.

That cold night we ran up against police who simply wanted to break heads and break spirits. Police who gave vent to the basest form of hatred – that based on ignorance, prejudice and contempt. Police who seemed to enjoy their work, and who quickly warmed up in the winter air with a spot of poofter bashing.

The two nights could not have been more different. It is confusing to think that each night is inextricably linked and that the glories of one were meant to commemorate the despair of the other. I find it impossible to fully understand the differences and to properly appreciate the continuities between those two nights. That, I guess, represents the wonder of what has happened to gays and lesbians in Sydney over the past twenty years.

But in a way the announcer was right. We did create Mardi Gras. It's just that none of us knew it nor could we guess what that night's parade would become. The 1998 Parade was far beyond our wildest expectations. We drifted away in the early hours of the morning from outside Darlinghurst Police Station feeling defeated. But as we did so, the future was with us even if its face was hidden. Such an eventuality makes a mockery of certainty. No one ever has the final word.

So I am grateful for having been given those 90 minutes in the Mardi Gras limelight. It's more that I ever expected. It's probably more than I actually deserve. Because when all is said and done the present owes nothing to the past. The present is forever fashioning itself, while the past is just the past. For me that night in 1978 is a memory, but for most of those who watched the veterans march in 1998 that night we were commemorating is a piece of history. That difference is a chasm which is unbridgeable.

L. P. Hartley wrote: 'The past is another country, they do things differently there.'

Yes, we did do things differently then. We thought differently, dressed differently, danced differently, read differently, listened to different music. We were very different and we have suffered the fate of all those inhabitants of the country of the past: we have grown up and grown old. We are living evidence of the saying: old radicals never die, they just become irrelevant.

As a citizen of Mardi Gras past I say thank you to the citizens of Mardi Gras present for allowing me an exhilarating 90 minutes of relevance. You have made an old radical happy.

*Robert Johnston is a native of Sydney who is becoming increasingly feral as he negotiates the shoals of middle age.*

# Rites of Passage

## So what does Mardi Gras mean to you?

## Ian Roberts

I'VE STARTED WRITING THIS so many times now if I don't finish it this time there won't be a next. Grammar and English diction aren't exactly what you would call my forte; shit, I'm flat out writing my own name and address, so please bear with me. Hopefully by the end of it you will have been able to piece all the pieces together and caught the gist of this story. (Fingers crossed.)

*Where do I start?*

Where does anyone really start, I suppose. I mean Mardi Gras is like that. It's a totally different concept for everyone. And when you think about it there are not too many other events on such a large scale that can bring such an incredible diversity of peoples together for a MONTH-long event, nationally as well as internationally.

I think back to my first Mardi Gras (although I'd sooner not, it's that long ago now). My virginal Mardi Gras. That's the way I like to think of it, kind of makes it sound sweet and innocent, don't you think? (I fucking wish!) Anyway, all those events, Fair days, film festivals, shows, etc, etc, that Mardi Gras organises and runs, and all those situations and experiences since that first time that I've been a part of. Remembering back stirs up an incredible amount of emotion inside me, good and bad, warm and cold, and all those beautiful friends we've lost and all the new ones we've made. It's kind of like a huge emotional whirlpool, although many people would call it more of a giant cesspool – I suppose it depends on your outlook on life.

That's another way Mardi Gras has affected my life. People have all these concepts of what Mardi Gras is and what it stands for and what it's about, and how it began all those years ago. It still amazes me that what was originally a demonstration for equal rights has turned into a month-long celebration for those same rights going into the new millennium.

I've just been looking back through all my pre-Party photos. It's strange because I can see the process of my total acceptance of my sexuality in those photos. Every year becoming a bit bolder and more adventurous in the way I dressed for each Party, trying to let those close to me really know the truth about me, without ever admitting it. The thing to me that is strangest of all, is that now I dress down to the Parties, because there's no one left that doesn't know I'm a gay man. It's kind of come full circle.

The one constant in most of the photos is the friends surrounding me. Being gay is a really good measuring stick to gauge your friends (or so-called friends) by – both straight and gay. I lived for a long time as a closet gay, but as the photos show, year by year, I slowly came out, a process that took close to ten years. And I'm glad to say that the majority of those friends early in the piece are still just that today – 'good friends'. I LOVE YOU GUYS.

Thinking about all the Parties I have been to, although they're all kind of just a blur – well mostly, anyway – it's strange the way people, myself included, absolutely exhaust themselves to extract every bit of thrill and fun out of the night of the party. Kind of like trying to wring out a sopping wet towel, and the way people try to do it harder every year. Thank God for the ageing process that slows us down naturally over time. I can't see myself doing things in the next ten years that I did in the last, although I was probably saying that years ago as well. Oh shit, scary, isn't it?

A lot of people see Mardi Gras now just as a big opportunity to party, and forget the real purpose of it and the reasons for it. I suppose as we move into the 21st century and admitting you're gay becomes more widely accepted, or should I say tolerated, then I suppose Mardi Gras has served one of its original purposes – in the fact that it was originally a march for equal rights and now, slowly, slowly, we may be gaining just that.

Christ, I'm no brain surgeon, I wish I were. I've been in an incredibly lucky situation, with family and friends, and the love and support that they have given me. I'm paid to play a game that I enjoy, and luckily I've had the opportunity to help so many people because of that. People may think I've had too many knocks around the head (although that's probably the safest place to hit me, you can't do any more damage) but if someone like me can put it together, and see how much Mardi Gras can help the individual and the community –

and I'm not talking just about the gay community, I'm talking about the greater community, with better awareness and understanding of gay people, against the prejudice, intolerance and discrimination we face daily – then here's to another twenty years. CHEERS!

*Ian Roberts told his very special story in Paul Freeman's remarkable biography* Finding Out. *His football talents are legendary.*

The Sydney Gay and Lesbian Mardi Gras is currently Australia's largest gay and lesbian organisation, supported by 7400 voting members, 13 full-time staff, 5 part-time workers, and approximately 1500 volunteers. The month-long Mardi Gras Festival is made up of over 100 events and is the largest gay and lesbian festival in the world. More than half a million people watch the Parade, which has over 200 entries. A further 1 million people plus watch the delayed telecast. Just under 40 000 people attend the Mardi Gras Party and Sleaze Ball.